WALES

A HISTORY

WALES

A HISTORY BY
WYNFORD VAUGHAN-THOMAS

MICHAEL JOSEPH

LONDON

First published in Great Britain by Michael Joseph Ltd
44 Bedford Square, London WC1
1985

British Library Cataloguing in Publication Data

Vaughan-Thomas, Wynford
    Wales: A History
    1. Wales—History
    I. Title
    942.9   DA714
    ISBN 0 7181 2468 5

Typeset and printed in Great Britain by BAS Printers,
Hampshire and bound by Hunter and Foulis, Edinburgh

Contents

List of Colour Illustrations

Acknowledgements

The author and publishers would like to thank the following for permission to reproduce illustrations on the pages indicated:
Aerofilms: 31, 69; Chris Barber: 25, 43 (l), 53, 61, 63; C. Batstone: 235; BBC Hulton Picture Library: 37, 39, 206, 210, 243, Derry Brabbs: 26 (r); The Trustees of the British Museum: 30, 75; Cambridge University Committee for Aerial Photography (Crown Copyright reserved): 41 (top); Messrs Collins, from *The Bayeux Tapestry: The Norman Conquest, 1066* by Norman Denny and Josephine Filmer-Sankey, 1983: 85 (l & r); Danish National Museum: 35; Mary Evans Picture Library: 158, 188, 203 (below); Gwynedd Archive Services: 197, 225, 241 (l & r) 246; HTV Stills Library: 182, 234; J. I. Jones: 255; The Dean and Chapter, Lichfield Cathedral: 77 (l); Mansell Collection: 165, 172, 175; National Library of Wales: 47, 77 (r), 90 (top), 97, 102, 107 (all), 115, 127 (r), 143, 150 (above and below), 153 (l), 155, 166, 167, 171 (l & r), 180 (below), 185 (all), 187, 190, 192 (l & r), 213, 215, 219, 221, 231, 238, 239, 252; National Museum of Wales: 19, 28, 33 (top & below), 34 (l & r), 49, 55 (top & below), 94, 109 (l & r), 127 (l), 181, 222, 232; National Museum of Wales/Archives Nationale Paris: 123; National Portrait Gallery: 128, 141, 145; Peter Newark's Historical Pictures: 248; Newport Museum: 208 (l & r), 209; Plaid Cymru: 259; Public Record Office, London: 121; Royal Commission for Historic Monuments, Wales: 24 (l), 79 (r), 88, 100, 126, 153 (r), 154; The Master and Fellows, St John's College, Cambridge: 162; South Glamorgan Library: 237, 242; South Wales Miners' Library: 249, 250; H. Tempest: 168; Welsh Folk Museum: 227; Welsh Industrial and Maritime Museum: 196, 198, 203 (top), 233, 236; Welsh Office: 24 (top), 41 (below), 56, 83, 90 (below), 105 (all), 137, 157; Welsh Tourist Board: 43 (r), 59, 79 (l), 87, 93, 113, 132, 136, 179; Western Mail: 258; West Glamorgan County Council: 149, 180 (top); Roger Worsley: 24 (r), 26 (l), 135, 195; Roger Worsley/Oriel Fach: 18.

Thanks are also due to Messrs Faber & Faber Ltd for kind permission to quote lines on pages 78 and 90, translated by Gwyn Williams from *Welsh Poetry: Sixth Century to 1600* and for the lines from W. H. Auden's 'O Love, the Interest' taken from *The English Auden: Poems, Essays and Dramatic Writings 1927–1939*; and to the Literary Executors of the estate of Dylan Thomas for permission to quote the lines on page 254 from *Under Milk Wood*, published by Messrs Dent.

Irish Sea

LANCASHIRE

HOLYHEAD
Cemaes
Parys Mt.
LIVERPOOL
BIRKENHEAD
Holy I.
Anglesey
Llanfaes
Deganwy
CONWY
LLANDUDNO
RHYL
Rhuddlan
Holywell
R. Dee
R. Mersey
CHESTER
CHESHIRE
Aberffraw
Llangadwaladre
Beaumaris
Penmaenmawr
Llanddulas
Dinorben
FLINT
NANTWICH
Penrhyn
Llandegai
BANGOR
Llanfair Talhaiarn
DENBIGH
Hawarden
MOLD
Caernarfon Bay
CAERNARFON
Dolbadarn
Waenfawr *Snowdon*
Llanrwst
Perfeddwlad
Brymbo
WREXHAM
Bersham
Marchwiel
Bangor
R. Conwy
Clynnog
CAERNARVONSHIRE
Dinas Emrys
Dolwyddelan
DENBIGHSHIRE
Corwen
Valle Crucis Abbey
Ruabon
FLINTSHIRE
Nefyn
Lleyn Peninsula
PORTHMADOC
Port Merion
Tremen-y-Mur
Trawsfynydd
Rhiwlas
Bala
Glynmydyfrdwy
Llangollen
Chirk
OSWESTRY
R. Dee
Bardsey Sound
CRICCIETH
Harlech
Llanfair
Rhinog Mtns.
R. Dyfi
Llanrhaeadr-ym-Mochant
L. Vyrnwy
Powys
SHREWSBURY
Cardigan Bay
MERIONETHSHIRE
Cymmer Abbey
DOLGELLAU
Cadair Idris
Castelly Bere
WELSHPOOL
SHROPSHIRE
BRIGNORTH
Llanegryn
MACHYNLLETH
R. Dovey
Llanbrynmair
Berriew
Ffridd Faldwyn
MONTGOMERY
MONTGOMERYSHIRE
NEWTOWN
R. Severn
Tywyn
Llandinam
Llanidloes
R. Severn
ABERYSTWYTH
Nanteos
Ysbyty Cynfyn
Devils Bridge
Plynlimon Fawr
Abbey Cwm Hir
RADNORSHIRE
LUDLOW
Bewdley
Wigmore
WORCESTER
R. Severn
Aberaeron
Cardiganshire
Strata Florida
Llangeitho
Llanddewi Brefi
LLADRINDOD WELLS
Disserth
Mortimers Cross
Mynydd Bach
R. Teifi
HEREFORD-SHIRE
CARDIGAN
Goodwick Sands in Fishguard Bay
Careg Wastad
LAMPETER
BUILTH WELLS
R. Irfon
Llanwrtyd
Merch
Strumble Head
Nevern
Newcastle Emlyn
Pencader
Pumpsaint
Epynt Hills
Hay-on-Wye
HEREFORD
R. Wye
St. David's Head
Pentre Ivan
Presili Hills
FISHGUARD
Carn Meini
LLANDOVERY
R. Cothi
Y Pigwn
Brycheiniog
R. Usk
Talgarth
Black Mountains
St. David's
Ramsey I.
PEMBROKESHIRE
Llanboidy
Abergwili
LLANDEILO
Carmarthen Vans
BRECON
Tewkesbury
St. Bride's Bay
HAVERFORDWEST
CARMARTHEN
Carreg Cennin
BRECONSHIRE
Brecon Beacons
GLOUCESTER
Broad Haven
Whitland
St Clears
Golden Grove
Carmarthenshire
R. Usk
ABERGAVENNY
MILFORD HAVEN
Norbeth
Laugharne
Dehenbarth
Dowlais
Brynmawr
Nantyglo
MONMOUTH
Dale
Kidwelly (Cydweli)
Pontardulais
Hendy
Hirwaun
MERTHYR TYDFIL
Ebbw Vale
Blaenavon
Raglan
Forest of Dean
Lydney
PEMBROKE
Carew
Pembroke Dock
Llanelli
Llangyfelach
Morriston
Loughor
ABERDARE
Rhondda
Abercynon
PONTYPOOL
Tintern Abbey
Llantrisaint
Berkeley
GLOUCESTER-SHIRE
Manorbier
Caldy I.
TENBY
Carmarthen Bay
Neath
Llansamlet
Baglan
Aberavan
Tonypandy
PONTYPRIDD
Senghenyd
Caerwent
Caerleon
Llanwern
CHEPSTOW
Beachley
Aust
SWANSEA
Llangennith
Gower
Ilston
PORT TALBOT
Margam
Coity
Vale of Glamorgan
LLANTRISANT
CAERPHILLY
R. Usk
NEWPORT
BRISTOL
Worms Hd.
Arthur's Stone
Pavyland Caves
GLAMORGANSHIRE
Bridgend
Llandaff
Ely
St. Fagans
CARDIFF
Penarth
BATH
Porthcawl
Ewenni
Llandough
Dinas Powis
R. Severn
R. Avon
Llantwit Major
Llanarfan
BARRY

Bristol Channel

DEVON
Wells
SOMERSET

KEY: ＊ Prehistoric or Roman site   ✠ Church or Abbey   Ⓗ Castle or fort
✗ Battle or siege   ∧∧ Mountain range   County border before 1974
Welsh border before 1974

WALES

Showing places and areas of
historic interest in Wales and
the Welsh Marches that are
— mentioned in the book —

Approximate scale
0   5   10   15   20   25 mls
0   10   20   30   40 kms

MERSEYSIDE
GWYNEDD
CLWYD
CHESHIRE
Shropshire
WALES
POWYS
HEREFORD AND WORCESTER
DYFED
GWENT
GLOS.
GLAMORGAN WEST MID SOUTH
AVON
DEVON
SOMERSET

County boundaries since 1974

CHRONOLOGY OF EVENTS

15,000BC	Paviland Cave burial
c. 6000	Arrival of Neolithic farming communities
c. 3000	Beginning of construction of megalithic cromlechs and stone circles
c. 2000	Blue stones from the Preseli Hills transported to Stonehenge
900	Llyn Fawr hoard
c. 700	Arrival of first Celts in Britain
AD43	Roman invasion of Britain under Emperor Claudius
51	Defeat of Caractacus in Wales
61	Invasion of Anglesey by Suetonius Paulinus, followed by the revolt of the Iceni
72	Conquest of the Silures by Julius Frontinus
74	Conquest of Anglesey by Agricola
c. 350	Fortification of Caerwent
383	Magnus Maximus (Macsen Wledig) leads troops from Wales to invasion of Gaul
410	Rescript of Honorius
423	Allelulia victory of Britons under St Germanus
c. 410	Vortigern
500	Battle of Mount Badon
500–50	St David and the Age of the Saints
547	Death of Maelgwn Gwynedd
602	St Augustine meets leaders of the Celtic Church at Aust
613	Aethelfrith's victory over the Welsh at Chester
634	Death of Cadwallon in battle of Heavenfield
c. 770	Construction of Offa's Dyke
856	Rhodri Fawr, King of Gwynedd, defeats the Vikings
950	Death of Hywel Dda
1052	Gryfydd ap Llywelyn killed
1066	Normans win Battle of Hastings
1067	William the Conqueror installs William Fitzosbern as Earl of Hereford. Norman incursions into Wales begin
1081	William goes on pilgrimage to St David's
1135	Death of Henry I of England

1171	'Strongbow' sails to Ireland from Pembrokeshire
1171	The Lord Rhys holds the first Eisteddfod at Cardigan
1173	Failure, in the Berwyn Mountains, of Henry II's expedition against Owain Gwynedd
1188	Geraldus Cambrensis accompanies Archbishop Baldwin through Wales to preach the Third Crusade
1200	Llywelyn ap Iorwerth (Llywelyn the Great) becomes master of the whole of Gwynedd
1204	Llywelyn pledged to the daughter of King John
1215	Llywelyn's rights recognised in Magna Carta
1240	Death of Llywelyn the Great
1244	Gruffydd ap Llywelyn killed trying to escape from the Tower of London
1247	Unequal Treaty of Woodstock
1255	Llywelyn ap Gruffydd seizes power in Gwynedd
1267	Treaty of Montgomery. Llywelyn acknowledged as Prince of Wales
1277	First Welsh war of Edward I
1282	Second Welsh war of Edward I and death of Llywelyn
1284	Edward I reconstructs administration of Wales by the Statute of Rhuddlan
1294	Revolt of Madog ap Llywelyn
1301	Edward I creates his son, Edward, Prince of Wales
1349	The Black Death reaches Wales
1346	Welsh bowmen serve at Crécy
1399	Richard II arrested by Henry Bolingbroke at Flint Castle
1400	Revolt of Owain Glyn Dŵr (Owen Glendower)
1404	Glyn Dŵr calls an all-Wales parliament to meet at Machynlleth
1408	English re-capture Harlech Castle. Decline of Glyn Dŵr's fortunes
1415	Welsh archers fight with Henry V at Agincourt
1455	First battle of St Alban's. Beginning of the Wars of the Roses

1890	Election of David Lloyd George as MP for Carnarvon Boroughs
1898	Formation of the South Wales Miners Federation
1900	Kier Hardie elected as the junior member for Merthyr
1908	Lloyd George becomes Chancellor of the Exchequer
1911	Investiture of the Prince of Wales at Caernarfon Castle
1914–18	First World War
1916	Lloyd George becomes Prime Minister
1925	Foundation of Plaid Cymru – the Welsh nationalist party
1926	Welsh miners stay out after the collapse of the General Strike
1930	Deepening depresssion in the South Wales coalfield
1936	Saunders Lewis and members of Plaid Cymru burn a building at the RAF bombing station at Penrhos in Lleyn
1939–45	Second World War
1962	Formation of Cymdeithas yr Iaith Gymraeg – The Welsh Language Society
1964	James Griffiths becomes the first Secretary of State for Wales
1966	Gwynfor Evans becomes first Plaid Cymru MP
1973	Creation of the new county system
1979	Wales voted to reject devolution

Introduction

The astonishing thing about the history of Wales is that it can be written at all. The very existence of this small country, tucked away on the western seaboard of the main island of Britain, can come as a complete surprise to many of the visitors who pour over the border for holidays in summer. Within seventy miles of vast English conurbations like Birmingham, Liverpool and Manchester, they can find themselves sitting in an inn in which every person around them is speaking a foreign language and has radically different traditions in politics and religion. The Welsh even sing, with impressive harmonic power, an entirely different national anthem.

How has this miracle occurred? For miracle it undoubtedly is. All History's cards seem to have been stacked against the survival of Wales as a separate entity. Again and again, the little country seemed about to be overwhelmed and absorbed by its powerful neighbour, England. For over four hundred years Wales has, by law, been part — and perhaps the least vocal and appreciated part — of that astonishingly successful amalgam of races (English, Scots, Northern Irish and Welsh) which we call Great Britain. By 1542, Wales had been incorporated into England by Acts of Parliament for all official purposes. We have to plunge back seven hundred years into the mists of medieval history before we find a part of Wales which was self-governing. After Llywelyn ap Gruffydd had been killed near Builth on that fateful December day in 1282, Edward I proceeded to stamp out the last embers of Welsh independence.

Wales, today, has no separate parliament, no official currency, no customs barriers on the borders, none of the outward trappings of nationhood as understood in the modern world. There seemed, at one time, to be complete justification for the notorious entry in one of the early editions of the *Encyclopedia Britannica* — 'For Wales *see* England'.

Yet Wales steadfastly refused to disappear politely from the map. If Welsh history has one underlying theme, that theme is surely survival. An old prophecy, none the worse for being written, like all good prophecies, after the event, described the fate in store for the old Celtic inhabitants of Britain:

> Their Lord will they praise,
> Their speech they will keep,
> Their land they will lose,
> Except Wild Wales.

Even after its official incorporation into England, Wales continued to exercise a surprising, if underground, influence on affairs in its bigger neighbour. Many of the archers who won Crécy and Agincourt came from Gwent and Glamorgan, the original home of the long bow; the private armies of the powerful barons of the Welsh Marches often turned the scale in the battles of the Wars of the Roses; and with the Tudors, Wales actually supplied one of the most successful dynasties ever to occupy the English throne. During the Civil War, Wales was the 'nursery of the King's infantry'. Even in recent years the secret influence of Wales has continued. Historians are still assessing the effect of the eruption of that extraordinary political volcano, David Lloyd George, on the life of Britain.

Today, as the tide of nationalist feeling rises in other parts of these islands, Wales has understandably begun to lay a new emphasis on its separate nationhood. Welsh men and women are taking an increasing interest in their past history, searching its pages for inspiration in facing the uncertainties of the future. Summer visitors also are showing a new desire to discover the story that lies behind the cromlechs, castles and chapels that litter the Welsh landscape. More specifically, viewers of television news bulletins may ask themselves what motives lead obviously high-minded young men to burn second homes in remote Welsh valleys. And what memories of the past have left their mark on the policies of Plaid Cymru, the Welsh Nationalist Party?

All this has led to a new interest in Welsh history, a new feeling of its relevance to contemporary life in Britain. It encouraged HTV to launch their television 'History of Wales'. The programmes were broadcast in thirteen episodes, not only in the HTV area of Wales and the West but also in the general network of Channel Four. This book was designed as a companion to the series, for the television image is powerful but transient. The printed page can fix it in the memory and act as a springboard for a wider exploration of the subject. Television and print are thus useful, even necessary, partners in presenting a popular history of Wales to a popular mass audience.

I was the co-presenter of the series with the distinguished Welsh historian, Professor Gwyn Williams of the University College of Cardiff. Let me say, straight away, that although I have taken a life-long interest in the history of my native land, I make no pretensions to being an expert. Throughout the presentation of the series, I leant heavily on the knowledge and advice, not only of Professor Williams but also of a host of other scholars in the field. Over the last fifty years the colleges of the University of Wales have produced a succession of brilliant historians who, between them, have revolutionised the study and writing of Welsh history. As a result, Welsh history has now been given its proper place in the schools of Wales; but I suspect that no such revolution has taken place in the schools of the rest of Britain. In our television series we had therefore to assume that most of our viewers would be unfamiliar with much of the basic framework of our subject. We had to take the risk of underlining the obvious. This volume is conceived in the same spirit. Its modest purpose is to excite the interest and stir the imagination of the man or woman who is coming to Welsh history for the first time.

I must confess that, as I am not a Marxist, my own view of History may seem a little conservative in these vociferous and progressive days. Professor Elton began his investigation of the Purpose of History with these eloquent words: 'The future is dark, the present burdensome; only the past, dead and finished, bears contemplation. Those who look upon it have survived it: they are its product and its victors.' But victors should be compassionate and understanding. It is possible to write a history of Wales – and, indeed, some have been written – in the spirit of a prosecuting counsel arraigning the culprits at the bar of History. There is no lack of candidates for the dock, from Edward I to the Elizabethan gentry and the Merthyr iron masters. The heroes depend on your own point of view. No one has yet succeeded in writing history with a God-like impartial judgment. However hard I may try, I am bound to see the march of events from a Welsh point of view. I am also old-fashioned enough to feel that personalities are still important in relating the story of Wales. I do not deny that there are deeper factors at work that ultimately shape the course of events. The very geological structure of the country has moulded its agriculture and its industry. Over everything looms the all-powerful presence of an ambitious England on the very border. Factors like these set the stage, but the actors also have some influence on the play. Would the Russian revolution have taken the course it did without being stamped with the iron personality of Lenin? Would there have been a rising in Wales at the beginning of the fifteenth century without the 'charisma' of Owain Glyn Dŵr?

Professional historians must avoid such speculation. They are dangerously close to the despised Cleopatra's Nose theory of History – the suggestion that the whole course of events would have been different if Cleopatra had been a long-nosed frump, incapable of enchanting Antony into believing that the Roman world was well lost for love. But in the story of small nations chance can sometimes play a decisive part. Who could have forecast the astonishing rise of the Tudors, or the advent of a Lloyd George?

Yet a continuity does run through Welsh history. In his stimulating book on the quest for the Welsh identity, Emyr Humphries defines it as the Taliesin Tradition – an indestructible feeling for the past as expressed in the survival of a poetic tradition that goes back unbroken to the sixth century. I feel with Emyr Humphries that our present conduct, the way we think and feel about the changing world around us, is profoundly influenced by what we know – or think we know – about the past. We neglect the study of History at our peril, but I do not think that the Past offers an infallible blue-print for the Future. History always holds unpleasant surprises for the prophets. For a thousand years the Welsh bards confidently expected the return of a new Arthur. Has he yet arrived?

Still, even these dreams are an essential part of the history of Wales. A small nation, even more than a big, powerful one, has need of its myths. I have therefore dwelt at some length on the origin of the Celts and on the Dark Ages. Out of this crucible came the 'mystique' of the modern Welsh nation – the feeling that they are different, a special group with its own right to nationhood. I return, in the end, to the modest aim of this book as a companion for the viewers to the HTV series on Welsh history. I hope it will help to fix the visual images and encourage the viewer to look with a greater interest at the complex and colourful tapestry of the history of Wales.

I must express my thanks to all who made the television series possible: to Ron Wordley, the managing director of HTV, who had the courage to back the project with generous finance; to Geraint Talfan Davies of HTV who guided it through all difficulties; to Professor Gwyn Williams, once again, for his endless patience with my somewhat idiosyncratic views; to Colin Voisey of HTV and Anne Jones for help with the illustrations; above all to my producer, Colin Thomas, who not only organised the complex schedule of film shooting but made visual sense of many of my more sweeping generalisations, and brought to each programme his own special insight into the history of Wales. His team worked with equal enthusiasm and I am especially grateful to cameraman Peter Thornton; sound recordist, Paul Gaydon; Medwen Roberts, researcher; Margaret Griffiths, production assistant; and Terry Elgar, film editor. My gratitude also goes to my wife who helped me in my research and prepared the index.

Finally, I owe a special debt to Alan Brooke, of Michael Joseph, for the way he has been so understanding about the delays inseparable in a work of this sort, and to Jenny Dereham and Clare Coney, again of Michael Joseph, whose skill and patience saw it successfully through the press.

Wynford Vaughan-Thomas
Fishguard, 1984.

Note   The place names in Welsh history present a slight problem to a writer who is aiming to interest a reader unfamiliar with Wales. The spelling on the early Ordnance Surveys left a lot to be desired. In recent years it has been corrected under the advice of scholars, and the approved Welsh spelling now appears not only on maps but on road signs. But the newcomer to Welsh history might still be puzzled by some of the changes. For example, he might not recognise Kidwelly under its correct Welsh form of Cydweli. I have therefore adopted the change where it is easily recognisable – Conwy for Conway – and retained the old anglicised form where the correct Welsh form may be confusing – Carmarthen not Caerfyrddyn. In general, I have accepted most names as they now appear on the latest edition of the Ordnance Survey.

There is a second problem. In the '70s the whole of the Welsh county system was re-organised, ostensibly in the name of economy and administrative tidiness, but both propositions may be of doubtful validity. The whole business has certainly caused problems for historians. The old counties were thrown together in shot-gun marriages which ignored the loyalties and interests built up through hundreds of years. To confuse matters still further, the administrators annexed the names of some of the ancient principalities of Wales and extended them into areas that they never covered in history. Thus Dyfed, which covered the area which later became Pembrokeshire under the Acts of Union, was now linked with Cardiganshire and Carmarthenshire. The old kingdom of Powys was resurrected in name to embrace the counties of Radnorshire, Montgomeryshire and Breconshire. Denbigh and Flint were joined to each other in a brand-new county called Clwyd. Gwynedd has more validity: the old counties of Anglesey, Merioneth and Carnarvonshire, now united in the larger county of Gwynedd, had all been created by Edward I, when he conquered Llywelyn the Last's principality of Gwynedd. Gwent, too, has strong roots in history. There had been an ancient kingdom of Gwent whose boundaries had roughly coincided with the old county of Monmouthshire created by the Act of Union. Gwent for Monmouthshire offends no one in the area. The strangest case of all was the old county of Glamorgan. There was an ancient kingdom of Glamorgan which disappeared with the advent of the Normans. But in the new re-organisation this convenient county, with a long tradition of unity, was divided into three – West, Mid and South Glamorgan! No one has yet explained how this makes for more efficient administration, and it certainly ensures a more puzzling history. I have retained the old names of the counties where it makes for clarity and allows the reader to be more precise in placing a name on the map.

Finally, a short word on Welsh orthography. It eases problems when you remember the 'w' is a vowel representing the sound of double 'o', and that 'y' is also a vowel, pronounced as 'er', or sometimes as 'e'.

1

Out of the Mists

Where should we ring up the curtain on the eventful drama of Man, as played out on that small but beautiful patch of the Earth's surface we now call Wales? I have chosen to begin our story at the foot of a precipitous cliff-face in West Glamorgan. The south coast of the Gower peninsula stretches westwards for sixteen miles from the industrial port of Swansea, in a splendid succession of golden sands and limestone crags, until they reach their impressive climax at Paviland. Here, below the 200-foot plunge of Yellow Top, is the well-hidden cave of Goat's Hole. It can be reached for a few hours at low tide by scrambling over the uncovered rocks, but when the tide rises the entrance can only be gained by a difficult traverse over the rock face with the waves roaring below.

Whenever I set out on that traverse I feel that, somehow, it symbolises the difficulties that beset Welsh historians, seeking to reach certainty about so many obscure parts of our national story. The local accounts of the traverse are inaccurate and misleading. On some sections the unwary can easily slip, and the main objective always seems to be hidden around a perpendicular corner. When at last Goat's Hole is reached, it still holds dark corners and inaccessible passages.

Yet, in 1824, a remarkable man made his way across the difficult cliff-face to this inhospitable cleft in the rocks. Dean Buckland was already famous as Oxford's

Opposite St David – an idealised portrait in St David's Cathedral

Below Goat's Hole, Paviland, where Dean Buckland discovered the so-called 'Red Lady' in 1821

first Professor of Geology when he came to excavate the contents of the cave at Paviland. He dug carefully, indeed more carefully than many archaeologists since his day, and he had his reward. He uncovered a headless skeleton, its bones daubed with red ochre and with a necklace of animal teeth.

It was the first find of its sort in Britain and it created not only a sensation but a problem. For the human bones had been found in association with those of animals long extinct in this country – hyaena, mammoth and woolly rhinoceros. Buckland was in a fearful quandary. He was a respected dean in the Church of England and naturally accepted the chronology of Archbishop Ussher who had used the narrative of the Creation in the Bible to maintain that God had brought the world into being in 4004BC. A successor, Dr Lightfoot, used Ussher's calculations to be even more precise and narrowed down the creation of Adam to 9 am on 23 October of the same year. Yet here at Paviland, before Buckland's very eyes, were the remains of animals which had not previously been known to exist in Britain. In 1823, only a year before this discovery, Buckland had published his monumental work, *Reliquiae Diluvianae, or Observations on the Organic Remains Contained in Caves, Fissures and Diluvial Gravels, and on other Geological Phenomena Attesting the Action of Universal Deluge.* In view of his published work, Buckland had no option but to conclude that the animal bones had been swept into Goat's Hole by Noah's Flood, where they had come to rest with a human skeleton which he thought was that of a woman, probably a priestess of the Romano-British period. 'The Red Lady' of Paviland hit the headlines!

It is easy to chuckle at Buckland at this distance of time, and to smile when, nearly a hundred years later, Professor Sollas proved that the 'Red Lady' was no lady at all, but the remains of a youth of the Cro-Magnon race, the first representatives of modern man as distinct from the parallel type of the Neanderthal. He had obviously been buried, with some ceremony, not in Romano-British times but well over 15,000 years ago.

Every archaeologist, and certainly every historian, profits by the mistakes of his predecessors. But what cannot change, even with the most radical revision of accepted ideas, is the emotion and sympathy with which we contemplate those sparse and pathetic remains at Paviland that have come down to us so haphazardly through the long ages. Did that little band of hunters in Goat's Hole cover the young man's bones with red ochre in the moving hope of giving him some life after death? Were his small possessions placed besides him in order to comfort him in his journey towards the unknown? We can only speculate, but we feel that we are in the presence of fellow human beings – the first in Wales with whom we can sense some affinity, whose thoughts we think we too can understand.

I have been tempted to call the youth from Paviland our first Welshman, but this is a pardonable exaggeration. It will be another fifteen thousand years at least before the Celts, the ancestors of the modern Welshmen, tread the soft turf on Yellow Top above Goat's Hole. We cannot know what tongue the young man spoke or to what sort of social organisation he belonged. We can only say that he was one of a tiny group of hunters who appeared in what we now call Wales round about 15,000BC, following the vast herds of game that roamed the tundras left behind by the melting glaciers. We cannot even say that the Paviland hunters were the first humans or hominids who set foot on Cambrian soil. An odd tooth, a few heavy stone tools, testify the presence, in some interglacial periods, of modern man's rival, *Homo neanderthalensis*. But whoever they were, those Paviland hunters were pathetically few in number. They were a mere handful of adventurers into a wilderness where the last glaciers of the final Ice Age were slowly retreating.

Far to the south of them, in caves on the Dordogne in France or at Altamira in Spain, their contemporaries were creating the first great art in the world, the marvellous animal paintings in the inner recesses of Lascaux or Les Trois Frères. The men of Paviland had the same motives for painting as the hunters of France and Spain. Could similar paintings be discovered in the bone caves of Gower or the rest of Wales? Excitement ran high in 1912 when strange cross-markings were noticed in the dramatic cavern of Bacon Hole, again on the south coast of Gower. Could these marks be the representation of a net or a trap for big game? The greatest contemporary authority, the Abbé Breuil, was summoned from France. He carefully examined the marks and uttered a qualified, 'Yes, they could be.' Welsh archaeologists were delighted. They put up an iron grille in the depths of the cave to protect this proof that Upper Palaeozoic man was as talented in Wales as he was in France. Alas, as the years passed, the marks slowly changed shape. They were natural oozings of iron oxide from the rocks. Wales had lost its chance of producing another Lascaux. The iron grille is now rusting and broken, a fading witness to the first, but not the last, illusion about the history of Wales.

Long thousands of years pass after that strange burial at Goat's Hole before we come to the next dramatic change in life as lived in Wales. During this slow passage of time, the landscape of the country took a shape we could roughly recognise if we looked upon it with the eyes of today. The climate improved and became warmer. The great ice-sheets melted. The smaller glaciers retreated into the rocky hollows they had carved in the high hills, and then disappeared. The swollen streams cut deeply into the boulder-clay that the ice had left plastered over the countryside. The salt waters, no longer locked up in the great ice-sheets, returned over the lowlands of the Bristol Channel and Cardigan Bay. The outline of the present coast appeared and the trees started to reclothe the hillsides. The waters also returned to create the North Sea, and cut the English Channel to separate Britain from the Continent.

The tide must have run furiously through that newly-formed passage through the chalk, yet the next settlers who followed the hunters to the westward edge of Europe dared the crossing, then spread out over the country and eventually came to Wales. We are in the presence of the world's first farmers, masters of a new technique that would eventually alter the whole face of the land. That great leap forward in the way man fed himself, which archaeologists rightly call the Neolithic Revolution, had at last come to Britain.

In truth, it had already been many thousands of years on the way. Somewhere in the Middle East men first learnt to cultivate and not merely collect the early forms of wheat and other grains, and domesticate animals. We know that in Palestine crops were being harvested with stone sickles around 10,000BC. By 7000BC the new farming technique had spread into Anatolia, then slowly westwards through Greece and the Mediterranean and up the valley of the Danube. When the farmers reached the more heavily forested and northerly lands of Europe, they had to make clearings in the woods with their stone axes – for metal smelting was not yet on the horizon – and burn out the stumps to fertilise the soil. They moved on when the soil was exhausted. By the fifth millennium the Neolithic Revolution had reached Britain. Curiously enough the earliest evidence for the presence of the new farmers comes from the most westerly section of these islands, Ireland. Carbon dating of materials from the settlement at Ballymagally, Co. Tyrone, take us back to 4580BC, and if the new technique had reached Ireland by that date it must also have reached Wales.

As the brave new farmers pioneer their small settlements in the wilderness, we can look closer at the Promised Land that lay virgin before them. These adventurous agriculturists, taming the wilderness during the centuries ahead, will alter the surface appearance of the land of Wales, but its main features, based on geology, will perforce remain unaltered and will continue to influence the course of Welsh history down to our own day. Wales, as all Welshmen are proud of proclaiming in song and verse, is a land of mountains and therefore, all through history, a natural stronghold into which a threatened people can withdraw and safely rebuild its forces. But this stronghold is not quite so strong as it seems. True, there are great tracts of high ground like Snowdonia, the Berwyn Mountains and the wilds of Plynlimon which have always remained hostile to the farmer and where the soil is rocky and the summits bog-laden.

In 1188, the celebrated Geraldus Cambrensis, Gerald the Welshman, made a tour through his native land with Archbishop Baldwin to preach the Third Crusade. He gives a vivid description of the countryside of Merioneth, which must have looked the same to the first Neolithic settlers who attempted to penetrate its fastnesses.

'The territory of Cynan,' says Gerald, 'and especially Merioneth is the roughest and rudest of all the Welsh districts. The mountains are very high, with narrow ridges and a great number of very sharp peaks, all jumbled together in confusion. If the shepherds who shout together and exchange comments from these lofty summits should ever decide to meet, it would take them almost the whole day to climb up and down again.'

But into these mountain strongholds great river valleys, like those of the Dee, the Severn, the Wye and the Usk, cut deep trenches which could be followed by invaders from the midland plains of England. The Welsh national redoubt has its weak points. The Southern Uplands of Scotland are a far more effective barrier since they run east to west across the narrow neck of land joining the two countries. They helped to keep Scotland independent long after Wales had been conquered. In addition to the rivers, there are the coastal plains of Wales, narrow in the north but wide in the south where they outflank the mountains. The lands of Gwent and Glamorgan, with the Vale of the Tywi and Pembrokeshire beyond, were comparatively low-lying and offered good, workable soil in many places. To the first Neolithic farmers, as to many subsequent arrivals, certain areas of Wales were by no means unattractive to the enterprising agriculturist.

Those early farmers were certainly enterprising. Their hunting predecessors may have already made a start in cutting back the forest to make clearings for game, and many of the larger animals – the lion, the mammoth, the woolly rhinoceros – had disappeared long before the agriculturalists arrived with their flocks of sheep and goats. The bear may have lingered on into Roman times and the wild boar still later into the early Middle Ages. Tradition maintains that the last wolf was killed in Wales when the Tudors were on the throne. But there were still plenty of dangers and difficulties facing those first Neolithic farmers as they prepared to penetrate the tangled oak thickets that covered places like the Tywi valley or plough the rocky soil of Lleyn. They had only stone tools to help them. They were the heroes who tamed the Welsh wilderness.

In Wales, one of the earliest settlements they created with such effort has been uncovered on the knoll of Clegyr Boia in Dyfed, within sight of the tower of the present cathedral of St David's. Here a small farming community lived in stone huts roofed with thatch, surrounded by their flocks and scratching a living from the virgin soil. Life was still hard by modern standards but we have come a long way from those Paviland hunters, crouching around their fire in a damp cave, only ten thousand years before. Can we get a fuller picture of the way man now organised his society? Are we, at last, entering the domain of the historian? Not yet. No writing, no recorded voice reaches us across the vast gulf of the past. The historian must perforce stand aside for the moment. The archaeologist alone can give us some of the answers, moving like a highly trained detective among the few clues to their presence left behind by the hardy Neolithic pioneers.

The story the archaeologists have to tell is fascinating, but it is also ever-changing as the experts continue to apply increasingly elaborate scientific techniques to the frail and scattered relics left behind by our remote predecessors. They show us how those early societies of primitive pastoralists became steadily more elaborate and better organised for the production of a food surplus.

It was these Neolithic farmers who brought Britain its first architecture. As they grew in wealth and power they started to bury their dead – or perhaps their more important dead – with impressive ceremony. They developed the technique of constructing burial chambers out of massive, undressed boulders – hence the term 'megalith' or 'big stone'. They covered the burial chambers with vast heaps of earth or stone to form a 'barrow'. Over the long passage of time, the mounds of earth and stone have been worn away leaving the great stones open to the sky to form a 'cromlech'.

These massive boulders, heaped one on to the other or tumbled in ruin among the heather, are the most compelling evidence we have of the achievements of our remote predecessors in Wales. Many of them stand in deeply impressive sur-

Top Pentre Ifan cromlech, on the slopes of the Preseli Hills, Dyfed

Above right The carved stones in the burial chamber of Barclodiad-y-Gawres, Anglesey

Above left The giant capstone of Arthur's Stone on the ridge of Cefn Bryn in Gower

Opposite page The stone circle on Penmaenmawr, Gwynedd

roundings. Carrig Samson, in Pembrokeshire, has the great sea-cliffs of Strumble Head as a background. Pentre Ifan is outlined against the moors of the Preseli Hills. The mound over the cromlech of Barclodiad-y-Gawres on the coast of Anglesey has been restored and you can grope your way down the dark passage to the burial chamber past great stones marked with mysterious carvings. These strange monuments have excited the awe and stirred the speculation of people through the centuries.

To the Welsh country folk of later years, it seemed that many of these structures could only have been built by giants. Barclodiad-y-Gawres means the Apronful of the Giantess, who must have emptied these stones from her apron. If they were not built by giants, then they must have been put up by King Arthur. Such a cromlech is Arthur's Stone on the ridge of Cefn Bryn in Gower, which was rumoured to go down to drink the waters of the Loughor River at midnight on Midsummer's Eve. In the eighteenth century speculation ran even wilder, and, as we shall see, led to a curious mix-up of later Celtic druidism with these far earlier megalithic structures; a concept which bedevilled Welsh history through the nineteenth century and is not extinct in certain quarters even today.

Side by side with the tombs, and rivalling them in mystery, stand the stone circles, represented in Wales by a series of strange rings of grey boulders scattered among the hills. The most impressive is, perhaps, the circle on the moors behind Penmaenmawr in north Wales. What were they? Temples, tribal gathering places, or even astronomical observatories, constructed according to the measurement of the 'megalithic yard'? We cannot tell with certainty. Writing in Wales is still over three thousand years in the future. No amount of scientific archeology can give us those human details that the historian longs to know – the language the builders spoke, the names of their great chiefs, what were the gods they invoked as they dragged the huge stones into place with back-breaking labour. We can only look at the tools they left behind and note that at last stone gave way to the far more flexible, practical and powerful material, bronze.

Copper smelting, like the art of farming, was first developed in the Middle

East, and may have been brought to Britain by the enterprising Beaker Folk, so-called from the characteristic shape of their pottery. They can also be distinguished from the older inhabitants by the shape of their skulls. These were round, and the Beaker Folk built round barrows. The Bronze Age brought a massive reconstruction in Neolithic society. Bronze spears and swords are far more efficient than stone axes when it comes to empire building.

In the barrows, avenues and stone circles of the chalk downs of Wiltshire and further west, we have impressive evidence of the great men of Wessex around 1470BC. These lords must have had command over a great area of southern Britain and certainly over its trade routes. The great circle of Stonehenge now reached its impressive climax, and it is a curious and intriguing fact that Wales had already played some part in the early construction of this circle, the finest megalithic monument in Europe. In 1922, the Welsh geologist, Dr H. H. Thomas, proved beyond doubt that the so-called Blue Stones, in the inner circle, were of a spotted dolorite which could only be matched by stones from the outcrops around Carn Meini on the lonely Preseli Hills of north Pembrokeshire.

They must have possessed some impressive religious significance for the lords of Neolithic society to go to the vast labour of transporting them the 135 miles – as the crow flies – from far-off west Wales to the chalk downs of Wiltshire. All this before the advent of the wheel. They must have been dragged to the shores of Milford Haven, floated on rafts along the Bristol Channel and then up the Avon, and finally dragged into position at Stonehenge. They had already been standing there for hundreds of years when the Wessex culture reached its climax.

Those Wessex overlords could now be buried with a host of rich possessions, with gold glittering among the earth of their barrows. Their trade extended from

Below left Stonehenge, showing one of the blue stones from Preseli in Wales standing before a giant sarsen trilithon

Below right The outcrop of Carn Meini in the Preseli Hill, the source of the blue stones of Stonehenge

Scandinavia to the Mediterranean. They wore daggers from Mycenae and their women took pride in their beautiful amber beads from the far north. Irish gold came into the hands of the Wessex princes to be fashioned into beautiful objects by native Wessex craftsmen, and the soil of Wales has yielded one of the finest examples of the British goldsmith's art. This is the beautiful Mold pectoral, a short cape-like breastplate of sheet gold leaf. The story of its discovery is as strange as any in the history of archaeology. It is related in 'Archaeologia' of 1836.

An elderly lady had gone to a tavern in Mold, Clwyd to escort her husband home, who was apparently the worse for wear. As they stumbled along, the lady, who was completely sober, and who clearly knew nothing about archaeological matters, saw what she said was a spectre cross the road before her and disappear into a nearby mound. This eerie vision was that of a very tall man dressed in a coat of gold, which 'shone like the sun'. She told the story to Mr John Longford, the very man, says 'Archaeologia', whose workmen drew the treasure out of the prison house.

But by the time the Mold pectoral had been fashioned with such care and skill, the glories of the high Bronze Age in Britain were already starting to fade. The stone circles slowly went out of use, burials were no longer conducted with the old reverence and the pride of the Wessex overlords passed into the shadows. We know that the climate started to change for the worse after 1200BC. Fringe land might become waterlogged and go out of cultivation. There would be increased competition for the still fertile areas. There was thus a steady increase in the number of hill-forts. Dinorben, in Clwyd, is typical. Carbon dating puts its construction around 1200BC and its walls were strongly built of clay, rubble and wooden rafts, in a style which might have been derived from the Continent. Britain, to the men of the last phase of the Bronze Age, must have appeared a less secure, less prosperous place. Great changes were in the air, and they could hardly have been welcome to the people of the old Neolithic stocks, who had held Britain unchallenged for over three thousand years. Neolithic society had remained remarkably undisturbed by violent change from outside over this extraordinarily long period. The Beaker people had certainly arrived and influences continually flowed in from the Continent but, somehow, all these new ideas had taken on a particularly insular pattern. Britain had remained a distinct cultural province.

All this has prompted the speculation, so attractive to earlier archaeologists, that it should be possible – at least in Wales, the one part of mainland Britain uncontaminated by Anglo-Saxon invaders – to trace elements of the original Neolithic stock in the present population. Sir J. E. Lloyd, one of the first and finest of the modern Welsh historians, could still speculate enthusiastically, in his *History of Wales*, published in 1911, that the early Neolithic-race type was 'represented in modern Britain by the short, dark Welshmen of south Wales, possibly its very qualities of soul and mind in the typical collier and "eisteddfodwr", impulsive and wayward but susceptible to the influence of music and religion'. In the same quest for our Neolithic ancestors, bands of energetic students set out from Aberystwyth to measure the heads of the farmers in the fastnesses of Plynlimon in the

The Caergwrle bowl, a superb relic of the Bronze Age in Wales

hope that the shape of their skulls – brachycephalic or otherwise – would prove that the direct descendants of our first farmers were still alive and well in the grassy wilderness of central Wales.

Skull measurement, however, was frowned upon by modern scientific archaeologists. Plynlimon Man remains lost and unproven among his hills! In any case, the old Neolithic order was to be violently challenged in the last millennium BC, and to sense the nature of that challenge we go to a lake in south Wales, set in a circle of cliffs, and, until recent times, a remote and rarely visited spot.

Today you can drive to Llyn Fawr over an exciting mountain road that climbs out of the industrial Rhondda Valley to a pass that approaches the 2000-foot mark. From the summit a great view is spread before you. All along the skyline runs an impressive range of Old Red Sandstone summits that culminate in the Brecon Beacons. Immediately below you is a dark tarn which still looks mysterious and forbidding, in spite of the proximity of the modern road and the pines of the Forestry Commission. In 1912 the tarn was being drained, prior to its use as a reservoir. As the water level sank a strange pile of objects came into view. The Llyn Fawr hoard is now on display in the National Museum of Wales at Cardiff, and a remarkable collection it is. There are bronze objects a-plenty, including great cauldrons, bronze chisels and axes. Even more interesting were parts of horse harnesses in bronze. But the greatest surprise of all was three objects – part of a sword, a sickle and a spearhead. Commonplace things enough to find in hoards such as that of Llyn Fawr. But there was one most uncommon thing about them. They were fashioned from a new metal, iron; and iron would mark the end of the old life as lived in Britain. We do not know who flung the hoard into the cold waters of Llyn Fawr. They could have been traders, or robbers, or even men from a little settlement nearby, although it is hard to think of agriculturalists at work in such a bleak spot. Another possibility presents itself: could the men of the Llyn Fawr hoard have been the forerunners of the next wave of settlers to arrive in Britain, the Men of Iron *par excellence*, the Celts?

2

Celts and Romans

Modern Welsh-speaking Welshmen are proud to call themselves Celts. They speak a variety of the old Celtic tongues and have a special affinity with their Celtic neighbours in Ireland and Brittany. They feel that they have inherited a whole series of characteristics from their remote Celtic ancestors – from eloquence to a soaring imagination – which mark them off from the sober, matter-of-fact English on their border. For them, the arrival of the Celts in Britain is the one basic, unalterable fact in Welsh history. Without the Celts there would have been no Wales.

In view of their vital importance in the mystique of the Welshmen of today, we must now take a long, cool look at the Celts. What do we really know about them? Where did they come from and when and how did they enter Britain? Even a decade ago, it would have been possible to give a confident answer to these questions. The Celts, claimed the experts, were a people formed in Europe around 1200BC. By 700BC they had already started to move out and take possession of much of Western Europe. By 500BC they had entered Britain. They came in a series of conquering waves, for they were a race of warrior aristocrats who were already in possession of superior weapons made of the new metal, iron. The Celts are the central figures in the Iron Age of these islands. The earlier waves reached Ireland, where they naturally retained an earlier form of the Celtic language, the Goidelic. Successive waves occupied the mainland, where the language became simplified into Brythonic, from which modern Welsh is descended. By the first century BC, a new wave of invaders, the Belgae, had become firmly established in south-east Britain, who had strong links with the Belgae of north-eastern France. With them we see the final flowering of that splendid Celtic art style that archaeologists associated with the name of La Tène. The stage is set for the arrival of the Romans and the next dramatic change in the life and politics of Celtic Britain.

This summary must, of necessity, be perfunctory, but it contains the one basic assumption of the long-established picture of the Celts – that they came to Britain in a series of invasions of varying strength and continuity. However, like so many other long-accepted views of pre-historians, this has been strongly disputed by the 'new archaeology'. The 'Invasion Thesis' seems no longer tenable. The method by which Britain became Celtic was obviously extremely complex. The 'Waves of Invasion Theory' simply will not do. Even the dates of the Celts' spread are now extremely flexible – some scholars going so far as to suggest that the Beaker

Above The flowing curves of Celtic Art on the shield found in the Thames at Battersea

Opposite The Celtic cult of the horse is expressed in the White Horse, cut in the chalk at Uffington

Folk were the first Celts. As the non-specialist picks his way among the learned and complicated arguments of the experts, he may be forgiven if he sees his solid Celts disappearing into a form of speech and an art style!

There is, however, a ray of hope on the horizon. With the Celts, for the first time in our story of Wales, the written words come to the aid of the excavator's spade. As the Celts embarked on their vigorous expansion they came into contact with the settled world of the Mediterranean. The Greeks and the Romans were compelled to take account of the Celtic newcomers and they have left descriptions of them. The archaeologist will be of vital importance for a long time to come, but from this time his work can be supplemented by evidence from contemporary observers. It is now possible to give names to places, and characters to names. But judgment must be exercised: the written record cannot be treated as infallible. Scholars have to check the sources and the prejudices of a writer as carefully as an archaeologist examines the artifacts that turn up in the trenches of his 'dig'. But the written word undoubtedly adds a new excitement to history. It makes the dry bones live! It has always been thrilling to look at the first map of the world as known to the ancients, the Ptolemy map produced in Alexandria in the second century BC, and to see that it includes an approximate outline of the coast of Wales. The far-off land on the edge of the world was beginning to emerge from the mists!

For all that, we must still turn to the archaeologists for our picture of the early Celts. They show us that the peoples we loosely call Celtic had their origin in the basin of the upper Danube, which includes modern Bohemia, parts of Hungary, Austria and Bavaria. This had always been a fecund crucible in the development of European culture, for it lay open to formative influences from many directions, not only from the older civilisations of the Middle East but also from the distant steppes of Russia. Around 1200BC these wide plains north of the Black Sea and the Caucasus nutured tribal movements that brought chaos to the old, settled world. The brilliant culture of Mycenae and Crete collapsed under barbarian pressure. The invaders smashed the empire of the Hittites in Anatolia and may thus have aided the spread of the Hittite monopoly of iron working into Central Europe. Out of this welter of races and cultures on the move the Celts were born.

Archaeologists had already distinguished the activities of a Bronze Age people in the upper Danube basin who buried their dead in urns. The Urnfield people were a warrior race, builders of hill-forts and delighting in battle. Pre-historians have labelled them 'proto-Celts'. In the chaos of end-of-Bronze-Age Europe, they may have come under the influence of the superb horsemen of the steppes, for when the dust raised by these vast folk movements settles, we see a new face of things in the Celtic homelands. At Hallstatt, near Salzburg in Austria, archaeologists uncovered a cemetery near ancient salt mines, which revealed a people who had now added iron to their economy. Iron tools made forest clearance more effective and warfare more deadly. Hallstatt men, under influence from the steppes, were also masters of the horse. The Celtic world had found its formula for expansion. The horse and iron were a winning combination, hard to beat in the hands of a people clearly conscious of a new power, a new vitality.

It was not long before the Celts were on the move. By 700BC they had swarmed over north-western Europe. They had a new power base in Burgundy. They had penetrated across France into northern Spain. By 500BC they had entered Britain. We now face the problem of the nature of their arrival. In solving it, we are deprived of the easy key of successive invasions. We have to visualise a steady extension of continental influence throughout Britain over many centuries at the end of which we have a whole country that spoke Celtic languages and shared in the later achievements of Celtic art that came to its climax at La Tène.

The first Celts may have come as traders. Small Hallstatt-type settlements around the coast may have followed. In one case, in east Yorkshire, we have evidence of a warrior people who had emigrated from Champagne, in north-east France. Whatever may have happened in the east and south, the original inhabitants seem

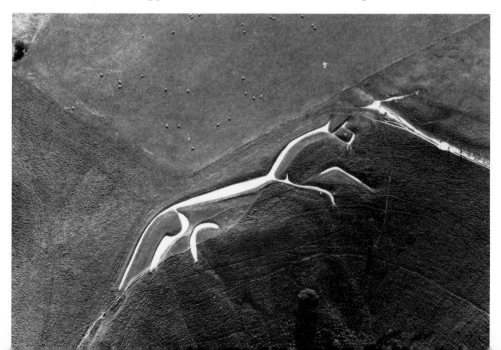

to have survived in some strength in the west and north. The transition from Neolithic and Bronze Age Britain to Celtic Britain was not accompanied by violent, wholescale elimination of the original inhabitants. However, the Celtic warrior class had power and prestige. It was their language that spread steadily among the native population. Modern Welshmen, watching the spread of English and the decline in Welsh speaking before the last war, are only too familiar with the insidious process.

The Celtic language, as it developed among the people of these islands, divided into two main groups. Irish is a Q-Celtic tongue, and due, no doubt, to the isolation of an island, retained several primitive characteristics. In Brythonic, from which modern Welsh is descended, the Q sound has been replaced by P. Welsh is therefore a P-Celtic tongue. Perhaps Brythonic simplified itself under continental influences. We are still in the field of speculation, however. All we can be sure of is that the whole of the British Isles was speaking some variety of Celtic when the Romans finally arrived.

The full splendour of the Celtic achievement was demonstrated by the discoveries at La Tène, on the lake of Neuchâtel in western Switzerland. Here a great heap of remarkable objects had been thrown into the shallows of the lake as an offering to the gods. They were decorated with patterns of great and sensuous beauty. The La Tène style was an individual adaptation of Mediterranean and eastern motives; it was the greatest barbarian contribution to the art treasures of Europe.

So the Celts swagger across the stage of European pre-history, madly brave and reckless, great talkers, great drinkers, possessed of their own brilliant art style and a source of anxiety and admiration to their neighbours. The La Tène aristocrats not only decorated their possessions nobly but had themselves buried with their new war-winning acquisition, the two-horsed chariot. They remind us of those Homeric heroes battling before the walls of Troy.

Wales can supply evidence for one of the darker aspects of our picture of the brave, vigorous, Homeric warrior Celts. In 1943, workmen were extending the runway of the Valley aerodrome in Anglesey over the dried-up bed of Llyn Cerrig Bach. They uncovered a long, linked iron chain. It was so strong that the workmen used it to pull a tractor out of the mud, unaware of what it was. It turned out to be a slave-chain or 'coffle', as the eighteenth-century slave-traders called it. It may have been thrown into the lake as a ritual offering. We cannot banish that slave chain from our minds when we look back, through the mists of history, to the Celts of Wales.

As we look at the strange, intriguing and beautiful objects from the Celtic past in the National Museum of Wales at Cardiff, we feel an irresistible desire to know the men who used and fashioned them, not as museum specimens, but as fellow human beings. We must now turn from the archaeologist to the writers, to the men who were actual contemporaries of the Celts and who set down their impressions of them.

★   ★   ★

Cerrig Samson cromlech,
Dyfed

BELOW The Llyn Fawr in
Mid-Glamorgan, where the
remarkable mixed bronze and
iron hoard was discovered

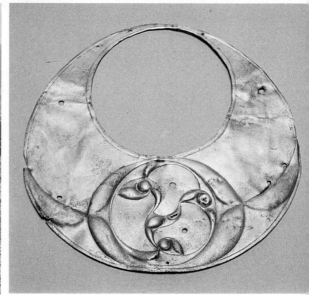

TOP Venta Silurium (Caerwent), a reconstruction by Alan Sorrell

LEFT The Celtic hill-top village of Tre'r Ceiri in North Wales. The Silures in South Wales may have abandoned similar villages to settle in Venta Silurium

ABOVE Golden treasure from the Llyn Cerrig Bach hoard

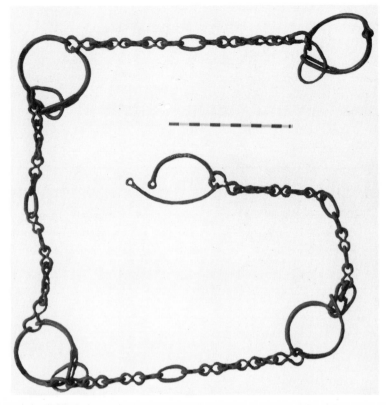

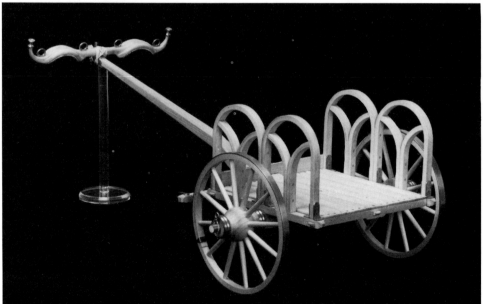

Above The slave chain found at Llyn Cerrig Bach, Anglesey

Below A reconstruction of a Celtic war chariot in the National Museum of Wales

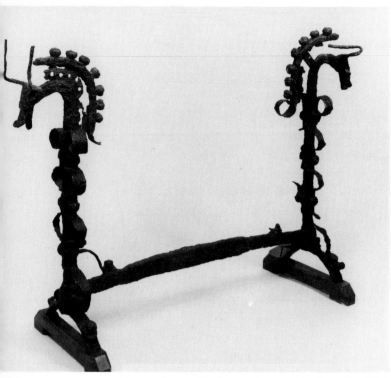

Masterpieces of Celtic craftsmanship found in Wales: the 'fire-dogs' from Betws Garmon and the Tal-y-Llyn plaque

The Celts enter literature when they came into violent contact with the old settled Mediterranean world to the south of them. Celtic war bands had penetrated into Greece and had sacked the sanctuary of Delphi in 270BC. It was the Greeks who gave them the name by which they are known to history – the 'keltoi'. Celtic tribes spilled over the Alps and destroyed the old Etruscan civilisation. In 387BC they threatened the Eternal City, Rome, itself. Livy's account of their terrifying leader, Brennus, may not be factually accurate but it is true to the spirit of the occasion. Brennus demanded his own weight in gold as the city's ransom, and then threw his sword onto his own side of the scales with the contemptuous words, '*Vae Victis*' – 'Woe to the Vanquished!'

In the end, it was the Celts who were the vanquished. Celtic élan went down before Roman discipline. The Romans drove the Celts out of Italy and then destroyed them in their heartland of Gaul, using the same tactics that had made the legions the masters of the Mediterranean world. In the course of this long struggle the Romans came to respect their enemies and were fascinated by their culture and religion. But when we turn to the classical writers, we must remember that they were looking at the Celtic world from the outside and did not always understand what they saw. They sometimes appear as tourists, looking at the curious customs of the natives with a sort of shuddering delight. And it must be admitted that some Celtic customs were very curious indeed!

'The whole race,' says Strabo, 'is madly fond of war, high-spirited and quick to battle.' Some of the warriors stiffened their hair with lime, so that it stuck out like a lion's mane; others came leaping naked into battle, confident that nakedness gave them magical protection. The sight of a Celtic army preparing to charge could strike terror into the most hardened Roman legionary.

Tacitus describes the hesitation of the soldiers of Suetonius Paulinus as they prepared to cross the Menai Strait to invade Anglesey:

> The enemy lined the shore with a dense, armed mass. Among them were black-robed women with dishevelled hair, like Furies brandishing torches. Close by stood Druids, raising their hands to heaven and screaming dreadful curses. This weird spectacle awed the Roman soldiers into a sort of paralysis.

In the end, the formidable Roman discipline prevailed, but the interesting thing about that account is the presence of women in the front line. Clearly the aristocratic Celts held women in high esteem and even welcomed them in a governing role, in a way that would have pleased the modern advocates of Woman's Lib.

The Romans, with their Mediterranean and restrictive attitude towards women, also looked with disapproval on the sexual freedoms permitted by the Celts, although Sulpicius Severus recorded the proud reply of the wife of a Caledonian chief to Severus's wife, Julia. 'We fulfil the demands of nature in a much better way than you do, you Roman women. We consort openly with the best men, while you let yourselves be debauched in secret by the vilest.'

The Romans were on surer ground when they looked with a prim shudder at certain aspects of Celtic religion. There can be no doubt that it involved human sacrifice. Indeed, this offering of victims to the gods may have had its origin in the earliest stages of Neolithic society, when the new farming technique made

The Gundestrup cauldron, which may depict human sacrifice among the Celts

it essential to secure fertility by any means. Greek and Roman legends reflect the inescapable fact that human sacrifice had once been a practice in the now respectable classical societies – a practice that they had firmly banished into the depth of their unconscious. The Roman Senate's decree finally prohibiting human sacrifice was passed as late as 97BC, and the bloodthirsty gladiatorial games were still taking place in the arena in Rome when Tacitus wrote his disgusted description of the sacred groves of Anglesey, destroyed by Suetonius Paulinus:

> The groves devoted to Mona's barbarous superstitions he uprooted. For it was their religion to drench their altars with the blood of prisoners and consult their gods by means of human entrails.

A religion, even if it includes human sacrifice, demands priests to preside over it. So, inevitably, we come to those enigmatic but ever popular characters from our Celtic past, the Druids. From the seventeenth century onwards, antiquarians had a delightful time in reviving and refurbishing the druidic image. And nowhere was this revival of interest in the Druids more popular or more potent than in Wales. Today, the Archdruid, wearing his crown of golden oak-leaves and a golden torc around his neck, leads his white-clad followers of the Gorsedd onto the National Eisteddfod platform, to the applause and approval of the packed pavilion. Of course, everyone knows that they are taking part in a revival, a symbolic pageant which has no direct connection with that long vanished druidic reality. Yet this modern Welsh Gorsedd embodies a legend, a long tradition which is even found in some classical authors and which sees the Druids as the embodiment of wisdom, the possessors of secret, esoteric knowledge and 'natural philosophers' of a high order.

Unfortunately, when we try to pin the Druids down in the accounts given of them in ancient literature, they prove disturbingly elusive. We have a whole string of distinguished names to quote from – Pliny, Lucan, Caesar, Cicero, Diodorus Siculus – but vivid as many of their descriptions may be, they present us with a problem. It seems that a great deal of what they say is second hand, and derives originally from the Greek teacher and Stoic philosopher Posidonius or from an even earlier Greek scholar and ethnographer, Timaeus. The original works of both of these men are lost and we only know of them through references in other writers, but it is clear that Posidonius may have projected something of his own philosophic attitude into his account of the Druids. Caesar was the only one of our authors who had direct and continuous contact with the Celts so we can at least trust his description of the Druids' place in Celtic society.

He shows us a rigid and aristocratic society, with the ruler and his or her associated families on top and only two classes of any account below them – the Knights and the Druids. The common people scarcely feature at all. 'They never venture to act on their own initiative,' says Caesar, 'and are never consulted at all.' The Knights, as Caesar calls them after the Roman pattern, were, no doubt, those proud, warlike nobles, splendid in their La Tène-style finery and riding into battle with reckless bravery. The Druids were equally a class set apart.

They were dignified with the title 'wisest of men', but we do not know the exact nature of that wisdom, for they had a strict rule that no part of their doctrine should be committed to writing. Their pupils had to memorise everything. The Druids were clearly not illiterate, for the Coligny calender, found in Gaul, attests their knowledge of astronomy and calendrical studies. No doubt they were equally interested in medical matters and the law, but the nature of their teaching in spiritual matters is still a subject for occasionally wild speculation. In the total absence of any written accounts from Celtic sources, we have to rely on the odd scraps of gossip picked up by the classical observers, who had their own philosophical axes to grind and tended to see in the lore of the Druids exactly what they, themselves, wanted to see. They tell us of the druidical doctrine of the immortality of the soul, but they leave us in some doubt about the relations of the Druids to the human sacrifices which lay at the heart of Celtic religious observance. Later admirers of the Druids would have these 'wisest of men' distance themselves from such barbaric rites. Professor Stuart Piggott makes a wise and witty comment on this view:

> It is sheer romanticism and a capitulation to the myth of the Noble Savage to imagine that they [the Druids] stood by the sacrifices in duty bound, but with disapproval on their faces and elevated thoughts in their minds.

Altogether a picture somewhat removed from the popular impression of grave,

The eighteenth-century romantic picture of a Druid bore no relation to reality

white-robed and white-bearded sages moving with quiet dignity under the trilithons of Stonehenge, mistletoe in hand! And whatever the scholars and philosophers may have thought or imagined about the Druids, to the hard-headed Roman soldiers and administrators they were simply a confounded nuisance. The imperial authorities were not interested in the cultural and philosophical aspects of druidism. They saw the Druids as the central inspiration of Celtic nationalism. The Emperor Tiberius published a decree against them and Suetonius Paulinus destroyed the sacred groves of Anglesey but modern historians tend to dismiss the idea that the Romans invaded the island to smash the power of the Druids. They deny that, by this time, the Druidic order had any power at all in Celtic society. The poor Druids are thus relegated to a shadowy role, a mere footnote to history. But the Empire had now embarked on the final period of its expansion. With or without Druids, the Celts were to be swept out of the way.

Celtic fire and dash was bound to give way before Roman discipline. The Celts might well lament with some of the native peoples who faced the expansion of the British Empire, 'They have the Legions. We have not!' The legion was a superb military machine. Caesar had used his legions with devastating effect in his final conquest of Gaul. It took the Romans time to absorb the conquest. Nearly forty years passed before they were ready to tackle Britain.

We have a chance to take a quick look at the island scene before Celtic Britain passed under the Roman harrow. We see a country where Roman influence was already well established in the south-east. Here the tribal kings had been drawn into the cultural orbit of Rome. Powerful rulers like Cunobelin of the Cantuvellauni, Shakespeare's Cymbeline, had his own coinage and his *oppida*, or capital, at Camulodunum near Colchester. There was a close connection between his kingdom and the continent. Luxury goods came from Roman Gaul and in return Britain exported grain, slaves, Cornish tin and Irish gold. Roman financiers were well aware of the commercial possibilities of Britain before their invasion was launched.

The tribes of the west and north were obviously not so opulent as their neighbours in the lowland zone, but at least we now know their names in Wales. The Silures held the south-east, modern Gwent and Glamorgan. To the west of them the Demetae occupied Dyfed. Central and north-west Wales was the land of the Ordovices and the Deciangli spread over the present Clwyd and the northern border. No name of any ruler of these tribes has come down to us, although the titles of the princes of the Dubunni, who held the Cotswolds and lower Severn valley, appear on their golden coins, while the reverse carries the characteristic Celtic image of a three-tailed horse. We can, however, assume that the tribes in Wales had the same social structure as Celtic society elsewhere. The ruler would come from a royal family of repute, but the eldest son did not automatically inherit. That was never the Celtic way. The prince would be surrounded by his nobles, who would each have their clientele of lesser folk. The family, in the widest sense of the word, was the social cement that held society together. It was the family

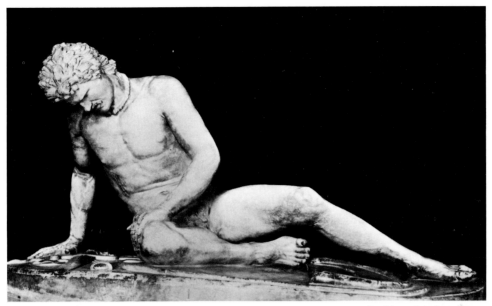

'The Dying Gaul' – the Roman view of the Celtic warrior, going naked into battle

which took responsibility for the conduct of its members before the law. Is it too fanciful to see a faint survival of this obligation in the interest modern Welshmen sometimes take in tracing their family connection back to second cousins twice removed?

So the tribes of Wales, and of the whole of Britain, awaited the arrival of the Romans in arms. This time there can be no question about any 'invasion thesis'. In AD43 the Romans were ready to launch a full-scale attack on the islands of Britannia. They did not underestimate the fighting qualities of the Britons and they made careful preparations. The troops must have felt that they were being ordered to sail across wild waters into a strange country on the very edge of the civilised world. Old soldiers who landed in the reverse direction, in Normandy on D-Day, will share their feelings.

The motives for the invasion were mixed. The new emperor, Claudius, badly needed a spectacular success to establish his prestige with the army, who had put him on the throne, and with the senators of Rome, who would have been glad to see him pushed off it. The existence of an independent Britain, ever ready to receive and aid discontented elements in Gaul, was a threat to the stability of the empire. And there was always the lure of gaining loot on a grand scale.

In AD43, the moment for action had come. The great Cymbeline had died and his sons were squabbling over the inheritance in the usual Celtic way. When the experienced commander, Aulus Platius, landed in Kent with a well-equipped and formidable force of 40,000 men, he was able to push the Britons back over the Medway and the Thames. Then he tactfully paused to allow the emperor to hurry from Rome in time to receive the credit for the storming of Camulodunum.

Claudius stayed in Britain for sixteen short days and then hurried back to Rome to celebrate his triumph. His commemorative inscription still stands in the capital city, with the proud boast that he had 'for the first time reduced trans-oceanic barbarians under the power of the Roman people'.

The trans-oceanic barbarians, however, were not so easily reduced. Some rulers of tribes in southern Britain hastened to come to terms with the new regime, 'following the long established Roman custom,' as Tacitus recorded with his usual irony, 'of employing even kings to make others slaves'. The tribes in Wales gave Tacitus no further opportunity for sardonic epigrams. Caractacus, the defeated leader of the Trinovantes, turned to them after the fall of Camulodunum. His military reputation and his courage impressed the Silures and the Ordovices. With their active help, he kept up British resistance for eight years along the Welsh border. In AD51, however, he risked a battle in a place somewhere in the upper valley of the Severn in the heart of mid-Wales. Inevitably he was defeated. The Romans always won these military set pieces. Caractacus fled for refuge to the Brigantes in the north, and their queen, Cartamandua, promptly handed him over to his enemies. The defeated British leader made a memorable appearance before Claudius and the Roman mob, when he behaved with defiant dignity. The Welsh remembered him with pride under the name of Caradog.

The tribes in Wales remained as defiant as Caractacus. It took the Romans more than twenty more years of hard fighting to subdue them, and the struggle ebbed and flowed with varying fortunes and packed with memorable incidents. In AD61, ten years after the capture of Caractacus, the governor, Suetonius Paulinus, resolved to break all opposition by driving straight into the very heart of the national resistance, the druidical centre in Anglesey. He smashed his way into the island and destroyed the sacred groves, but as if in answer to the Druids' curse, wild revolt broke out behind him in distant East Anglia with the rising of the Iceni, under their formidable leader Boudicca. The Romans came near to losing their control over the whole island. Suetonius saved the situation by desperate courage and bold generalship, but it was many years before the Romans could renew their advance.

North Wales was eventually recovered by Agricola, the father-in-law of Tacitus, and the historian has naturally painted him in glowing colours as a model of military virtue and administrative tact. There can be no question, however, that Agricola did a first-class job from the Roman authorities' point of view. He crushed the Ordovices so thoroughly that north and mid-Wales took centuries to recover. 'He made a desert and called it peace.' Other generals undertook the even more difficult task of overcoming the Silures. Unfortunately they did not have literary sons-in-law like Agricola. The Silures put up a desperate and prolonged resistance, carrying on a guerrilla warfare in the defiles of the Forest of Dean and the Black Mountains of Gwent. But at last even the Silures were worn down by methodical Roman pressure. The triumphant legions now set about holding down the tribes of Wales in an iron network of forts and military roads.

Even the tangled Welsh mountains could not stop the remarkable Roman mili-

Top Old Oswestry – a great Celtic hill fort which would have been a centre of resistance against the Roman advance

Above The Roman amphitheatre at Caerleon

tary engineers. Their roads ruled straight lines across the rugged landscape. The fort of Y Pigwn, a thousand feet up in the shadow of the Carmarthenshire Vans, or Tomen-y-Mur on the bleak moorlands behind Trawsfynydd, must have seemed cold and inhospitable indeed to legionaries from Spain and northern Italy who had to man them. The system was serviced from two great bases – Chester in the North and Caerleon (Isca) in the south. At Caerleon you can still see the strong, defensive walls and the amphitheatre just outside them, which was used for military exercises and displays. A similar amphitheatre has recently been uncovered at Carmarthen, the Roman Maridunum and the capital of the Demetae. It is curious that there seem to be no forts or Roman roads further west in Dyfed, or at least none have been discovered. Were the Demetae the only Welsh tribe who broke ranks and joined those Britons who, again according to Tacitus, 'are gradually led to those amenities that make vice agreeable – arcades, baths and sumptuous banquets? They speak of such novelties as "civilisation", when really they are only a feature of enslavement.' We can hardly picture the Demetae staging sumptuous banquets in little Maridunum, away in the west, or civilised vice flourishing in the small native settlements clustered near the fort at Brecon Gaer.

All of which brings us to the key question about the Roman occupation of Wales – how far did it submerge the original Celtic social structure, or profoundly alter it? The Celtic world of Gaul became completely 'Romanised'. The tribes who fought Caesar so furiously ended up proud of being citizens of Rome and part of her Empire. Did the same thing happen in Wales?

The Roman presence in Britain has been described as an interlude in our history. If so, it was a remarkably long interlude. It lasted at least twice as long as the British 'Raj' in India and, like the Raj, it was outwardly accepted over most of the country, although some tribes might have been less enthusiastic than others about their leading men 'donning the toga' and hurrying to learn Latin. Clearly Wales did not continue indefinitely to be the North-West Frontier of the province of Britannia. That honour was reserved for Scotland. The Romans failed ever to solve their Scottish problem. They alternately advanced and then withdrew their frontier, which finally settled at the line first drawn by the Emperor Hadrian. His wall still wriggles like a vast stone snake across the moors of Northumbria. The continual and pressing needs of this northern frontier had their effect on the strength of the garrison in Wales. Many of the Welsh forts were eventually abandoned, although others were reoccupied. The evidence is still confused and more excavation is necessary before we can get a clear-cut picture of what exactly happened in the Welsh military establishment. As Professor Jarrett pointed out, 'Wales was not a geographical or political entity in the Roman period . . . . Nor should we see the Romans treating Wales as a whole; the problem of the Roman governor was how to use a small army to the best advantage.' All governors, however, seem to have retained the firm bases of Chester and Caerleon. Mountain Wales may not have been uniformly happy under Roman discipline.

The southern and eastern areas of the country – Gwent, the Vale of Glamorgan and the lowlands further west – were another matter. Here the civilisation of Rome took deeper root. The Celts could not help being impressed by the most obvious and spectacular achievement of Roman culture, her architecture. They had never seen building on such a scale before. They had built their hill-forts, some large and complex; but towns laid out with straight streets, columned temples and baths and piped water were a revolutionary concept to the Celts. And an exciting one as well. Even the warlike Silures were tempted to abandon their fort on Llanmelin hill and descend to the fleshpots of Caerwent. This veterans' colony became Venta Silurium, the market town of the Silures. The villas (big, landed estates) at Ely and Llantwit Major in the Vale of Glamorgan had elaborate mosaic pavements, laid down by imported craftsmen. All the evidence shows Roman culture put down deep roots in the lowlands of the south-east. Even in the mountainous parts of

Left Maen Madoc – a Roman milestone on the mountain road leading towards the fort of Brecon Gaer.

Right The fourth-century walls of Caerwent still stand

Wales the Romans left their mark. They mined copper on Parys Mountain in Anglesey and gold in the valley of the Cothi in Dyfed. No natural obstacle deterred the Roman civil engineers. At Dolau Cothi, near Pumpsaint, the hillside is still honeycombed with the shafts they dug in their eager search for the precious metal. They brought water to the gold mines through a long aqueduct stretching along four miles of mountainside above the rushing waters of the Cothi. Celtic smiths and miners had never worked on such a scale.

The memory of the Roman achievements lingered long in the Celtic imagination. The fort of Caernarfon reappears in the Mabinogion as the glittering palace seen by Macsen Wledig, the great Emperor of Rome, in a dream – an architectural marvel with walls of solid gold. Seven hundred years after the legions of Isca had become a faint memory, Geraldus Cambrensis walked through the ruins of their headquarters at Caerleon. Even in the twelfth century Geraldus could still see the remains of 'immense palaces formerly crowned with gilded roofs in imitation of Roman magnificence . . . a town of prodigious size, remarkable hot baths, relics of temples and theatres, enclosed within fine walls, parts of which remain standing.'

The Roman occupation left a firm imprint, not only on the Celtic landscape but upon the language as well. Words were borrowed and the nature of this acquisition was interesting. Many of the military weapons – sword, javelin and shield – stay Celtic, but 'saeth', an arrow, comes from the Latin *sagitta*. Many of the words connected with writing are taken from the Latin, but poetic terms remain Celtic. Words about building are obviously Roman borrowings, like 'ffenestr' from the Latin for window. But surprisingly enough the natives clung to their own law terms. Professor Piggott may have been guilty of some picturesque exaggeration when he wrote that 'the Celtic cowboys and shepherds, footloose and unpredictable, moving with their animals over rough pastures and moorland, could never adopt the Roman way of life.' The Silures and the Demetae were hardly cowboys, but, certainly, a great deal that was intrinsically Celtic survived under the protective cloak of Rome.

Were the old Celtic religious observances among the survivors? The Druids certainly disappeared. Human sacrifices went the same way. The Romans, however, had no objection to local gods. The nominal cult of the divine Emperor was sufficient to symbolise publicly the unity of the empire. After that, it was left to the individual or to the local community to decide for themselves the deity or the ritual that best suited their needs. Thus, the exclusive cult of Mithras was popular in the army, and it came as no surprise when a Mithraic temple was uncovered just outside the walls of the fort at Caernarfon (Segontium). It was under the Romans, too, that Christianity first entered Britain. Once the Christian cult had been officially recognised by the Emperor Constantine after his victory at the Mulvian Bridge in AD312 the once-persecuted church had money behind it. In spite of the Emperor Julian's desperate attempt to reverse the triumphal onward march of the Church, the fourth century saw the bishops and clergy firmly placed in the administrative structure of Britain.

The early church had already produced its martyrs in Britain. It now sealed its success by producing its first heretic – not for the last time in our island history. The monk Pelagius propounded a complex interpretation of the term 'gratia', at a time when the minute analysis of the meaning of words was of vital importance to the well-being of the Church. Pelagius maintained, in principle, that by obeying the laws of God, Man could come to grace by his own individual efforts, a doctrine which might have found favour with the eighteenth-century Welsh Methodists but was anathema to the orthodox view represented by the powerful St Augustine. The two men clashed in one of those furious and acrimonious debates which enliven the history of the early Church. Pelagius eventually left Rome for the more friendly Jerusalem, but he naturally had strong support in his native land. Britain long remained a stronghold for the heresy propounded by one of her sons.

Unfortunately, we have no hard facts about the spread of early Christianity in Wales, for we must discount the later accretion of pious legend. The little reliable information we have comes, as was to be expected, from the south-east of the country. The remains of a small church are claimed for Caerwent, but its date is uncertain. Certain graves at Llantwit Major seem to have been oriented according to Christian custom, and a plausible case has been made out that St Patrick himself may have come from Gwent. A very small bundle of facts, indeed, on which to construct a picture of Christianity in Wales during the Roman period, but if we can follow the example of neighbouring Somerset and southern Britain it is possible to speculate that in Wales, too, organised Christianity was strongest in the towns and among the rich proprietors of the villas. Paganism had not been eclipsed among the hills and we know that it still had strong roots in the lower Severn valley.

At Lydney, on the Severn, Sir Mortimer Wheeler excavated the remarkable temple dedicated to Nodens, the Celtic god of hunting and healing. The elaborate temple complex was actually expanded between AD360 and 380, as a place of pilgrimage where grateful sufferers could offer gifts to Nodens in recognition of a cure. A dedicatory tablet set up soon after AD367 acknowledged the gratitude of T. Flavius Seculis, who describes himself as 'praefectus reliquationis', or head of the navy repair yard.

'Praefectus reliquationis' – those two words seem to bring a sudden shadow across the confident, sunlit façade of Roman power in Britain. What was a fleet doing in the tidal waters of the Severn and in the Bristol Channel? Against what threat was T. Flavius Seculis repairing his galleys? Had the Pax Romanum ceased to operate in the western seas? The unthinkable was about to happen. The strong, generative power of Rome was starting to crumble at the centre. The Roman Empire was not going to come to an end in one dramatic crash. It was a long decline rather than a fall. Like Charles II, 'it was an unconscionable time a-dying'. But die it did, and out of its long death throes came a country that we can now clearly call Wales.

Into the Darkness

There used to be what we might call an official date that marked the collapse of Roman rule in Britain, after which the so-called Dark Ages begin and last for the next two hundred years. The date is AD410. This was the moment when the Emperor Honorius sent an imperial rescript to Britain, formally severing the official links with Rome. In it he advised the Britons that, henceforth, they should look after themselves. Three years before, the usurper Constantine had withdrawn troops from Britain to support his bid for the imperial purple. The usurper was killed, but the legions never returned. From that time on, the Britons had to face the barbarian onslaught alone.

The Emperor Honorius certainly sent his rescript, but did it mean exactly what it said? Was he putting a brave face on a situation that had already gone beyond his control, and which he had no power to change? The Britons, themselves, may have decided to 'go it alone'. There had been a long history of usurpers using the safe base of the island of Britain as a springboard for an attempt at the imperial throne. At the end of the third century, Carausius had held Britain for years as an independent province. He issued his own coins, many of which have turned up in Wales. The latest came to light in recent excavations in Loughor in South Wales. The usurper Magnus Maximus nearly pulled it off. He held a great deal of north-west Europe before he was defeated and killed by Theodosius in AD388.

Magnus Maximus is an intriguing figure who has recently attracted a great deal of attention, especially from Welshmen who feel deeply about their national identity. It has even been suggested that he should be regarded as the real 'founding father' of the Welsh nation. This special 'Welsh connection' of a tough and successful professional soldier from Galicia in Spain is based on his suggested identification with Macsen Wledig, the hero of a haunting story in the great medieval collection of romantic tales known as *The Mabinogion*.

The Dream of Macsen Wledig relates how the Emperor, asleep on the banks of the Tiber, saw in his dream the vision of a maiden of surpassing beauty in a splendid castle at Caernarfon in far-distant Wales. The maiden's name was Elen, the daughter of Endaf. Macsen cannot rest until he makes the long journey to claim her. They marry and Elen builds great castles at Carmarthen and Caerleon and links them with Caernarfon with a series of splendid roads, still known in modern Welsh as 'Sarnau Helen' – Helena's causeways. The Romans revolt in the Emperor's long absence, but he returns and reconquers his realm with the help of Elen's two brothers. They take possession of Brittany on the way.

Magnus Maximus, known to the Welsh as Macsen Wledig

The whole story is rich in word magic and the exuberant fancy of the Middle Ages, but how much does it reflect the memories of the power and splendour of the Roman empire in Wales, dimly recollected after the eclipse of the imperial glory in the Dark Ages? How much hard fact is still embedded in the word tapestry of the old story teller?

As we might expect, the historian Edward Gibbon, in his account, *The Decline and Fall of the Roman Empire*, takes a cool view of the claim that Magnus Maximus had a special contact with Caernarfon or Wales. In a characteristic footnote he remarks, with a cultivated sneer: 'The prudent reader may not perhaps be satisfied with such Welsh evidence'! Yet there are some odd facts about the story that set the imprudent reader's fancy wandering. A unit of Seguntienses is noted as serving in Illyria after Magnus's defeat by Theodosius. Could they have been soldiers from Segontium (the Roman name for Caernarfon), brought there originally by Magnus because of his special connection with north Wales? Why were the Welsh so specially interested in this one usurper when there was a succession of them? And what about Elen? Was she a real British princess who married Magnus, or was the old story teller confusing her with Helena, the mother of Constantine the Great, who, after all, had been proclaimed as Emperor in Britain at York? We may never be certain, but perhaps we should be more sympathetic to the story than Edward Gibbon. At the least, it shows the powerful impact left by Rome on the tribes of Wales.

These usurpers seemed to have gained their support from the discontent in Britain, as in many of the outlying provinces, with the ever-increasing burden of taxation involved in the upkeep of the Roman administrative superstructure. The Empire had overstretched itself, like so many other empires before and after it. The army was expensive, and it cost money to keep the boundaries of the Empire – the 'limes' – safe from the barbarians outside. All through the fourth century the pressure from these barbarian tribes increased. The Alans, the Franks and the rest of the tribes beyond the Rhine were probably under strong pressure themselves from people like the Huns.

The islands of Britain were not immune from these increasing dangers. The Picts had always been a menace in the north, and now the Saxon raids increased along the east coast of Britain. The Romans set up a new line of fortifications under the control of the Count of the Saxon Shore. The same thing was happening in Wales, but here the danger came not from Saxons but from fellow Celts. Ireland had never been conquered by the Romans. Agricola once told Tacitus that he thought he could easily have over-run it with only a single legion and some auxiliaries, but generals sometimes become over-optimistic when there is a chance of military glory. Even in Agricola's day, the central authorities at Rome may have begun to feel that the resources of the Empire were being overstretched. Ireland thus remained a stronghold of untouched, unchanged Celticism lying off the coast of Wales. This would have important implications for the history of Wales as the protective power of Rome slowly waned.

The Roman authorities set up the same defensive counter-measures in Wales as they had on the Saxon Shore. New bases for the fleet were constructed at Cardiff and Holyhead, and the fort at Caernarfon was enlarged. Away in the south-east, Caerwent hurried to equip itself with walls. By AD340, the citizens felt uneasy enough to strengthen their walls with strong bastions which could act as platforms for *ballistae,* machines capable of throwing heavy stones with accuracy for four hundred yards. The walls of Caerwent can still be seen, and form some of the most impressive Roman remains above ground in southern Britain.

Yet still the Irish raiders kept coming. Gildas, writing in the sixth century, gives us a vivid picture of them, for they were not cleared from the scene even in his day. Every calm summer morning brought its dangers: 'Their hulls might be seen creeping across the glassy surface of the main like so many insects awakened from torpor in the heat of the mid-day sun and making with one accord for some familiar haunt.'

As the official defences weakened, the Irish seized the chance to make permanent settlements on the land of Wales itself. They moved into the Lleyn peninsula and Anglesey, where they left a strong mark on folk memory. Even today, any collection of ruined, round huts on a lonely headland or mountainside, although they date back to the Iron Age, are christened 'Cytiau Gwyddelod' – Irishmen's Huts.

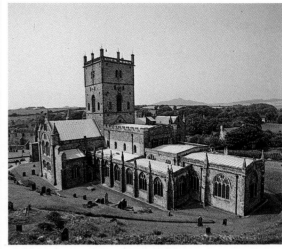

ABOVE St David's Cathedral, Dyfed

LEFT The coronation of King Arthur as painted by Matthew Paris in the thirteenth century BELOW Le Mort d'Arthur by James Archer, a contrasting Pre-Raphaelite view of early Welsh history

A light in the Dark Ages, the glory of illuminated manuscripts from Welsh monasteries: the
Rhigyfarch Psalter (LEFT) and the Lichfield Gospel

Ogham inscriptions side by side with a Roman one on a memorial stone

In south-west Wales, the Irish tribe of the Deisi, evicted from their original home in Meath, crossed the Irish Sea and settled in Dyfed. Their influence extended still further eastwards. The petty kings of the little kingdom of Brycheiniog were proud to trace their descent from the royal Irish house. An even more curious piece of evidence testifies to the Irish presence in South Wales: strange markings occur on many of the more ancient memorial stones in this area. Groups of small, straight lines have been cut along the edges, forming the letters of the Ogham alphabet, the earliest form of Irish writing.

There are markedly fewer Ogham inscriptions in north-west Wales, where the Irish also attempted to settle. A strong Welsh tradition offers a tempting, if unsupported, explanation. This tradition maintains that, at the end of the fourth century, a chieftain called Cunedda and his numerous sons came from a district called Manau Gododdin, in the lowlands of Scotland. Together they drove out the Irish, who, thereafter, never dared to try and settle in north Wales. Some of the sons gave their names to districts of north Wales. Merioneth comes, for example, from Cunedda's son Meirion. We need not take this nomenclature business too seriously but it is possible that Cunedda was the leader of a tribe from beyond Hadrian's Wall which was friendly to the Romans. According to a long-established Roman practice, they were deliberately brought into north Wales as *foederati* – friendly barbarian troops who were used to supplement the fading manpower of the Empire. In Cunedda's case it is claimed that the man who invited him to Wales was none other than Macsen Wledig (Magnus Maximus) himself. Magnus was taking the experienced legionaries with him as part of his preparations for his bid for Imperial power. He needed the *feoderati* of Cunedda to maintain the defences of north Wales until his return.

Magnus Maximus, as we know, never returned, but – again according to tradition – Cunedda remained to become the founder of the royal house of Gwynedd; and it is certainly curious that the Gwynedd dynasty seems to have long maintained a strong connection with the Britons of the north. When disaster finally overtook the northern British kingdoms, their epic poetry was preserved in the memory of the Gwynedd court bards. This northern connection gave a special prestige to Gwynedd and buttressed its claim to a vague overlording over the rest of Wales.

The Cunedda story seems so attractive that we instinctively feel it must be true, but historians can only repeat the remark of the Abbé Breuil when he was shown the supposed pre-historic painting in the Gower cave, 'Yes, it is possible, but . . .' That last word, 'but', is the important one. For at least one hundred and fifty years after the departure of the legions we have no reliable account written by a contemporary Briton of the state of affairs, not only in Wales, but in the rest of the country. The Dark Ages are dark indeed when it comes to documentation.

The few documents we have are the fortuitous survivors of ordeal by war, fire, pillage and the dissolution of monasteries, fluttering down to us through the centuries, borne on the winds of chance. It is a marvel that they reached us at all, and we can be thankful that, when the supply of papyrus failed with the collapse of Rome, scribes turned to using the carefully-prepared animal skin known as vellum. Even so, the actual script the historian has to work on is usually a late copy of an earlier work. As Professor Alcock has written, with resignation, 'We normally find that we are dealing with copies of copies . . . of copies', and Dr Wendy Davies has stated categorically that it is not possible to write a history of early medieval Wales which will stand up to the requirements of modern scholarship. Nevertheless, we must make the attempt to peer back into the mists of the fifth and sixth centuries, for it was at some point in this dark tract of time that changes occurred which still affect the way we live and think in Wales today. It was during the Dark Ages that Wales became distinctively Welsh. It was then that the Welsh language emerged in a recognisable form, and the boundary slowly took shape between the lands that were to become English and those that were to remain Welsh. This was also the period when Wales became a completely Christian community. We are thus desperately in need of a guide, however unreliable, who can lead us through the story of these uncertain but vital centuries.

So inevitably, if reluctantly, we come to the writings of Gildas – inevitably, because, of all our verbal sources, he stands nearest to the dark fifth century, and reluctantly, because his testimony creates as many mysteries as it solves. Professor Alcock has labelled Gildas as 'prolix, tedious and exasperating', and anyone who has struggled through the *De Excidio et Conquestu Britanniae – Of the Ruin and Conquest of Britain* – will heartily endorse the professor's verdict. Gildas may be prolix but, at least, he writes as a man who feels that Latin is the medium of culture and who still feels that he shares the inheritance of Rome, although he is writing a hundred and fifty years after the departure of the legions. He appears to have been a monk who lived somewhere in western Britain between about 500 and 572. His contemporaries called him Gildas Sapiens, Gildas the Wise. Whatever we may think about his wisdom we can have no doubts about his irascibility. The *De Excidio* is a rip-roaring denunciation of the sins of the rulers of his time, but in the course of emptying his verbal vitriol over their hapless heads, Gildas also gives a short account of events in Britain in the fifth century. It is this section of Gildas's work that has passed into received history because of its use later on by the Venerable Bede in his celebrated *Ecclesiastic History of the English People*.

Gildas shows us a Britain which, according to him, had been under severe pressure from the barbarians since the time of Magnus Maximus. His credibility is undermined almost at once when he assumes that Hadrian's Wall and the Antonine Wall were both built by Magnus! The northern and western barbarians kept on increasing their raids and in AD440 the Britons appealed for help to Aetius, the Roman commander in Gaul. Aetius had his hands full with the new threat posed by the Huns and failed to answer 'the groans of the Britons'. Whereupon, the ruler of Britain decided to call in German mercenaries, Saxons, to meet the menace from the north. Gildas does not name this ruler but simply calls him the 'superbus tyrannus' – usually translated as the 'proud tyrant' but more correctly as the 'supreme ruler'. Eventually the Saxons revolted, and then ravaged the whole country with fire and slaughter. The cities were destroyed and many of the hapless Britons fled overseas to found a new Britannia in the sparsely-populated lands of modern Brittany in western France. At last the Britons rallied, led by a general with the Romanised name of Ambrosius Aureleanus. 'From that time forth,' says Gildas, 'sometimes the Britons were victorious, sometimes the enemy, up to the year of the siege of Mount Badon, which was almost the most recent but not the least slaughter of the gallows-crew'. He also adds that the siege of Mount Badon occurred in the year of his birth, and that he was forty-four at the time he was writing. These forty-four years had been free of barbarian attack though not from internal strife. When the Venerable Bede came to use Gildas, he added – perhaps from Anglo-Saxon sources – that the name of the 'superbus tyrannus' was Vortigern and that the Saxon mercenaries were led by Hengist and Horsa.

The great difficulty about this version of the 'Adventus Saxonum', the coming of the English, as related by Gildas and embellished by Bede, lies in its startling contrast with the archaeological evidence. Here the spade contradicts the pen. Many of the city sites in southern Britain seemed to have remained in some sort of occupation up to the middle of the fifth century. They came to their end by steady decay and not, in many cases, by fire and destruction. Even the skeletons found in the multi-angular tower of Caerwent could have been placed there by a deliberate burial at a later date. The reasonably trustworthy Life of St Germanus of Auxerre in Gaul shows us a part of Britain in AD429 where romanised patricians still seemed to be in control and even living in some sort of style. The saint, according to his admiring biographer, put new courage into them, and led the Britons to a victory over the barbarians, when a shout of 'Allelulia' struck terror into the hearts of the heathens. An ancient tradition in Wales claims the victory for a site called Maesgarmon in Clwyd, but somewhere in the Chilterns is more likely. The interesting thing about St Germanus's visit, however, is not the 'Allelulia' victory but the impression it gives of a Britain which was still striving to continue the traditions of Roman government after the departure of the legions. This could not continue indefinitely once the barbarians had interrupted the flow of coinage from the mints of Gaul. The monetary economy of Britain collapsed, and with it went the ability to pay for defence on a large scale. Housman's *Epitaph on an Army of Mercenaries* ends with the ringing lines:

> What God abandoned, these defended,
> And saved the sum of things for pay.

When the pay did not come, however, the sum of things could not be saved.

Something might yet be rescued from the wreckage. We have had to abandon Gildas's picture of general fire and slaughter sweeping Britain. The Adventus Saxonum, like so many other invasions of Britain, was a gradual affair, with changing fortunes and moments when the Britons felt that they were at least holding their own. One such moment came around AD 500, and here we can surely trust Gildas. The British victory at Mount Badon must have checked the Anglo-Saxon advance for Gildas's lifetime and given the Britons a valuable breathing space. The great question now arises – who won Badon? Who was the general who led the Britons to success in the many battles which, according to Nennius, preceded it? The Ambrosius Aurelianus mentioned by Gildas is the obvious candidate, but if he was a contemporary of Vortigern, the dates rule him out. At this point, a figure steps out of the shadows, a mysterious and powerful personality carrying a special aura of high romance but also a troublesome ghost whom serious historians have long striven to exorcise but who persists in returning to haunt the Dark Ages. We have come to King Arthur!

Gildas makes no mention of Arthur, but in fairness to him, he was not writing a narrative history. To discover the name of Arthur actually written down on a piece of vellum we have to go on in time around four hundred years beyond Gildas. Among the numerous manuscripts in the British Library collected under the laconic heading of 'Harlean MS 3859', there is a special section of importance to the student of the Dark Ages. This section is known as the *Historia Britonnum* or History of the Britons, and is usually ascribed to one Nennius. Nennius is as infuriating as Gildas but in a different way. His 'History' is not a carefully constructed narrative but the raw materials of history – a medley of documents gathered together almost haphazardly. Nennius himself was well aware of his limitations. He confesses: 'I have heaped together all I have found, from the Annals of the Romans, the writings of the Holy Fathers, the annals of the Irish and the Saxons, and the traditions of our own old men.'

The contents of Nennius's 'heap' are of unequal value. Some of it is mythology and not history, such as the celebrated story of Vortigern's flight to north Wales after his defeat by the Saxons. He determined to build a citadel on the wild rock of Dinas Emrys in the heart of Snowdonia, but the timber and stone gathered for its construction during the day mysteriously disappeared overnight. Vortigern's magicians declared that only the blood of a fatherless child, sprinkled over the rock, would prevent the disappearance. The fatherless boy was the young Ambrosius, but when he was brought to the rock he confounded the magicians by explaining that there was a well nearby where two fierce dragons, one red, one white, were imprisoned. The well was uncovered and the two dragons immediately rose into the air and grappled in fight. The red dragon overcame the white, a sign that the Welsh would eventually be victorious. The red dragon became the symbol of Wales.

Dinas Emrys – the reputed site of Vortigern's fortress

Alongside this sort of folk-tale, however, lie other stories only to be found in Nennius and which would be far more credible if they were not mixed up with his Vortigern fantasies. Foremost among this unique material is the list Nennius gives of the battles of Arthur. It begins with the clear-cut statement: 'Then Arthur fought them in those days with the Kings of Britain but he himself was leader [Dux] of Battles.' There follows a list of the twelve battles fought by Arthur, but the place-names are hard to interpret. They seem to cover the whole country, down from Scotland through Lincolnshire to the Cotswolds and the West Country. The twelfth battle was Badon 'in which nine hundred and sixty men fell in one charge by Arthur, and no one overthrew them but himself. And in all these battles he stood forth as victor.'

This is Nennius's most important statement about Arthur, but the remarkable Harlean miscellany contains one other vital piece of Arthuriana. Alongside certain dates in the Easter Annals are cryptic notes of Arthur's part in the battle of Badon and this mention against a date which could be AD539, 'The strife of Camlan in which Arthur and Modred perished. And there was plague in Britain and Ireland.'

On these entries in Nennius and the Easter Annals a vast structure of speculation has been raised, some of it sheer fantasy. The figure of Arthur was seized upon in the Middle Ages as the embodiment of the ideal of Chivalry. Hence the King Arthur of Camelot and his queen, Guinivere, surrounded by his Knights of the Round Table. All this has nothing to do, of course, with a possible Arthur who fought in the rough and tough sixth century. But serious Arthurian scholars are steadily building up a more acceptable picture of a possible Arthur and the age in which he might have lived.

There was certainly no Arthur who bore a title of king. Nennius simply calls him Dux or leader, and he could have been the professional general of the combined forces of the petty kingdoms of the Celtic world which had decided to fight together after the end of Roman rule in Britain. He was thus not in a position to found a dynasty as Cunedda was supposed to have done. If he was the commander at Mount Badon, his victory led to a temporary and not a permanent peace. Why, then, did his name remain in folk-memory and continued to gather a special aura of romance down the years? The answer must lie in the desperate need of the Welsh for a hero. Welsh history, like Irish history, has had more than its share of defeats and disappointments. Welshmen needed continual reassurance that someone would appear in the future who would reverse the tide of present defeat. Arthur was only the first in a long line of heroes – from Owain Glyn Dŵr and Henry VII on to David Lloyd George – who would minister to this deep need in the Welsh psyche. Thanks to modern scholars, Arthur is slowly but steadily creeping back into historical credibility.

The mists of history start to thin a little after Arthur and Badon, and for this we have to thank prolix old Gildas. He may have gone wildly astray in his account of the arrival of the Saxons, but we can surely read him with profit when he writes about his contemporaries, even though we must still read him with care. We must always remember that he was an ecclesiastic and therefore had a professional interest and even a professional expertise in lashing the sins of the rich and powerful.

Britain was now split into a mosaic of petty kingdoms, mostly at war with each other. The Scotti, from northern Ireland, had crossed the Irish Sea to establish themselves around the Firth of Clyde and the Isles. They would eventually eliminate the Picts and give their name to most of the country north of Hadrian's Wall. There were still Brythonic kingdoms in the Lowlands, in Cumbria and along the Pennines, but they were beginning to feel the threat of the constantly advancing Anglo-Saxons, who were already firmly established in the south and east of Britain and in the midlands. The intruders had now no hesitation in regarding the people they had ruthlessly displaced as the foreigners or 'Wealas' (the Welsh). They were beginning to approach the Welsh borderland, but, as far as Gildas could see, the political situation in Wales itself was stable, if sinful!

The leading figure on the scene was Maelgwn of Gwynedd. Gildas stigmatised him as 'the Island dragon . . . first in evil, mightier than many in power and malice', and accuses him of 'closing his ears to the music of Heaven and listening only to the flattery of the bards'. But behind the diatribes of Gildas we can clearly discern an outstanding prince, holding his court in his fortress on the rock of Deganwy above the estuary of the Conwy, a patron of music and poetry and a generous giver – a quality always admired in a Celtic ruler. Maelgwn probably died in AD547 from the great plague that had swept the whole of Europe; or, as the chronicler put it more vividly, 'And Maelgwn of Gwynedd beheld the Yellow Plague through the key-hole of the church door and forthwith died.' He left a strong kingdom to his successors who had no difficulty in maintaining the special position of Gwynedd. Early in the seventh century the subjects of Cadfan of

Gwynedd set up a memorial to their king, which is now in the church at Llangad-waladr on Anglesey. On it they had no hesitation in describing Cadfan as 'rex sapientisimus opinatisimus omnium regum' – 'the wisest and most renowned of all kings'. All exaggerated perhaps, but it shows that sense of superiority that Maelgwn bequeathed to Gwynedd.

Dyfed, in the south-west, was ruled by a king named by Gildas as Vortipor, ruler of the Demetae. Poor Vortipor cannot escape from the Wrath to Come! He is described as like a leopard in his behaviour, covered with the spots of sin. 'The end of your life is drawing near,' warns Gildas. 'Why can you not be satisfied by the surges of sin, which you suck down like vintage wine.' After this verbal violence, it comes as a mild surprise to find that, on a memorial stone to Vortipor from Castelldwyran in Dyfed, he is described as a Protector. 'Memoria Voteporigis Protictoris' reads the Latin inscription – which doesn't sound undignified. There was clearly a well-established, orderly state in Dyfed.

The memorial to King Cadfan of Gwynedd.

The Vortipor Stone, Dyfed.

We know from sources other than Gildas that there were small kingdoms in the rest of Wales as well. The interesting little state of Brycheiniog (Brecon) embraced the country between the upper reaches of the Usk and the Wye, and the dynasty of Brycheiniog, like that of Dyfed, seems to have been of Irish origin. There were also kingdoms in Gwent and Ceredigion (Cardigan). On the northeastern border the dynasty of Powys survived fierce English pressure to play an important part in the subsequent history of Wales.

All these petty kings had their fortresses on hill-tops or convenient promontories, where they were surrounded by their war-bands. The walls of the fortress could be of timber, backed with earth or stone, and the life of these little courts centred around the wooden hall, where the mead flowed and the bards praised the generosity and courage of the ruler, or recited epics celebrating the heroic deeds of their forebears. Thus many characteristic features of the old Celtic way of life re-emerged relatively unchanged once the trappings of Rome were removed. Post-Roman society in Wales was still aristocratic, and below the aristocracy the ranks were carefully organised, with the lowest ranks of the peasantry, as usual, tied to the land. In all ranks, however, the claims of the family, and the obligations of kinship, were vitally important. Birth, even more than wealth, gave a man status.

Wealth, in early Welsh society, was a relative term. The men and women at the top had their elaborate ornaments and weapons, their rich clothing and their assured food supply, but excavations in such post-Roman princely strongholds as Dinas Powis, Deganwy and Dinas Emrys reveal no great store of earthly treasure. The diet, even of the wealthy and powerful, was monotonous. The draughty,

The hilltop of Deganwy, the stronghold of Maelgwn Gwynedd

wooden hill-top residence of the ruler who lived at Dinas Powis near Cardiff is in startling contrast to the Roman villa at Ely only a few miles away. Gone are the stone walls, the mosaic floors, the heating chambers and the piped water supply. The collapse of the Roman economic system, based on the money supply, had compelled a return to the basics of life.

The people who lived at Dinas Powis had not returned to barbarism, however. The simple life does not imply a loss of quality. The arts that do not require cash – music, oratory and poetry – could still be cultivated. In the most important of the Welsh courts, the court of Gwynedd, a whole body of epic poetry, common to the Brythonic people in northern Britain as well as in Wales, was carefully preserved. The names of many of the bards have come down to us. Outstanding among them were Aneirin and Taliesin. Later bards looked back on Taliesin as their master in technique but Aneirin is credited with the most impressive of the semi-epic poems that have survived, the *Gododdin*. This describes the fate of a band of British warriors who set out from Manau Gododdin, the country around Edinburgh, to check the Saxon advance near Catterick in Yorkshire. The poem had a Homeric ring about it:

> The men who went to Catraeth,
> Merry was the host; the grey mead their drink.

Inevitably the British war-band met with heroic death. This was the period, in the late sixth or early seventh century, of the successful Saxon advance towards the north, and the bard could only celebrate dauntless courage in the face of defeat. The *Gododdin,* it has been well said, is the poetry of a nation with its back to the wall.

> Men went to Catraeth with battle-rank and warcry,
> Power of horses, blue armour and shields,
> Shafts held on high and spearheads . . .

Only one of the band returned.

The poem has come down to us in two versions contained in a single manuscript preserved in the Public Library in Cardiff. Once again it is the case of a 'copy, of a copy . . . of a copy.' The late Sir J. E. Lloyd described the *Gododdin* as 'a genuine relic of a long-forgotten strife – a massive boulder left on its perch by an icy stream that has long since melted away.' But the poem, as we have it, presents an important problem. It is written in Welsh; an archaic Welsh it is true, but, in essence, the same language that we speak today. The events and material of the poem are generally agreed to date back to the seventh century, but was the Welsh language then in existence? What tongue did Maelgwn Gwynedd or Vortipor speak? Can a language simplify itself and radically change its structure in the short space of, say, two hundred years? Apparently it can if its speakers are subjected to dramatic social and political pressures. After the Norman Conquest, Anglo-Saxon went underground and emerged a few hundred years later as the English which would be used with such splendid effect by Chaucer. The Brythonic-speaking inhabitants of Wales had certainly been subjected to a series of traumatic shocks. They had seen the withdrawal of the legions and the replacement of the authority of Rome by the re-emergence of a series of petty Celtic kingdoms. They had seen their lands steadily shrink under the Saxon advance. It is no wonder that their language simplified itself under strain. Welsh, like Wales itself, was born in the turmoil of the Dark Ages.

Whatever language they spoke, the inhabitants of Wales took a conscious pride in the one thing that, they felt, marked them off from their Saxon enemies – they were Christians. They may have been cut off from Rome itself by the barbarian flood, but they regarded themselves as the guardians of the precious heritage of Christianity, even though they were but a small, threatened people on the western edge of the old Roman world. The question immediately arises – did Welsh Christianity descend unbroken from the Christian Church that we know was well established in Britain in the last stages of Roman rule? Or did the Church collapse in the troubled world that followed the departure of the legions, to be later re-introduced into Wales from Gaul, by missionaries travelling from the western coasts and using the old Roman roads? We are again in the midst of one of those fascinating controversies among Welsh historians which are at once the delight and the anxiety of the layman, stumbling in search of certainty amid the darkness of the Dark Ages. Continuity or discontinuity – that is the question!

The defenders of the orthodox view of continuity point to the undisputed fact that after Constantine, at the beginning of the fourth century, the Christian Church had received the official backing of the state until the end of Roman government in the province. It was certainly well established in south-eastern Wales, an area which may have been harassed by Irish raiders but was never over-run by the Saxon invaders. The beleaguered Britons, in this area at least, were hardly likely to abandon their faith lightly, their sole comfort in adversity. And when, over a hundred and fifty years later, St Augustine tried to make contact with the leaders of the Celtic Church, he found that these men had no doubt that their traditions, so zealously guarded through trial and tribulation, went back in unbroken succession to the fountain-head of the Faith.

The champions of discontinuity took a careful look at their map and plotted the position of the memorial stones which are unquestionably the oldest Christian monuments in Wales. They showed that these rough but moving memorials are heavily concentrated in the west of the country near the coast, and are especially numerous on the western peninsulas of Lleyn in the north and Pembrokeshire in the south. Furthermore, the inscriptions on these stones are carved in the vulgar Roman cursive hand – the same hand as the inscriptions in the Roman catacombs and retained by later Christians as a matter of pride in their lowly origins. Thus, as the late Professor Nash-Williams suggested, 'the early Welsh inscriptions are not in the direct line of succession from the pagan monuments of the Roman period in Wales'. The supporters of discontinuity could also stress the fact that Christianity in Britain, as in Gaul, was essentially an urban creed. The countryside, especially the more remote and mountainous part of the Welsh hinterland, may have

St Govan's Chapel in Dyfed, on the site of the cell of the saint

remained pagan. The work of conversion was yet to be done.

This, surely, is the key point, and may lead us to an acceptable compromise between the two embattled sides. Christianity may have survived in some quarters in the south-east, but it may also have been 'refreshed' by influences entering Wales through the western sea-ways.

So begins that remarkable period, around the later half of the fifth and the beginning of the sixth century, which is usually known in Welsh history as 'The Age of the Saints'. Whatever may have happened before, at the end of it all Wales was certainly Christian. Was this work of conversion completed by the saints, and who exactly were they? Tradition presents them to us as men of special sanctity who wandered through the country, impressing all who met them with their holiness and asceticism, and founding monasteries and churches that still bear their names; men who bravely travelled along the abandoned Roman roads spreading the faith of Rome.

Once again, as so often in early Welsh history, we have to fall back on tradition and legend, backed by manuscript accounts written several hundreds of years after the event. There are very few accounts of the lives of the saints that date from earlier than the eleventh and twelfth centuries, when the cult of saints took on a new importance. The Celtic saints were never formally canonised by authority. The monkish chroniclers who wrote the *Lives* were naturally motivated by a desire to enhance the importance of their own local saint, especially if it would also support claims to the church's land. We can get a good idea of the difficulties in interpreting these saints' *Lives* and of distilling the small residue of fact from the mass of legend and miracle, if we look at the account of the obscure St Cenydd, the only saint produced in the Gower peninsula.

Cenydd was born, according to his *Life*, of royal stock, the son of Dihocus, a prince of Brittany, but by 'a most unnatural sin'. Dihocus had seduced his own beautiful daughter and made her pregnant. King Arthur happened to be holding his court at the time in Gower, and he ordered his vassal to bring his unhappy daughter to court. When the child was born, King Arthur ordered the babe to be cast adrift in a Moses-like basket. The tide wafted the infant saint to safety on the wild headland of Worms Head, where the birds and animals immediately looked after him. The gulls protected him from the wind and the snow 'with the shelter of their wings'. On the ninth day an angel of God descended and placed a bronze, breast-shaped bell in the infant's mouth through which a kindly doe miraculously fed him 'with the sweet savour of infant nourishment . . . for in Welsh it is called to this day Cloch Tethan, or the Titty Bell. But the secretions which childhood naturally discharges in its retirement, he never did for he was fed with a more subtle food, which has no secretions.' As he grew older, an angel looked in at regular intervals to complete his education.

The birds and the wild deer were determined to look after him as if he were one of their own. When he was unexpectedly found by a passing kindly farmer and taken home to his wife, the gulls immediately tore all the thatch off the farmer's roof, until little Cenydd was restored to his cosy nest on Worms Head. At eighteen, he was ready for his saintly life. His angel directed him to the spot which is now the village green at Llangennith, where a stream sprang out of the ground to form a well that refreshed him. His fame spread throughout Gower and his Titty Bell had surprising power. One touch of it forced an evil-doer to repent and gave the sinner the power to skip across the waves into exile with St David in Pembrokeshire. The kindly saint used it to restore stolen booty and convert thieves. At last, the good St Cenydd died, 'Leaving the earth however to receive reward in Heaven, he departed on the calends of August'. His birthday, or Mapsant, was riotously celebrated by an annual three-day festival at Llangennith, which was not discontinued until the early years of the present century. To echo a celebrated comment from one of the *Lives of the Saints* undertaken by the Oxford Movement, 'This is all, and indeed more than all, that is known about the life of the Blessed Cenydd.'

The life of St Cenydd can be paralleled by numerous lives of equally obscure saints, and strict scholarship demands that we treat these productions with caution. They are evidence for eleventh- and twelfth-century attitudes, with no real relevance to the facts of life in the fifth or sixth century. Yet we can surely gather some crumbs of detail, or at least some sense of the atmosphere of the so-called Age of the Saints, from this curious corpus of pious hagiography. The chroniclers generally insist that their saint had royal connections. There are links with religious

The stones in the churchyard wall of Yspytty Cynfyn.

life in Brittany, and the holy men, each with his bell, his well and his special powers over birds and beasts and nature, seem to carry some faint trace of old pagan Celtic practices. None of them seem to have gone in for painful martyrdom in the continental style, and their miracles again have a touch of old Celtic magic about them.

They are also depicted as constantly on their travels, busy founding the churches that bear their names. Of course, many of these dedications are of a later date, but most saints had their 'patria', the area where they had first impressed the people by their special holiness. Thus St David had his first strong following in Dyfed, the cult of St Beuno spread from Clynnog in Gwynedd, while St Illtud had special connections with Glamorgan. The saint is usually described as a monk, for monasticism's powerful appeal had affected Wales at the same time as it had reached the rest of Western Europe.

The traditional accounts show the leader setting up a cross at a chosen spot and, if the people were responsive, a little church would be built of wattle and daub, with some simple cells for the company. The whole settlement would then be surrounded with an earthern rampart against wild beasts – maybe against wild humans as well. Such a settlement was known in Old Welsh as a 'llan', and eventually 'Llan' was used for the church itself. On a few occasions, the church may have been deliberately sited to exorcise the last traces of pagan worship. The little church of Yspytty Cynfyn in the lonely country near Devil's Bridge in Dyfed is built in the centre of a churchyard, the walls of which contain several giant stones which could have formed part of a prehistoric circle.

We can see some of these saints more clearly than others. St Illtud is depicted in one of the few *Lives* that is known to be from an earlier date – that of St Samson of Dol in Brittany – as the most learned of the Britons, a philosopher, skilled in rhetoric and, curiously enough, as a man gifted with the power of foretelling the future. One is suddenly reminded of the old Celtic diviners. Perhaps in that uncertain world, compounded of the new Christianity, the learning of pagan Rome and the living memory of Celtic lore, a holy man could draw on all three sources of inspiration, and be all the better for it.

Near St Illtud's monastery, St Cadoc is reputed to have set up his own seat of learning at Llancarfan. Cadoc's family is boldly claimed to have descended from that of the Emperor Augustus and he was famous for his love of Virgil and the pagan poets. In St Cadoc, St Illtud and St Dubricius we sense a deep respect for the achievements of Rome. These men were the bridge over which the best of the ancient world was carried to the newly-emerging Celtic Church.

If we can trust the stories about them St David and St Teilo in the south, and St Beuno in the north, were men of a different stamp. By the eleventh century the cult of David was already beginning to eclipse those of all rivals in south Wales and his growing importance is reflected in the life of him written by Rhygyfarch; again, we must remember, five hundred years after the saint's reported death. Rhygyfarch does not picture David as a man of learning. He won fame for his asceticism and his gentle but persuasive character. The monastery he founded in a remote corner of west Wales was noted for its hard discipline. Dewi Sant (St David) drank only water. He was Dewi Ddyfrwr, David the Water-drinker, the first Welshman who is known to have been pledged to teetotalism. His monks had to harness themselves to the plough. All work was carried on in religious silence. No one claimed any property for himself. The man who actually said 'my book' or 'my plate' had to expiate the offence with a severe penance. Yet, in spite of this stern discipline, disciples flocked to David.

We hear of David being summoned to combat heresy at the Synod of Brefi in northern Dyfed. (Could the Pelasian heresy still claim adherents at this time?) None of the bishops there assembled could make themselves heard amid the vast throng. St David, who seems to have been a stocky little Welshman, had no trouble at all. He produced a miracle. The ground on which he stood conveniently rose into a little hill (the church of Llanddewi Brefi is built on it) and his voice penetrated into the furthest recesses of the crowd. St David died on 1 March and this has become the National Day of Wales.

The mention of bishops at this Synod of Brefi shows clearly that the Welsh church was not an exclusively monastic one, but our records are too few and obscure to give us a precise picture of ecclesiastical organisation in Wales in the Age of the Saints. Some churches were clearly more important than others. They were the 'clas' or 'mother churches'. But we are uncertain about the authority they could or could not exercise over the smaller establishments. One thing seems clear, however: the Welsh saints were not imbued with a burning desire to carry the gospel to the heathen Saxons, however zealous they might have been about

The church at Llanddewi Brefi

the conversion of their own countrymen. Bede reproaches them for this failure, but it is surely easy to understand. Irish and Scottish saints were more active in this matter, but they were not in direct contact with the barbarians. The Welsh were right next door to the invaders, who were steadily pushing them off their lands. There were barriers of battle between the races which were almost impossible to traverse, even with Cross in hand.

The story goes that St Beuno, in his cell at Berriew not far from the Severn, one day heard a Saxon voice on the other side of the river, urging on his dogs in chase of a hare. Beuno hurriedly called his monks together and ordered instant departure. 'The kinsmen of yonder strange-tongued man will surely obtain possession of this place.' A Saxon of any sort was held to pollute the very air of Britain.

A man who preached to these invaders was no religious hero. He was a traitor to his race and to civilisation!

This, then, was the position when St Augustine landed in Kent in AD597, sent by the Pope to convert the Anglo-Saxons to Christianity. He had an impressive success. Clearly a meeting between himself and the leaders of the Celtic Church could not be long delayed. According to Bede, it came in about AD602 at Aust (Augustine's Oak) on the Severn estuary. The usual picturesque legends have gathered around this important meeting. The British bishops are supposed to have consulted a hermit as to the line of action they should follow at the meeting. The hermit bade them take their cue from Augustine's own actions. If he rose courteously from his chair to receive them, he should be heard with attention as a true servant of God. Augustine failed to rise and remained seated. A subsequent meeting, perhaps in north Wales, failed to correct the painful first impressions. The Celtic bishops saw him as a man who had come to them from the hated enemy, and who stubbornly stood on the authority of Rome. Bede's stories may not be accurate but they symbolise the underlying reasons for Augustine's failure. Augustine may have been a saint and a first-class organiser, but tact has never been a prerequisite for sainthood.

The ritualistic differences between the two churches over such things as the shape of the tonsure and the correct date of Easter were, after all, trivia which could easily have been adjusted. What stuck in the gizzard of the leaders of the Celtic Church was Augustine's tone of superiority, his demand for submission to Rome when co-operation would have been gladly given. The Celtic leaders retired in distaste, and, although some branches of the Celtic Church were later to enter into renewed communications with Rome, Wales was the last to do so. The Welsh Church remained in isolation for nearly two hundred more years. It was not long before religious isolation was followed by political isolation as well.

4

The Age of Isolation

For the four hundred and fifty years between the visit of St Augustine and the arrival of the Normans on the Welsh border, Wales was cut off by the steady advance of the Anglo-Saxon invaders, not only from the Continent but also from all those small fellow-Celtic kingdoms to the north and south which had sprung into being with the collapse of the Roman imperial power. Nora Chadwick has pointed out that, as late as the time of Maelgwn Gwynedd in the early sixth century, a traveller could set off from Edinburgh and journey through Cumbria, Lancastria and the western Pennines, along the Welsh border and so on down through Somerset into Cornwall, and order his meals in Welsh (or, perhaps, still in a form of Brythonic) along the whole length of the way. He could also have crossed the sea from Land's End and found a warm welcome in Brittany, which was being settled by colonists from southern Britain and Cornwall. The victory at Mount Badon seemed to have given Celtic Britain a new chance of survival even though the Anglo-Saxons were now well-established in the eastern and southern lowlands.

But as the sixth century progressed into the seventh, the Anglo-Saxons resumed their steady gnawing into the Celtic heartlands, and we can begin to see the dim forms of later kingdoms that were to rise into greatness. The founders of the future kingdom of the West Saxons were starting their drive towards the lower Severn valley and Somerset. The East Angles had consolidated their lands under the successful kings whose pagan funeral rites revealed rich treasures when the ship-burial was excavated at Sutton Hoo. The foundations of the future kingdom of Mercia were being laid in the Midlands. There were smaller kingdoms in Kent and Lindsey (Lincolnshire) which would be soon absorbed into larger and more successful units. All this boded ill for the Celtic kingdoms which still held the west and north.

The most immediate threat to them from this Anglo-Saxon revival came from the invaders who had advanced up the north-east coast with apparently irresistible force – an advance so eloquently lamented by Aneirin in the *Gododdin*. Already the kingdoms of Deira and Bernicia stretched from the Humber to beyond the Tweed. At the end of the sixth century Bernicia found a ruthless and formidable leader in Aethelfrith, who inflicted a crushing defeat on Aidan, the leader of the Argyll Scots, at Dagestan, probably somewhere in Lidderdale. 'From that day to this,' says Bede with some complacent satisfaction, 'no king of the Scots dwelling in Britain has dared to take the field against the English race.'

Dagestan probably allowed Aethelfrith to take over Deira as well, and thus Northumbria enters history. Deira also brought him in contact with the Britons on his new border – the men of Gwynedd, Powys and Lancastria. In AD613, according to Bede, he dealt them a blow as severe as the one he had inflicted on Aidan and his Scots. At Chester the leader of the Welsh was Selyf, the ruler of Powys, the state that guarded the entrance to the valley of the Dee and still extended well into the Midlands. Powys, of all Welsh kingdoms, had the most to lose by the Anglo-Saxon advance and would be in the forefront of the resistance for the next hundred years, often losing ground yet never completely overcome. At Chester, however, Selyf was killed and so, according to Bede, were hundreds of monks from the nearby monastery of Bangor-upon-Dee, who had come to support the Britons' army with their prayers. The pagan Aethelfrith, so the story goes, asked his advisors what monks were doing near the field of battle and on being told burst out, 'If they cry to their god against us, they fight against us as surely as those who bear weapons.' His men rushed on the unfortunate ecclesiastics and the 'saints' suffered immediate and involuntary martyrdom. Thus, says Bede, the prophecy of Augustine was fulfilled, that those who did not join him in bringing Christianity to the Anglo-Saxons would, themselves, be the victims of the pagans' rage. Welsh readers may feel that this prophecy reflects an interesting light on Augustine's failure to charm the Celtic clerics into acknowledging Rome.

Aethelfrith's triumph did not immediately separate Wales from her northern Celtic neighbours. In some respects it proved to be a hollow triumph. Not long afterwards, Aethelfrith himself was killed in battle against Raedwald of East Anglia. In the murderous mêlées that passed for battles in those days, all leaders were expected to be right in the forefront, and the chances of war could cause dramatic changes in the fate of kingdoms.

Aethelfrith's death sparked off a revolution in Northumbria. Edwin, a scion of the eclipsed royal house of Deira, grasped power and proved as stern an enemy to the Britons as his predecessor. He finally eliminated the little Celtic kingdom of Elmet, in the country around modern Leeds, and drove King Caredig from his throne. This opened up the way to the west for him. Aethelfrith's attack at Chester had been a foray in force. Edwin was able to consolidate his conquests in the Pennines and Lancashire. It was probably now that the breach between the Welsh and the northern Britons was made permanent.

The Welsh in North Wales had, up until then, regarded themselves in some respects as natural 'blood brothers' to the Celts to the north of them. They were both 'Cymry' – fellow-countrymen. Edwin's advance made it certain that, as the centuries progressed, the Cymry would be confined to Wales. Not yet, however. Edwin may have met with a resounding success in the north – he even embarked a force in a fleet from Chester that over-ran Anglesey, and he became converted to Christianity by missionaries from Canterbury, thus earning Bede's approval. But once again the Wheel of Fortune turned. Edwin might have taken Anglesey but he could not take the whole of Gwynedd. The remarkable dynasty that looked back to Maelgwn Gwynedd, and further still to Cunedda, once more produced a man to match the hour.

Cadwallon was the son of the King Cadfan, whose memorial in the church of Llangadwaladr in Anglesey had proclaimed him to be the wisest and most renowned of kings. Edwin's invasion of Anglesey had eventually forced Cadwallon to take refuge in Ireland – always 'a very present help in trouble' to Welsh princes. Cadwallon, in his extremity, made a remarkable and desperate move. He allied himself to Penda, the heathen ruler of Mercia. Penda was now struggling to establish the ascendancy of Mercia in the midlands, and regarded Edwin, for the moment, as a far greater threat to his interests than the Welsh. Cadwallon felt the same way. The struggling Mercia did not seem to him to present a serious danger as yet to the Welsh kingdoms, and Penda's heathenism was no barrier to co-operation. A Canterbury convert had no special claim on a follower of the spurned Celtic Church. The alliance was an early example of Bismarkian *realpolitik*. Across the wide gulf of the ages, Cadwallon and Penda would have understood the motives of the Hitler–Stalin pact over Poland!

The alliance had a swift success. Cadwallon marched eastward under his dragon standard, and Penda hastened to join him. Together they inflicted a defeat of Chester and Dagestan proportions on Edwin. The king of Northumberland was slain and the whole of his country now lay at the victor's mercy. For one intoxicating moment it seemed as if all the miseries of the hundred and fifty years that had followed the tragic mistake of Vortigern had been avenged. The Britons might yet regain their lost lands. It was an illusion. Cadwallon was far from his real power base. There was no possibility of him holding down his conquest, even if he could enlist the help of the remaining and weakened small Celtic kingdoms. He chose the only course open to him. He ravaged the enemy lands to destroy their potential for recovery and did his best to eliminate all the members of the old Northumberland ruling house.

His very violence produced its natural reaction. A second son of Aethelfrith, Oswald, had been in long exile in the Scottish court of Argyll. There he had been converted to Celtic Christianity. He gathered a small but devoted body of troops around him and took courage to march south to confront the conquering Cadwallon. Bede tells of Oswald reaching the Roman Wall and somewhere near it, probably at the spot still marked by St Oswald's chapel, setting up a wooden cross, the first ever seen in those parts. He and his war-band knelt before it and prayed. Then, after a swift night march, they surprised Cadwallon's army at dawn, utterly defeating it. Cadwallon himself was killed and with him went the last practical chance of the Britons regaining their lost lands.

Oswald restored the power of Northumberland, but he still had to contend with the implacable enmity of Penda. In 642AD, the Mercian leader was able to avenge the death of his ally, Cadwallon. He attacked and slew Oswald at Maserfield. The site of the battle has been claimed for Oswestry on the modern Welsh border. The identification is not impossible, for the armies of those days ranged far and wide into enemy territory, before their opponents could gather sufficient strength to oppose them. Cadwallon had met his death far from home, along the Roman Wall. Oswald might, equally, have met his fate in the foothills of mid-

Wales. The head and hands of the unfortunate Oswald were nailed by his enemy on to Oswald's Tree; Oswestry is 'Croes Oswallt', or Oswald's Cross in Welsh. Oswald naturally became a saint as well as a martyr. He was succeeded in Northumbria by his brother Oswy.

Welsh hopes of revival flickered again when, in AD655, Penda decided to deal as decisively with Oswy as he had dealt with Oswald. Cadael of Gwynedd was among the Welshmen who marched north with Penda. At first, all went well. Oswy was compelled to take refuge in his fortress somewhere near the Firth of Forth and had to buy the enemy off by surrendering his royal treasure, including the loot gained in years of war with the Britons. Penda and his allies started home in triumph, but Oswy followed them. He burst in on them at Winwaed Field, probably somewhere in Yorkshire. Penda was killed, and Cadael, to his shame, seems to have beaten a quick retreat even before battle was joined. The only consolation for the Welsh lay in the fact that Cadael was not of the noble direct line of Gwynedd. Cadwallon's son, Cadwaladr, was a child and Cadael may have been a stop-gap, described with contempt in the Triads as one of the Three Peasant Kings of the Isle of Britain.

The death of Cadwallon had been the real turning point. The bards kept alive the hope that, one day, a new hero would arise, a second Cadwallon who would sweep the hated Saxons from the lands they had treacherously stolen from their rightful owners. This was now merely a pious hope, and the practical rulers of Wales knew it. From now on, the main theme in Welsh history would be the presence of powerful enemies on the very borders of Wales.

We can now talk with accuracy about a border and about a well-defined territory we can call Wales. That border took shape in the long years that followed the death of Cadwallon and Penda, as the result of a constant series of small encroachments, border forays and minor clashes in which the Anglo-Saxons were generally successful. The beleaguered Welsh could no longer turn for help to their fellow Britons. Even in the south, the West Saxons had been busy pushing towards the Severn estuary. They had established themselves in Somerset and around the Devon border, and the days of the small Celtic kingdoms in the south-west peninsula were numbered. Penda's death had removed the last chance of a deal with Mercia over the border. His successors were converted to Christianity, and more ominously for the Welsh, converted by Canterbury.

Mercia now embarked upon a policy of expansion which was to make its rulers the most powerful princes in southern Britain and even win a grudging acknowledgement of their superiority from their old enemies in Northumbria. The king of Mercia was the *Bretwalda*, or Overlord, of the English. The new rulers of this successful kingdom had little use for the old pagan Penda's policy of 'live and let live' along the border.

The very name of Mercia, comes from the 'march' or 'borderland', and implied an obligation on its rulers to defend and expand the frontier. Cheshire, Shropshire and Hereford were all lost to the Welsh, and the bards could only pour out their grief in poetic lamentation:

> Dark is Cynddylan's hall tonight,
> With no fire, no songs.
> My cheek is worn out with tears.

So the Welsh were driven from the fertile lands of the plains towards the foothills of the central mountains, but there they made their stand – stubbornly, desperately but successfully.

Their success is reflected in the remarkable barrier line known as Offa's Dyke, that runs over hills and valleys for over a hundred and twenty miles, from the Severn Sea to the estuary of the Dee. It is one of the most impressive monuments to come down to us from this dark, troubled period in Welsh history, although the Welsh had no hand in building it and probably regarded it with the deepest suspicion. To this day, Welsh people talk of the adventurous journey into England as going 'dros Clawdd Offa' – crossing Offa's Dyke. There can be no question about its name. It was undoubtedly built, late in the eighth century, by Offa, the most powerful and successful of all the Mercian kings. He dominated England, and his power was acknowledged on the Continent by the great Charlemagne himself. Offa had led many expeditions into Wales, but in his later years he decided upon a policy of stabilising or at least permanently marking the frontier. His Dyke

The great earthwork of Offa's Dyke along the Welsh borderland

was not intended to be a second Hadrian's Wall, manned with permanent garrisons, although it could certainly act as an obstacle to raiding parties driving back their booty of stolen cattle. It was a boundary, marking the land on either side which remained in undisputed possession. The deep ditch lay facing the Welsh side and the line of the barrier was skilfully selected to take advantage of the lie of the land. At certain points, like Gop Hill, Selatyn Hill and Bakers Hill, the Dyke gave the Mercians wide views into the country held by the Welsh, although the equally strategic hilltop of Ffridd Faldwyn near Montgomery lay on the Welsh side.

The Dyke is not continuous. There are gaps in the line, but some of these may have been covered, in Offa's day, by dense forest tracts which rendered the passage of armies extremely difficult. At the northern end lies a secondary dyke, known as Wat's Dyke. This may have been constructed by Offa's predecessor, Ethelred – a sort of rehearsal for the greater work that was to follow. The main dyke is a spectacular achievement, as anyone will testify who has walked the modern Offa's Dyke Path. Only a ruler of Offa's power and determination could have imposed such a task upon his ealdormen and peasants.

Of course, the creation of the Dyke did not lead to a permanent separation of the two peoples. There are villages beginning with 'llan' on the English side, and ending with 'ham' or 'ton' on the Welsh. It did not stop border warfare. Both the English and Welsh were to make forays across it in the years to come. Offa, himself, is supposed to have died at Rhuddlan, near Rhyl, in AD796 after a battle with the Welsh. The oft-told story that a Welshman found on the wrong side of the Dyke could have his hand cut off seems to be a later invention. In spite of the legends that inevitably gathered around it, this great earthwork, climbing high over the moors and dipping down into the secluded valleys of the borderland, symbolises a permanent difference between national characters, and, in a curious way, seems to guarantee the separateness of Wales.

But as we now peer westwards across the newly-constructed dyke, do we see any significant change from the Wales depicted by Gildas over two hundred years before? We still see a mosaic of tiny, independent kingdoms, sometimes at war with the Anglo-Saxons, sometimes feuding among themselves. To Dyfed and Gwynedd, mentioned by Gildas, we can add Powys, still manfully struggling for survival along the border. Brycheiniog held the area of the upper Usk, but we also have glimpses of more shadowy kingdoms such as Ceredigion, along the western coastline between the rivers Dovey and Teifi, and Builth in the valley of the upper Wye. The modern counties of Glamorgan and Gwent fell within the boundaries of Glywysing. This area had a complicated history of shifting frontiers and changing rulers. In the early part of the tenth century the land was held by a Morgan, who made such an impression on his contemporaries that the western section became known as the Land of Morgan, Gwlad Morgan, or Glamorgan.

We call these small territories kingdoms, for their rulers styled themselves kings, but in truth their kingdoms were barely the size of a modern county. In the days when travel was difficult in wild, mountainous country, these small units were probably the largest areas over which rulers could exercise effective control. Their history is hard to recount in detail. The written evidence is still sparse and difficult to interpret. Scholars have had to piece the story together from a complex corpus of genealogies, collections of charters copied by clerics centuries later, rare inscriptions on stones and monuments, references in Anglo-Saxon sources and marginal notes on illuminated manuscripts. This is the province of experts only, but one of the documents can give the average reader the strange flavour of this dark period. The *Annales Cambriae*, or *Welsh Annals*, were probably first compiled in the episcopal community of St David's. The purpose of these Annals was chronological in origin, but there are terse entries in Latin opposite certain dates, that record events that seemed memorable to the clerical compiler. Thus, in the year AD798, the Annals note, 'Caradog, King of Gwynedd, was strangled by the Saxons', and under AD910, 'St David's was burnt.' These laconic comments present us a picture of a society in which violence and warfare, plague and death, were the common background to life in the little kingdoms of Wales.

Yet we must not think that Wales was exceptional in this regard. The Anglo-Saxon kingdoms were also at constant war with each other. Mercia strenuously resisted the rising power of Wessex. David Hume, looking back from his vantage point in the seventeenth century, may have felt that these struggles were but 'the scuffling of kites and crows', but one of them eventually came that united, relatively well-organised Anglo-Saxon kingdom which fell so conveniently into the grasping hands of William the Conqueror. The same thing might have happened in ninth- or tenth-century Wales. The kingdom of Gwynedd had always been among the most powerful and well-organised of the little Welsh states. It seemed to have inherited a special aura from its past. Its rulers claimed descent from the legendary Cunedda and had the prestige of long connections with the British kingdoms of the north and with the heroic exploits of Cadwallon. Gwynedd could make some claim to the overlordship of the whole country, on the lines of the Irish *ard-rhi* (High King) or the Saxon *Bretwalda*.

At some time around AD825, Merfyn Frych (Merfyn the Freckled) seized power in Gwynedd. He may not have been of the direct descent from Cunedda, but he was clearly a ruler of exceptional ability. He ruled unchallenged for nineteen years and handed on a strong kingdom to his son, Rhodri. Merfyn's court was a surprisingly cultivated one, and it was probably at this time, in Gwynedd, that the old Brythonic epics were preserved in permanent form, and there were close cultural links with Ireland and the Continent.

Merfyn's son, Rhodri, is the most notable figure in the history of Wales before the advent of the Normans. He succeeded in uniting most of Wales under his overlordship, the first Welsh ruler to do so. Much of his success in this was due to a series of opportunist marriages. The House of Gwynedd could echo, in a modest way, the proud boast of the House of Habsburg, 'Others wage war. You, happy Austria, marry.' In this way, Rhodri came to power in Powys and Ceredigion as well as in Gwynedd. His contemporaries had no hesitation in hailing him as Rhodri Mawr – the Great, the first Welshman to earn this honorific. But he also had to earn it the hard way.

His reign coincided with the rise of the Viking menace to serious proportions in Wales. The assault of these Nordic raiders came at an unfortunate time for Europe as a whole. The great Charlemagne had succeeded in reimposing some sort of unity on the continent for the first time since the disintegration of the Roman Empire. A similar political unity was slowly emerging in Anglo-Saxon England, and there were even tantalising glimpses of such a possibility in Wales. The advent of the raiding Norsemen put an end to these dreams. The Viking swarms may have been set in motion by a whole variety of causes – overpopulation in the harsh northern lands, political troubles and even a desire for trade, albeit with sword in hand. Once the raids began, they were fuelled by the loot offered by the richer lands of Europe that lay to the south of Scandinavia.

The 'black gentiles' appeared in Wales as the ninth century began and their forays steadily increased in strength and in the damage they caused. In their long-boats, the Vikings possessed the most efficient and mobile war-machine in the western world. It was impossible to defend the whole coastline of the British Isles. Even with their fleets and shore-line forts, the Romans had found this task beyond them. The little Welsh states – and even the larger English ones – could not hope to ward off the sudden descents of these formidable free-booters. Later historians may have cast an air of heroic glamour over the Vikings. Beyond question, they were brilliant seamen, who ventured boldly out over the wild Atlantic to discover Iceland, Greenland and Newfoundland. They had their own stern code of honour among themselves, reflected in the sagas. But the hapless farmers in Anglesey who saw their cattle driven off and their houses burnt, or the unfortunate monks on Caldy Island who cowered hidden in their caves as the invaders made off with their precious gold altar pieces, were hardly likely to appreciate the moral qualities of these ruthless despoilers. The damage to the monastic communities was particularly serious since they were the cultural pace-setters of Wales. The country was to suffer from increasingly severe Viking raids as the ninth century progressed. They became even more destructive after the Norsemen had succeeded in establishing a permanent Irish base in Dublin. But there is one interesting and surprising aspect of these Viking attacks: savage and destructive as they were – and many of the forays through the more fertile Welsh lands of the northern and southern coastal plains were on a grand scale – yet the invaders never took permanent possession of great tracts of the country, as happened further east in England. There was no Danelaw in Anglesey or Glamorgan.

There may have been some later trading settlements along the south coast, and the name of Swansea is claimed to have developed from 'Sveinn's ey' or Sveinn's island. The headlands along the western peninsulas of Wales received Norse names, for they marked the favourite routes by which the raiders sailed to their prey; hence Bardsey and Anglesey in north Wales, and a whole string of Norse names along the Bristol Channel, from Ramsay Island to Worms Head. But, again, there was no settlement on a big scale.

Could the stubborn resistance of north Wales under the great Rhodri have had something to do with this? Rhodri gained a notable success in AD856 when he slew the famous Viking leader Horn in a battle in Anglesey. His victory was hailed in the court of Charles the Bald, the descendant of the great Charlemagne, for the courts of Gwynedd and those of the Carolingians had been in contact since the days of Merfyn Frych.

Rhodri's success raises the fascinating question which was to haunt Welsh history for the next five hundred years. Could he have created that strong, united Wales which had been the bardic dream – a national state under a native ruler – admittedly a primitive state, by modern standards, for bureaucratic efficiency lay far in the future, but still a state which would have safeguarded the special social and cultural traditions of Wales? What would have been the course of Welsh history had Rhodri established a truly united Wales? There were always formidable difficulties in the way of Welsh unity. The great mountain wilderness of Plynlimon and the lonely heights of the Berwyns were barriers to easy communication between north and south. Welsh custom approved of the sharing of the ruler's heritage between his sons – there was no rule of primogeniture in Wales. Yet these difficulties could have been overcome by a resolute and ruthless ruler, operating without outside interference.

That is the very thing that did not and perhaps could not happen in Wales. A powerful England lay on its borders, ready to nurse rival claimants to the throne and to actively interfere if necessary. Unity was possible in England. A generation after Rhodri, Wessex produced a whole succession of efficient rulers, the descendants of Alfred the Great. Under Edward the Elder, Athelstan and later under Edgar, the unity of Anglo-Saxon England was firmly established. It is tempting to think that Rhodri could have done the same thing, but in AD878 the great Welsh leader was slain – by the English. We do not know exactly how he met his death, but the Welsh chronicles noted that a signal Welsh victory over the English a few years later was hailed as 'God's vengeance for the slaughter of Rhodri'. Rhodri's fate emphasises the axiom that England's difficulty was Wales's opportunity, but a strong England brought trouble to the Welsh. The pattern became well established almost immediately after Rhodri's death.

His realm, as was usual when a Welsh king died, was divided among his sons. They were a vigorous brood, who caused deep anxiety among their neighbours. Dyfed, Brycheiniog and Morganwg all looked eagerly around for help, and they found it in England. Alfred the Great was now starting his remarkable career in Wessex. In the very year after Rhodri's death, he won his resounding victory over the Danes at Edington. He did not free Wessex completely from the Danish menace, for the invaders were already founding a permanent settlement in the north-east, but he had driven them out of southern Britain. He had begun to extend his authority over what was left of Mercia after the Norse invasion. He was the obvious man of power to whom the minor Welsh kings had to turn. Their change of policy was made easier by the character of Alfred. He was a ruler of exceptional probity, a man whose word could be trusted. It was, after all, a Welshman who wrote Alfred's biography and gave us a picture of the king, replete with those personal details which are so rare in the accounts of this troubled period. Would that we had a Bishop Asser at the court of Rhodri Mawr!

Asser's account of Alfred shows us a man who was determined to inspire his countrymen, not only in their fight against the Danes but in the revival of culture and religion. He shows us a ruler touchingly eager to lure learned men to his court, pursuing them, as Asser says, as a bee pursues honey. The minor kings of Wales had no hesitation in overcoming their traditional distrust of the English and placing themselves under Alfred's protection. In the end Anarawd himself, Rhodri's son, ruler of Gwynedd and the principal cause of the tumult, felt compelled to submit himself to Alfred. He even came in person to the court of Wessex, the first ceremonial visit ever made by a Welsh ruler to an English king.

Alfred died around AD901, but after his death the power of Wessex steadily increased while Wales fell equally steadily into confusion. From this confusion the country was rescued by a remarkable man, Hywel ap Cadell, the grandson of the great Rhodri, and the only ruler in Welsh history to be distinguished by posterity with the title of Hywel Dda – Hywel the Good. He inherited the energy of his famous ancestor, and like Rhodri he was helped in his rise to power by a successful marriage policy. His career seems to have begun in Ceredigion but through his marriage to Elen, the daughter of Llywarch ap Hafaidd, king of Dyfed, he gained a firm grip on the south. Gwynedd and Powys fell into his hands on the death of Idwal the Bald in AD942. Hywel was then regarded by the English as 'the king of all the Britons'. Not quite. Morganwg and Gwent remained independent. Indeed, this south-eastern part of Wales remained curiously detached from the general run of Welsh politics. Its annals may be obscure, but there is no doubt that it succeeded in holding itself apart from the dynastic tangles that enmeshed the rest of Wales.

How 'Good' was Hywel Dda? Again, we have curiously few personal details about him, and we must lament the absence of a Bishop Asser from Hywel's court. The ephithet 'good' was attached to his name many years after his death, and it was certainly not given as a tribute to a saintly, gentle character. No prince could have come to power in Wales at this time without a ruthless streak in him, and it does not do to look closely at the way Hywel dealt with his rivals before he married into power in Dyfed. But we know enough about Hywel's achievements to realise that we are in the presence of an exceptional figure among the long roll-call of Welsh rulers. He was the first Welsh king to issue his own coinage. His celebrated silver penny was minted for him in the English mint at Chester. He reigned for over forty years and felt safe enough on his throne to go on pilgrimage to Rome. More important still, his name is inseparably connected with the codification of the Welsh laws. Hywel Dda has passed down into history as the first and greatest lawgiver of Wales. Was he also a statesman, aiming at building up a united, independent Wales?

Questions have been raised by later historians, and even by some of Hywel's contemporaries, about his status as a pure Welsh patriot. Was he too much of an Anglophile? Sir John Lloyd stated firmly that Hywel was a strong admirer of English methods. 'There is good reason', he wrote, 'to believe that he [Hywel]

The silver penny of Hywel Dda

made Alfred, in whose reign he was born, his model and exemplar'. Hywel had certainly to take a good look across his borders at what was happening in England. During his reign, the heirs of Alfred – Edward the Elder and Athelstan – were raising the power of Wessex to new heights. When he came to plan his policy, Hywel had only two alternatives before him. He could either come to terms with the Wessex kings, or look around for strong allies who could help him to defy them. The author of the interesting poem entitled *Armes Prydein*, written in Hywel's reign, had no doubt that alliance and defiance was the right course. He advocated a grand alliance between all the surviving Celtic rulers, and even with the Danes of Dublin. 'There will be a reconciliation,' he sang, 'between the Cymry and the men of Dublin. The Irish of Ireland and Anglesey and Scotland, the men of Cornwall and of Strathclyde shall be made welcome among us.'

Hywel rejected this course and submitted himself to the English, with as good grace as possible. There is no need to think that he actually did so with enthusiasm, or in deep appreciation of the achievements of Alfred. In the circumstances, it was the wisest thing to do. Athelstan demonstrated the futility of any other course when he won his smashing and celebrated victory over the alliance of the Danes and Constantine, King of Scotland, at Brunanburgh. Accordingly, we find Hywel paying his tribute and, along with the minor Welsh princes, appearing regularly at Athelstan's court. We have his name as witness on numerous charters granted by Athelstan, and he obviously became familiar with the administrative procedures at the Wessex court. Athelstan was also a great legislator, and Hywel must have taken a special note of this, for he too saw the urgent need for some unification of law-giving in his own territory. He had acquired Dyfed, Gwynedd and Powys, each with their own customs. If there was to be any hope of permanent Welsh unity, it had surely to start with the unity of Law.

The traditional story relates that at Lent, Hywel summoned six wise men from every cantref to his hunting lodge at Ty Gwyn ar Dav (The White House on the Taff), the modern Whitland in Dyfed. They laboured for six weeks, and at the end of the session, the Laws were solemnly proclaimed and a firm malediction pronounced upon any evil-doer who should dare to break them. For good measure, it was decreed that no portion of the Code could be altered except by a body as large as that which had assembled at Hywel's command.

So runs the popular story, but as with so many well-loved stories in Welsh history – and, for that matter, in English and Scottish history too – it must be received with caution. We have about forty medieval manuscripts of the Laws in Welsh and five in Latin. Many of them have a preface describing how this particular text had been collected, and ascribing the work to some particular person, such as Iorwerth ap Madog, or, in many cases, to a mysterious and untraceable figure entitled Master Blegywryd and described as an Archdeacon of Llandaff and a Master of Law. The later the manuscript, the more elaborate the details in the preface. In truth, the contents of these manuscripts are not a legal 'code' in the strict sense. They are, rather, a lawyer's guide to aspects of Welsh law and custom, which would be of practical service to him in the courts in the thirteenth century and later.

How many of the details of the Laws go back to Hywel's day is a complex question still being investigated by scholars. Much intensive and difficult work remains to be done before we have a definite answer. But there was undoubtedly a body of law in existence in the tenth century, and we should be reluctant to deprive Hywel of the credit for first attempting to bring it to some sort of order and reconciling one code with another. For this alone he deserves his proud title of Hywel Dda.

The rare interlude of peace and order under Hywel Dda tempts us to take a brief look at the way people lived through these obscure centuries in Wales. As we peruse the endless tales of war, plague, and murder and mayhem in high places, we may easily forget that we are dealing with real people and not with terse entries in dry annals. It demands an imaginative effort to cross the vast gulf of Time Past and put ourselves in the place of the average Welshman — if there was such a man. For the society reflected in the Laws of Hywel Dda was a highly stratified one. As in the far-off days of Gildas and Maelgwn Gwynedd, the king and his court were still at the top of the social pyramid. The king was surrounded by his nobles, on whom he hoped to rely in war. They also expected him to do his duty by them. The king was the giver of gifts, the ultimate controller of the distribution of the available surplus wealth. A king's success was judged, among other things, by his generosity to his entourage, and the presentation of gifts was a constant feature of the higher society.

Not that there was a vast surplus to give away! The Welsh economy was totally an agricultural one. It depended directly on the land in a way that we, who have been brought up in a modern industrial society, find it hard to understand. There were no towns in the modern sense in early Wales. The land was grouped in units which were largely self-supporting. Many of them were worked by bondmen. There is even talk of slaves. It is idle to picture early Welsh society as a collection of pastoralists wandering over land held in common, operating some sort of Celtic democracy. Early Wales was the home of a privileged aristocracy with the king at the head.

We have to count the clergy among the privileged. By Hywel's day the enthusiasm that fired the early Celtic saints had faded into the light of common day. The monastery still lay at the centre of church organisation but the ideal of celibacy seems to have little attraction for many of the clergy. Bishops of St David's had no hesitation in marrying and acknowledging their sons. But it would be wrong

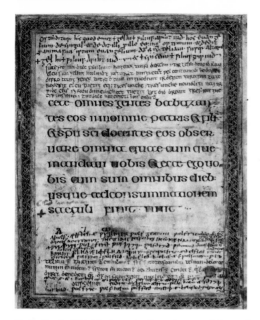

Left Early Welsh inscriptions inserted into the Lichfield Gospel. They record the manumission of bondsmen

Right Hywel Dda pictured in a later manuscript of his Laws

to regard the Welsh Church of the ninth and tenth centuries as debased. Alfred the Great turned to it for Bishop Asser's help in reviving the culture of Wessex. But compared to the Irish Church in the same period, the Welsh Church seems somewhat lack-lustre. Ireland was a richer land; it had not undergone the discipline of Rome and had no powerful Anglo-Saxon kingdoms on its doorstep. The art of the Irish church, in its stone crosses, its altar ornaments and its manuscripts, could draw on an uninterrupted Celtic tradition. This tradition had been broken in Wales.

Does no sound of pleasure, no laughter, reach us from the Past? Is History only the sad record of the Martyrdom of Man? Were the Dark Ages so dark that no one could express himself except in wailing and lamentation? No, all was not lost. The Welsh Church could also produce monuments of sinuous beauty. The Celtic crosses that still stand at Carew in Dyfed and in the churchyard at Nevern may show Irish and Norse influences in their style, but the artist that carved those entwining curves must surely have delighted in his task. And, as if to reassure us that Welshmen or Britons in the far-off past were as human as ourselves, we find, wedged among the stern stanzas of the *Gododdin* that celebrate the heroes who went to their death at Catraeth, a stray verse which the monk who was copying the early manuscript may have included because he did not understand the nature of the material or perhaps because he understood it too well and needed some human touch to break the endless solemnity of the epic. He wrote out this little lullaby, sung by a mother to her baby while father was out hunting. We

read it, and the Dark Ages seem no longer quite so dark. The translation is by
Gwyn Williams:

> Dinogad's speckled petticoat
> was made of skin of speckled stoat:
> whip whip whip along
> eight times we sing the song.
> When your father hunted the land
> spear and shoulder club in hand
> thus his speedy dogs he'd teach
> Giff Gaff catch her catch her fetch!
> In his coracle he'd slay
> fish as a lion does his prey.
> When your father went to the moor
> he'd bring back heads of stag fawn boar
> the speckled grouse's head from the mountain
> fishes' heads from the falls of Oak Fountain.
> Whatever your father struck with his spear
> wild pig wild cat fox from his lair
> unless it had wings it would never get clear.

We have good reason to bear in mind *Dinogad's Lullaby* and the rich pattern on
the Carew and Nevern crosses as we contemplate the next century in Welsh history.
They will cheer us through the hundred years of feuding, inter-kingdom warfare
and fierce raids by both the English and the Danes that were the only too familiar
sequel to the passing of a powerful personality in Welsh politics. Hywel Dda, 'the
head and glory of the Britons', died in 950AD and the unity of his realm died
with him. His descendants immediately started to carve up his possessions between
them. In the chaos that followed, those forty years of Hywel's reign must have
seemed a happy dream, never to be repeated.

Some of his heirs struggled to restore the lost unity. His grandson, Maredudd ap
Owain came near it and held Deheubarth (Dyfed combined with the lands eastwards from the Tywi to the Tawe), Gwynedd and Powys for thirteen years. The
chroniclers remembered him as 'the most praiseworthy king of the Britons', but
there was precious little to praise in the tumultuous years that followed. Professor
Gwyn Jones, looking through the record in *Brut y Tywysogion*, the Chronicle of
the Princes, found that between the death of Hywel and the Norman Conquest
– just over a century – thirty-five Welsh rulers died by violence mostly at the
hands of their fellow-countrymen, four were blinded and yet another four were
cast into prison by their enemies. After this grim roll-call of regicide, the *Brut*
recorded, almost with astonishment, that in 1043, Hywel ap Owain, King of
Glamorgan, died peacefully in his old age. A rare end, indeed, to the career of
any Welsh king!

Welsh affairs may have been chaotic, but when we look back across the border at Anglo-Saxon England, we see English affairs starting to take a similar turn. The line of strong Wessex kings had continued after the death of Athelstan. Edgar, for example, had kept a firm grip, not only on the Danelaw but on the petty kings of Wales. He was anointed and crowned in 973, and in the same year the Welsh rulers paused for a moment in their perpetual feuding and hastened to Chester to pay homage. There is a picturesque story that Edgar had himself rowed on the Dee by seven kings, including a regal contingent from Wales. True or not, the tale emphasises the continued control of the Wessex kings over the Welsh.

By the turn of the millennium, however, the dynamism of the line of Alfred was beginning to falter and die. The advent of Ethelred to the throne in 978, after the murder of his brother Edmund, marks the beginning of troubled times. Ethelred has gone down in history as 'The Unready' – more correctly, the man of 'evil counsel'. Medieval kings were expected to be just but also firm. Successful rulers, including those in Wales, had an aura not only of admiration but of fear about them. It was dangerous to cross their path. Ethelred had none of this quality. He may have been 'The Unready' but he was also Ethelred the Unlucky. His reign coincided with a revival of Viking power. The Danes resumed their raids on a big scale. A resolute Wessex ruler of Athelstan's class would have made short work of them, but Ethelred was no warrior. He resorted to the expedient of buying them off. His notorious Danegeld did, however, keep his enemies at bay for thirty years.

Welsh kings could not afford Danegeld and the Danes therefore kept on helping themselves to the loot of Wales. There were savage and continuous raids on the country throughout the period when Ethelred the Unready was only too ready with his cash in England. Anglesey was continually ravaged and Welsh monasteries

Left The Celtic Cross at Carew, Dyfed

Right St Brynach's Cross in Nevern churchyard, Dyfed

were favourite targets. The raids continued until the end of the tenth century and
beyond. In 999, St David's was pillaged once again and its bishop, Morganeu,
killed. The ultra-pious regarded his fate as God's judgment upon him for being
the first man to break St David's strict rule against eating meat. The poor bishop's
ghost appeared to a fellow bishop in Ireland lamenting, 'I ate flesh and am become
carrion.'

In 1003, the Danes decided to finish off Ethelred. Swein, King of Denmark,
led an overwhelming force to England. Ethelred fled to Normandy and years of
tumult followed out of which Cnut (Canute), Swein's son, emerged victorious.
He was a man of impressive power, king not only of England but also of Denmark,
and for a time ruler of Norway and part of Sweden. He was the most powerful
figure in the northern world and he controlled England firmly until his death in
1035. His manifold duties obviously prevented him taking a special interest in
Wales and this state of affairs continued for most of the reign of Edward the Confessor. Once again, it was a case of England's difficulty being Wales's opportunity.
The man who seized the opportunity was one of the most ruthless and spectacular
figures in the story of medieval Wales.

Gruffydd ap Llywelyn was the son of a Llywelyn ap Seisull who had seized
the throne of Gwynedd in 1018. Llywelyn proved himself an efficient ruler but
was himself violently removed in 1023. Apparently Gruffydd was a sluggard in
his youth. We have a picture of him from the vivid pen of Walter Map who,
although he was writing in the next century, was a Herefordshire man, who
recorded the traditions of the border, which played such a prominent part in Gruffydd's career. Young Gruffydd, at first, was a disappointment to his family. One
New Year's Eve the taunts of his sister drove him out of doors. He crouched against
the walls of a house, where the company were boiling beef in the family cauldron.
'It is curious,' said the cook, 'but there is one piece I keep pressing down with
the fork but it keeps coming to the top.' In an age when signs and omens were
an integral part of men's thinking, Gruffydd recognised this immediately as a sure
promise of future success.

He seized power in Gwynedd and Powys, and soon showed that he was a worthy
son of his father. In 1039, he fell upon an English army at Rhyd-y-Groes, a ford
on the Severn near Welshpool. He won a crushing victory, in which the brother
of the Earl of Mercia was slain. Rhyd-y-Groes marked the rise of a new power
in Wales. Gruffydd was ruthless and allowed no man to stand in his way – either
in love or war. Any young man who might have a claim to the throne was marked
for destruction. Walter Map reports Gruffydd's grim witticism. 'I kill no one.
I do but blunt the horns of the offspring of Wales, lest they should wound their
dam.' Like many other ruthless men, he possessed a charm of manner which he
could use with irresistible effect to encompass his ends.

He engaged in constant warfare, not only along the border but in Wales itself.
He made himself master of Deheubarth. His victories in Herefordshire forced the
English to come to terms with him and the terms were favourable indeed. Gruffydd
became the master of the whole of Wales, the first and only Welshman to do

LEFT Gerald Cambrensis at work

BELOW Valle Crucis Abbey near Llangollen, North Wales

LEFT Coity Castle in the Vale of Glamorgan

ABOVE Carreg Cennen Castle in Dyfed

BELOW The great concentric castle of Caerphilly, near Cardiff, built by Gilbert de Clare

so. He also made important gains along the border itself. When, later, the warlike Bishop of Hereford endeavoured to reverse the position by a surprise attack. Gruffydd won another outstanding victory, and the bishop and the sheriff were left dead on the field. The great men of England were now forced to come westward to deal with a serious situation. They included Earl Harold, who was then shouldering his way to the highest position of power. There were ominous signs that the days of Welsh opportunity were passing. The vacillating Edward the Confessor had a man of steel behind him.

For the moment peace was patched up, and a celebrated meeting took place between Edward and Gruffydd, which was probably the meeting so vividly described by Walter Map. According to him, Edward came to Aust on the English side of the Severn Estuary while Gruffydd was at Beachley. The mind goes back to the meeting between Augustine and the Welsh clergy four hundred and fifty years before on the same spot. Both sides debated as to who should cross to whom. Both sides were fearful of losing prestige. At last, Edward generously got into the ferry-boat. As it approached the Welsh side, Gruffydd was overcome by the humility of the king. He plunged into the water, lifted Edward out of the boat and carried him ashore on his shoulders. As Sir John Lloyd said, 'One whose better nature can be aroused by the sight of virtue in others was clearly not altogether the tyrant and the man of blood.'

One man was certainly not impressed by this sudden display of generous feeling on the part of Gruffydd. Earl Harold must have taken a cool look at the scene at Beachley – if indeed it took place – and decided that, sooner or later, he would have to deal firmly with Wales. He bided his time. By 1062, there were changes along the border. Harold judged that his opportunity had come. He persuaded the malleable Edward to let him try a surprise attack in the depths of winter on Gruffydd's headquarters at Rhuddlan. Gruffydd escaped to his boats, but the die had been cast. Harold now brought the full strength of England to bear. In the spring, his brother Tostig pressed along the northern coast toward Anglesey with a powerful force. Harold sailed with his fleet from the Bristol Channel right around the western coast of Wales to unite with his brother in a brilliant campaign that penetrated deep into the wilds of Snowdonia. Gruffydd's support fell away. In August 1063, his men betrayed him. He was murdered and his head was sent to Harold as the price of peace.

The chronicler of *Brut y Tywysogion* broke into an eloquent lament: 'And now was left in a solitary glen the man erst deemed invincible, the winner of countless spoils and immeasurable victories, endlessly rich in gold and silver and precious stones and purple apparel.' Three years later, Harold's beautiful mistress Edith Swan Neck, in tears and despair, was searching for his dead body among the heaps of his slain haus-carls on that fatal field of Hastings. The triumph of William the Conqueror was to change Wales as violently as it changed England.

5

The Coming of the Normans

The Welsh may have rejoiced at the news of the battle of Hastings. Earl Harold had been a sore trial to them along the border. He had overthrown the Welsh champion, Gruffydd ap Llywelyn; now he had been ruthlessly overthrown in his turn. Once more England lay weak and helpless before a conqueror. Maybe the Welsh, as so often in the past, could turn the troubles of England to their advantage? If they ever thought so, they were soon bitterly undeceived. The men who now arrived on the borders of Wales were the toughest warriors and the most brilliant organisers in the Europe of their time.

The Normans were the descendants of the Vikings who had permanently settled in northern France after the great raids of the eighth and ninth centuries. They made a deal with the French kings and Normandy became a French version of the English Danelaw. These Norse settlers rapidly assimilated all that was modern and forward-looking in the military techniques of contemporary Europe. This, coupled with the adventurous spirit of their Norse ancestors, made them formidable foes. The chronicler Oderic Vitalis, who was born on the Welsh border near Shrewsbury although he became a monk in Normandy, summed up the character of his adopted countrymen:

> When under the rule of a strong master the Normans are a most valiant people, excelling all others in the skill with which they meet difficulties and strive to conquer every enemy. But in all other circumstances they rend each other and bring ruin upon themselves.

As the eleventh century developed, Normandy produced just the sort of leaders who could harness the unruly energies of this restless people to great ends. Robert Guiscard, Roger, Count of Sicily and Bohemund of Taranto led comparative handfuls of Norman warriors to astonishing success in the south of Italy and then to crusades in the Holy Land. And William the Conqueror scored the greatest triumph of all when he seized England itself in one of the greatest smash-and-grab raids in history.

The struggle for England did not end at Hastings. There were revolts and rebellions, and the Normans had to resort to extreme measures to counter them. The Harrowing of the North long remained as a deep scar in English folk-memory. But in England William could claim to be the legitimate heir of Edward the Confessor and had taken over a well-organised administrative structure. Things were different in Wales. Here he had to deal with a separate race, and difficult mountainous country.

The first Norman barons arrived on the Welsh border not long after Hastings. It was likely that they were well-informed about Welsh affairs for there had been Normans on the Welsh border under Edward the Confessor. Ralph, son of the count of the Vexin and of King Edward's sister, had been set up in Hereford and Richard, son of the curiously-named Scrob, was building a castle south of Ludlow. Gruffydd ap Llywelyn had sensed the dangers they spelt for the future and had succeeded in defeating them. Now far more formidable adversaries had appeared in their place. William still had his hands full in establishing complete authority over England. He had no plans for an immediate Norman Conquest of Wales. For the moment he could only hope to pin the Welsh back into their mountain fastnesses – a task he had perforce to leave to certain of his most trusted great subjects.

The men he selected had all had previous experience of the problems of a border, for their estates lay in those edges of Normandy subject to constant pressure from the King of France and the Count of Anjou. They took up their new duties at a time when Welsh politics were in disarray. Gruffydd ap Llywelyn had gone, and the newcomers were not confronted with an united Wales. No Norman baron could resist such a temptation. Almost at once they cast their rapacious eyes on Welsh lands. Offa's Dyke meant nothing to them. As they conquered the Welsh areas opposite them, and dispossessed the original rulers, they also appropriated the legal rights and powers of the men they displaced. Power in Wales had always been broken down into smaller, more localised units than in semi-centralised Normandy. The newcomers were thus able to assume almost regal rights in Wales that would never have been countenanced in England. William and his successors did not approve. No Norman king ever gave away even a tiny portion of power

The motte at Tomen-y-Mur in Gwynedd, constructed by William Rufus on the site of a Roman fort during his invasion of North Wales

except under extreme pressure. However, for the moment William had to turn a blind eye to some of the things that were going on in the frontier society that was growing up along the Welsh border.

We are now face to face – from the earlier days of the Norman assault on Wales – with the Lords Marcher, men with private armies and private justice, who were to have a powerful influence not only on Welsh but on English history throughout the Middle Ages. The March comes from the French word meaning 'the border'. The Lords Marcher were the bold barons of the borderland, whose rights far exceeded those of their fellows in England. These were the people who now advanced on Wales with immediate and startling results.

In the south, at Hereford, the Conqueror placed one of his ablest lieutenants, William FitzOsbern, lord of Breteuil, hereditary steward of Normany and William's own cousin. His first task was to secure his base at Hereford against a rebellion in which the displaced English earls of Mercia made common cause with the Welsh. He crushed the revolt and made his base even more secure by a grant of certain liberties to the citizens of Hereford based on the customs of Breteuil. These became the model for subsequent charters granted to the embryo towns that grew up in Wales in the wake of the Norman advance. FitzOsbern also established a string of new, strong castles along the border, including the powerful fortress of Chepstow, the first of the Norman castles ringed with walls of stone in Wales. He pushed further west still to the lower valley of the Usk and eliminated the old kingdom of Gwent. But he was killed in a feud after returning to Normandy, and when his strong hand was removed after only five years as Earl of Hereford, the Norman advance into the south Wales coastal plain faltered and lost its impetus. Oderic Vitalis lamented FitzOsbern's passing in terms that seem a macabre echo of the cry of the Welsh chroniclers over Gruffydd ap Llywelyn.

> Truly the glory of this world falls and withers like the flower of grass; even as smoke it fades and passes. Where is William FitzOsbern, earl of Hereford, regent of the King, steward of Normandy and gallant leader in battle? . . . For alas! see how the brave warrior William fell and received just retribution. He who slew many by the sword has himself perished by the sword.

In the north the cruel and rapacious Hugh of Avrauches led the push along the north Wales coast from Chester. His lieutenant, Robert of Rhuddlan, built his castle on the banks of the Clwyd and pushed steadily westwards. He was able to capture the legitimate ruler of Gwynedd, Gruffydd ap Cynan, and by 1081 Norman power had reached Caernarfon itself. North Wales looked as if it might fall permanently into the hands of the invader. South of Chester, Montgomery was the chief base for the Norman advance into central Wales. Here in 1070 William the Conqueror had established Roger, the Earl of Shrewsbury, and the Normans began to penetrate towards the regions of the upper Severn.

Naturally the Welsh resisted. This Norman penetration was no walk-over. But the Normans commanded a military technique which was new to Wales and which

The charge of Norman knights on horseback and building a motte-and-bailey castle, from
the Bayeux Tapestry

the Welsh found extremely difficult to counter. Norman success was based upon
two great advantages; they commanded bodies of disciplined armoured horsemen
and they had mastered the art of castle building. The tactics of their advance soon
became standardised. The armed men and their followers would push their way
up the wide valleys or along the coast and their advance might follow the lines
of the old Roman roads. The lightly-armed Welsh might harass them or even
ambush them from time to time, but as long as they stayed away from the higher
hills, the mailed Norman knights could always get through to some strategic point.
Here they constructed a castle.

The Welsh were not alone in finding these military techniques almost impossible
to cope with. Similar methods swept the Normans to spectacular conquests in
Sicily, in eastern Europe and, eventually, the Holy Land. The Norman knight
on horseback in his coat of mail, with his sword, conical helmet and kite-shaped
shield, became the champion warrior of the western world. A concerted charge
by even a small number of these highly-trained Norman knights was widely held
to be irresistible. In the vivid words of Anna Comnena, the learned daughter of
the Emperor of Byzantium who observed the Normans at close quarters during
the Second Crusade, the crunch of a Norman charge 'might make a hole through
the walls of Babylon'. Of course the knights had their following of foot-soldiers,
but the concentrated impact of a band of trained knights was the Norman
equivalent of a Panzer division.

The castles thrown up by the first Norman invaders were not, of course, elaborate stone affairs. Those came much later. The first castles were of the 'motte and
bailey' variety. The bailey was an enclosure formed by a high bank of earth surrounded by a ditch and topped with a strong wooden palisade. This enclosure
would be big enough to contain a hall, a stable, a well, a workshop for the smith,
a storehouse, and if possible a chapel, for the Normans always believed that a sword
would cut more keenly if there was a prayer behind it. Attached to the bailey
was a high mound or 'motte', on which was perched a watch-tower or final keep,
a strong-point for a rally if the enemy broke into the bailey. In the early days
of the Norman advance, the whole structure of the motte and bailey would be
of earth and wood and constructed in a comparatively short time. You can see
what the whole thing was like from that earliest and most vivid of strip-cartoons,

the Bayeux Tapestry. The remains of these mottes and baileys, in various shapes and varieties, can be found in large numbers along the whole length of the Welsh borderlands and along the south Wales coastal plain into Pembrokeshire.

We can be sure that the Conqueror tried to keep a stern eye on the men who were now rising to power. He himself came to south Wales and visited St David's. The Welsh almost welcomed him as someone who could keep a check on his formidable barons, but with his death in 1085 and the accession of William Rufus the 'gnawing process' went on at an even faster rate. The little kingdoms of south Wales bore the full brunt of the attack. Philip de Braos occupied Radnor and moved down into the valley of the Wye at Builth. Bernard de Newmarch ended the long history of the little Irish-founded kingdom of Brycheiniog. Henceforth the valley of the upper Usk would be the Lordship of Brecon. Abergavenny became Norman. Robert Fitzhamon defeated the last Welsh ruler, Iestyn, and overran the Vale of Glamorgan. More surprising still, the Montgomery Normans swept down into the valley of the Teifi, through what the Welsh might have been pardoned for regarding as the impregnable mountain area south of Plynlimon. They established themselves at Cardigan and went on, deep into the western homeland of the Welsh, to build a castle at Pembroke on the very shores of Milford Haven.

Around the conquest of Glamorgan in particular, a whole mass of picturesque legends have gathered. Fitzhamon is supposed to have had twelve knights with whom he shared his loot. One of them, Payn de Turberville, cornered a leading Welsh prince named Morgan in his stronghold at Coity, near Bridgend. Confronted by Payn's men-at-arms, Morgan appeared leading his daughter by one hand and carrying a naked sword in the other. 'I am old,' he said to Payn. 'If you marry my daughter, you will have all my land without bloodshed when I die. If you refuse, we will fight to the last drop of our blood.' Payn naturally accepted the offer, although history does not relate if the maiden was as desirable as the castle. In fact history knows nothing at all about this remarkable encounter, although Payn himself is real enough. The Coity story, and many other similar delightful stories about the Conquest, seem to have originated in Tudor times, when the new Tudor nobility were anxious to lend a little antique distinction to their parvenu families.

The tide of Norman advance seemed irresistible. Gower was invaded probably from the opposite shores of Somerset and Devon and the peninsula ever since has been English-speaking. The whole of southern Pembrokeshire was so thoroughly settled by English immigrants, together with an intermixture of Flemings, a little later, that the very place-names were changed and a language frontier, now known as the Landsker, runs to this very day north of Haverfordwest and splits the county into a Welsh Pembrokeshire and a 'Little England beyond Wales'. The Welsh struck back wherever they could, and with great success in north Wales where Gruffydd ap Cynan drove the Normans completely out of Gwynedd.

In Cardigan too, Cadwgan ap Bleddyn recaptured the land of the Teifi and swept south into Dyfed to pen the Normans under Gerald of Windsor into their

The round keep of Bronllys Castle, Powys

new castle of Pembroke. Cadwgan's son Owain was the hero of one of the most celebrated romantic stories in the medieval history of Wales. In 1109, Gerald of Windsor was the custodian of Pembroke Castle. He had married Nest, the daughter of Rhys ap Tewdwr, for even in those early days of Norman aggression, marriages and alliances were arranged between the newcomers and the old rulers of the land. The beauty of Nest had become a legend throughout the country. The brave and dashing Owain attended a feast given by his father on his lands in Cardiganshire and heard the bards singing the praises of 'The Helen of Wales'. He determined to see for himself if the beauties of Nest lived up to the bardic eulogies. He discovered that Gerald and his wife were visiting the castle of Cenarth Bychan. Owain gazed on Nest and fell madly in love with her. Like Paris in Homer's story he seems also to have found favour in the eyes of Nest. Owain determined to abduct her. On a dark night a few days later, he returned to Cenarth Bychan with fifteen determined companions. They burrowed under the threshold of the gate, rushed in on the sleeping household, placed a guard on the bedroom of Nest and then added to the confusion by setting the rest of the castle on fire. Gerald of Windsor escaped through the unromantic exit of the garderobe – in other words the latrine. Owain carried off Nest and her children and began a war which set the whole of Wales in an uproar.

The shell keep of Cardiff Castle constructed on the earlier motte

In spite of frequent periods of exile in Ireland, Owain eventually succeeded his father as Prince of Powys and made a reasonably successful one as well. He even gained the favour of Henry I. But Gerald of Windsor had never forgotten the abduction of Nest. At the height of his success Owain was lured into an ambush and slain by one of the Flemings of Pembrokeshire. At last Gerald was avenged.

So fortune swayed between Welsh and Norman. The reign of Henry I marked a period of severe strain for the Welsh. The king had a personal interest in the conquest of the country. He himself led expeditions against Gwynedd and Powys. Pembroke was held in his name and there was a royal castle at Carmarthen. Norman rule seemed to be firmly riveted onto a great part of the land, and the contrast – which endured for the next hundred years – was firmly established between the lands where the Welsh held sway (Pura Walia) and 'The Englishry'.

The Norman-dominated areas had become strongly feudal in character. The castle was the centre of administration. Here the great lord not only had his safe refuge in a hostile sea, but also his seat of justice. Around him were the holdings of his vassals, bound to him by duties of military service in exchange for land. Soon little towns were to spring up under the castle's protection, in which the traders might go safely about their business. The lord would encourage them by granting charters and guaranteeing trading rights. The town was never a Welsh concept in origin, and most of the older towns of Wales – Swansea, Cardiff, Carmarthen, Haverfordwest, Montgomery and the like – all grew up in the shadow of the Norman castle.

With the town came new churches and abbeys. The Welsh had always had their monastic establishments, but they had retained many peculiarities of organisation. The old Celtic Church had long ago fallen into line over such matters as the date of Easter and the tonsure and had placed itself in full communication with Rome. But the Welsh might still be regarded as lax in such matters as clerical chastity. The sons and grandsons of Sulien, who was Bishop of St David's up to 1085, were the leading clergy of the diocese for the best part of the succeeding century and the canons lived with their wives in the shadow of the cathedral. In the monasteries the old austerities practised by St David had faded. Indeed, the Welsh establishments would hardly have been regarded as such by disciples of St Benedict. The hermit, the lonely anchorite, made much more impression on the faith of the ordinary people. The Welsh did not return to the monastic ideal until later, when they took the Cistercians to their hearts.

The Normans found all these manifestations of the wayward Celtic spirit in religion unacceptable. They had orderly minds. The old structure of the Welsh bishoprics was briskly broken up. Norman bishops sat in St David's and Llandaff, while the church was brought under the control of Canterbury. The old Welsh church organisation centred around the institution of the 'clas', a body of canons, usually hereditary, attached to a 'mother church'. The Normans broke up the 'clasau' wherever possible and their endowments were transferred to English or even Continental monasteries. The 'clas' at the ancient Glamorgan monastery of St Illtud in Llantwit Major, for example, was abolished and all its possessions granted to the abbey of Tewkesbury. Churches founded by Celtic saints were rededicated to James, Michael or Mary, names more in keeping with Catholic devotion on the Continent.

The churches built or rebuilt by the conquerors seem at times to have a double purpose – to minister to the service of God and protect the populace from the raids of the Welsh. Witness the towers of the churches in Gower and Pembrokeshire, and the strong battlements and defences of the austere priory of Ewenni in the Vale of Glamorgan. This Norman transformation of the church – the imposing of the authority of Canterbury and the steady reorganising of the church structure in the countryside into territorially-defined dioceses and on downwards into our present rural deaneries and parishes – was not without its advantages to Wales. The pre-Norman church had felt its isolation; it was in need of a new, fresh influence. The Normans brought the church back into closer touch with a papacy which was reformed and vigorous. Active young Welsh clerics could now look to Rome for their inspiration. Wales was in touch with the Continent again.

Such was the position when, on 1 December 1142, Henry I died from his celebrated surfeit of lampreys. Nowhere was the news received with such lack of grief as in Wales. Henry's death meant a disputed succession with Stephen fighting for the crown against the Empress Matilda. The Marcher lords, led by Robert of Gloucester, backed Matilda. The Welsh gleefully backed themselves. Once again England's difficulty was Wales's opportunity. In north Wales Gwynedd was now ruled by a man who knew how to make the most of his opportunities. Owain

Gwynedd had eliminated ruthlessly all his rivals and he now advanced eastward, profiting by the general anarchy in England. By 1153 he was almost in sight of Chester.

In the south, the Welsh returned to rule in Cardiganshire and the Vale of Tywi. The Norman grip on Pembroke, Gower and Glamorgan was too strong to be shaken but there was no question that the Welsh had recovered confidence. They felt that piecemeal conquest by the Normans was not the inevitable order of things. Even the accession of Henry II in 1154 did not shake their morale.

Henry II was a strong, vigorous king and took an interest in Wales, but the Welsh revival had altered the position since Henry I's day. Owain Gwynedd in the north and Rhys ap Gruffydd in the south were not men who could lightly be brushed aside. Henry naturally tried the orthodox solution to the Welsh problem by leading strong military expeditions into the hills. He tamed Owain Gruffydd for a period but an all-out effort to break him in his mountain stronghold in 1165 ended in a disaster which was long remembered in Wales. Henry, 'with a host beyond number', as the chroniclers recorded, led his army up over the high range of the Berwyn Mountains. He had reckoned without Welsh weather. As the army approached the 2000-feet level, at a point known to this day as Heol-y-Saeson (The Englishman's Road), the heavens opened and the great armament literally foundered in the bogs and rain-sodden moors. The Berwyn disaster was the graveyard of Henry's forward policy in Wales. Owain Gwynedd died five years later, a man full of honour after thirty years of service to his country. In the south, the Lord Rhys was equally successful.

Henry had his hands full of trouble. The murder of Becket in 1170 left him in need of friends and he had an additional anxiety in the success of that enterprising Lord Marcher, the Earl of Pembroke, Richard de Clare – the famous 'Strongbow' – who had led a mixed force of Normans, Flemings and Welshmen into Ireland in 1169, in response to an appeal from King Dermot of Leinster. A sort of gold-rush of Pembrokeshire knights followed him to carve out new estates in southern Ireland. De Clare's strong castle of Pembroke gave him an excellent springboard for his operation. So successful was he that he practically had the crown of Leinster within his grasp until Henry II came hurrying down to control his over-proud vassal.

In the middle of such harassing problems Henry II was glad to come to some accommodation with the Welsh. With the death of Owain Gwynedd the Lord Rhys had become, unquestionably, the leading figure in Welsh affairs. Henry established close relations with him and recognised him as 'Justice' of Deheubarth (south-west Wales). Rhys led a delegation of Welsh lords to confer with Henry at Oxford in 1177, and his prestige allowed him to become a major patron of the arts. At his seat in Cardigan he held a meeting of the bards which might be regarded as the first Eisteddfod.

Opposite above The Norman arches in the nave of St David's Cathedral

Below Church and castle stand together in Kidwelly, Dyfed

Thus as the twelfth century drew to its close, the Welsh could feel a new hope. Wales was not to be eliminated from the political maps. Welsh principalities would survive, even though surrounded by Norman lordships. And with survival came a new sense of pride in the old Welsh cultural heritage, a new artistic achievement. True that after the death of Owain Gwynedd and the Lord Rhys there were the usual troubles of disputed succession, but the Welsh revival had been too firmly-based to disappear. In the coming century it would lead to spectacular attempts to create a permanently-united Wales under the two Llywelyns, based on Gwynedd.

There had now been over a hundred years of struggle between the Welsh and the Normans – we should now call them the Anglo-Normans since the advent of the new Plantagenet dynasty under Henry II. Inevitably a pattern of living had been established between the two races. There would always be war from time to time since the very presence of alien elements around the Welsh heartland created tension, but there would also be marriage alliances and cross-fertilisation of ideas which led to a remarkable flowering of literature and the other arts on both sides.

In the Welsh principalities, rulers like Owain Gwynedd and the Lord Rhys had warmly welcomed the Cistercian monastic movement. The white-robed monks with their austerity of life, which seemed to reflect the early ideals of St David, made a strong appeal to the Welsh. They settled in the lonely places and they brought a pastoral skill as well as a spiritual message. The Lord Rhys was proud to endow the monastery of Strata Florida in its lonely valley amongst the Cardigan-shire hills and the monks developed the surrounding moorlands into one of the largest sheep-walks in Europe. In the later Middle Ages Welsh wool would have a special place in the Continental markets for its consistent quality.

Monasteries like those of Strata Florida, Cymmer, Valle Crucis, Neath and Margam became centres of learning and the arts. The princes themselves encour-aged the bards, who thus had an established position and special duties at court. The 'pencerdd', or chief court poet, was allotted a place next to the prince's heir and was regarded as socially equal to a judge. He had the task, in his song, of praising and encouraging the ruler and of reminding him of the long and heroic traditions of the past, of the claims of justice and honour. Below the 'pencerdd' was the 'bardd teulu', who performed the same function for the household and the prince's special group of men-at-arms.

Meilwr, Gwalchmai, Cynddelw, and Hywel the son of Owain Gwynedd him-self, are some of the great names amongst the 'gogynfeirdd' – the bards of the second generation, as it were – who were worthy to be ranked with the 'cynfeirdd', those noble poets of the sixth and seventh centuries, Aneirin, Taliesin and the rest of them, whose fame and example were still cherished by the 'gogynfeirdd'. These were the men who now began the perfecting of that complex and remarkable system of musical alliteration, of giving pattern to a line by means of echoing vowels and consonants, which the poets call 'cynghanedd'. Harmony is a rough and inadequate translation of the word, but this system of versification is the unique glory of the poetry of Wales.

The gateway to Strata Florida, Dyfed

This poetry is not solely concerned with politics and praise. It is alive with a new appreciation of nature, with a delight in the sheer joy of living. Listen to a part of Gwalchmai's *Beast* in a modern translation by Gwyn Williams. It catches the spirit of the poet's utterance but no translator, however skilful, can convey in English the brilliant word–juggling of the 'cynghanedd'.

> Quick rises the sun, summer hurries on,
> Splendid the song of birds, fine, smooth weather,
> I am of golden growth, fearless in battle,
> I am a line, my attack a flash against a host.
> I watched through the night to keep a border.
> Murmuring ford water in heavy weather,
> The open grassland green, the water clear,
> Loud the nightingale's familiar song:
> Gulls play on the bed of the sea,
> Their feathers glistening, their ranks turbulent.

A new note in Welsh literature, reflecting the new confidence of the Welsh political revival.

The same colour, gaiety and verbal splendour runs through that remarkable collection of prose tales, to which Lady Charlotte Guest added the title of *The Mabinogion* when she translated them into English in the early nineteenth century. But it was now, in the twelfth century, that they began to assume their final shape, although – as is the case for so many of the masterpieces of Welsh literature – the earliest manuscripts that have survived date from the fourteenth century. The binding of these manuscript collections gave them their picturesque titles – *The Red Book of Hergest* or *The White Book of Rhydderch*. But *The Mabinogion* is more than a book, it has been said. It is a complete, portable library. The tales are of infinite variety. Some of them, like that of Pwyll, Prince of Dyfed, incorporate strange, pagan elements from the pre-Christian past and memories of the old Celtic Homeric society. Others are linked with the development of the Arthurian legends, or – as in the story of the Dream of Macsen Wledig – with the lost glories of Roman rule. These stories must have been developed, elaborated and handed down through the ages, perhaps by professional story-tellers – the 'cyfarwyddau'. But the man who gave them their final shape, or perhaps we should say men, for there may have been many of them, were matchless artists in Welsh prose. The tales show speed of narration, irony, a tender lyricism. Wild jesting and grave tragedy all are there. *The Mabinogion* is one of the finest products of that world when the Welsh and the men of the Marches confronted and yet inspired each other.

These poets and story-tellers worked for an aristocratic society. It may not have been as strictly organised as the feudal world established in the territories of the

A mounted knight from a tile in Neath Abbey

Lords Marcher, but by no stretch of the imagination could it be called tribal. We cannot think of 'Pura Walia', Welsh Wales, as a sort of 'surviving pastoral reserve where Welsh patriarchs roamed at will through the Late Middle Ages'. Land tenure systems in Pura Walia and in the Marches were far closer than was previously realised.

So, too, were the contacts between these two divisions of the land of Wales. The clash between the Anglo-Normans and the Welsh was not simply a tale of bloodshed and burning, although there was always plenty of that. In 1175, for example, William de Braos, the Lord of Brecon and upper Gwent, who was to become an important figure in the Marcher world in the reign of King John, began his career by inviting Seisyll, the leading Welsh prince of the area, together with the most prominent Welshmen of upper Gwent, to his castle of Abergavenny for a friendly meeting. He and his men suddenly fell on the unsuspecting guests and massacred the lot. Worse still he sent his followers racing into Seisyll's country before the news of the treachery could spread. His armed men seized Seisyll's wife and then killed her seven-year-old son, Cadwaladr, in his mother's arms. This was barbarity of a high order. Yet the same William de Braos would never pass a wayside cross without stopping to pray, and spoke to children in the street in order to hear them murmur 'God bless you' in answer to his greetings.

Not all the boldness and ruthless initiative lay on the Marcher side. Welshmen could be equally daring. In 1158 a dramatic incident occurred which became one of the great legendary exploits of the Marches, and it took place in the heart of territory which had long been regarded as a completely Norman stronghold. In the hills of Glamorgan at Senghenydd lived Ifor ap Meurig, who was short of stature and was therefore called Little Ivor (Ifor Bach) by the Welsh. He was, however, great in courage and daring. He had a territorial grievance against his overlord Earl William, the ruler of Glamorgan. Ivor resolved to do the impossible and kidnap the Earl in his own castle of Cardiff. This must have seemed a mad escapade, for not only was the castle guarded by the earl's men-at-arms, but he had a strong body of archers in the little township now established in the shadow of the castle. Ivor however succeeded in climbing the huge motte which still exists in the centre of the castle grounds. He scaled the wall, got into the earl's apartment, seized him and his wife Hawise together with his young son, Robert, and whisked the family away to the hills before the alarm could be raised. He got all the concessions he asked for before he released the earl.

Such was life in the Marches of Wales – rough and always with a threat of danger, but still full of colour and even stimulating to men of imagination. It is more than likely that the Celtic stories about Arthur were transmitted to the Anglo-Norman barons through the medium of the 'latimers', or interpreters, in the castles of south Wales and so passed on into the literature of Europe to be developed in France into the full-scale Arthurian saga.

The Marches moreover produced two remarkable writers in whom we can see, without any doubt, the fruitful result of the cross-fertilisation of Welsh Wales and the world of the Anglo-Normans. Both obtained European reputations. The first was Geoffrey of Monmouth, who wrote what we must regard as one of the greatest best-sellers of the Middle Ages, the celebrated – or perhaps notorious – *Historia Regium Britanniae, The History of the Kings of Britain*, which burst on an astonished world around 1136.

Geoffrey frankly admitted that the sole purpose of his work was to glorify the Britons, to show that they, too, had a long and noble history. In this he may have been acting in the spirit of the Welsh revival. He also seems at times to assume a prophetic role. Once, Geoffrey claimed, the Welsh dominated Europe; let them remember the prophecies of Merlin about their triumphs yet to come. Let them draw the inspiration for their recovery from their glorious history. Another interpretation of the motive behind the *Historia* suggests that Geoffrey was a Breton by descent, who was yet fully aware that the Bretons and the Welsh were once the same poeple. The Normans, to whom the book might have been primarily addressed, would feel pride that they had conquered, and were thus the heirs, of a people with such a glorious past. The Welsh as well would delight in the *History*.

But what a history! Geoffrey produced a breathtaking narrative full of colour, drama and spectacular incidents. He relates how the British, in fact, were originally descended from Brutus, the Trojan, and how under Prince Belerius they captured and sacked Rome. He tells of the tragedy of King Lear; of the giants Gog and Magog; of Lud who built London, and a host of other dubious heroes, who have become so firmly fixed in our minds that it is difficult to believe that Geoffrey simply invented them. Above all we encounter Arthur and Merlin. Geoffrey could claim to have brought this famous pair to the notice of the intellectual world of Europe.

He also claimed that he had based his history on a mysterious ancient manuscript, a very old book in the British tongue lent to him by Walter, Archdeacon of Oxford. Geoffrey ultimately became Bishop Elect of St Asaph and, although some of his contemporaries early expressed their doubts, most of his fellow-countrymen swallowed the book's stories wholesale. Geoffrey, after all, was a great literary artist, and in the midst of a mass of obvious romance, some nagging little probabilities emerge. What are we to make of his story that the stones of Stonehenge were brought there from afar, or of the discovery of skeletons on the banks of the Thames at the very spot which Geoffrey, and Geoffrey alone, had indicated as the site of a great battle? Geoffrey's version of the early story of the British race, 'the Matter of Britain', passed as serious history and continued to bedevil historians down to the days of Charles II.

Our second man of the Marches is far more respectable from an historical point of view. He is Gerald de Barri (Geraldus Cambrensis or Gerald the Welshman). He was born about 1146 at the castle of Manobier on the south coast of Pembrokeshire, from the mixed Norman-Welsh stock which played such an important part in the history of the Marches, and his maternal grandmother was none other than the famous Nest, 'the Helen of Wales'. On his Welsh side he was related to the Lord Rhys while his father's family linked him with the Fitzgeralds and 'Strongbow'. Gerald was a scholar and a cleric who was frustrated in his great

The costumed splendour of medieval chivalry

longtam voyage. quil souffira de porter seulemet ung
lac de soye a ung ymage de samct george pendat a icellui.
Aussi se ledit colier dor auoit besoing de reparacion il pora
estre mis en la main de souurier iusques a ce quil soit
repare. Lequel colier aussi ne pourra estre enrichy de
pierres ou dautres choses reserue ses ymage qui pourra
estre garny au plaisir du cheualier. Et aussi ne pourra
estre ledit colier vendu engaige donne ne aliene pour
necessite ou cause quelconque que ce soit

Alexander Rey
Scotorx

Lewellin
princeps
wallie

Edward I presides over Parliament, attended by Llywelyn, the last native Prince of Wales ambition of succeeding to the see of St David's and of making it independent of Canterbury and the true centre of an autonomous archbishopric of Wales. But he was also a born writer with a sprightly pen. He was not afraid to record his own little vanities, his hopes and disappointments, his boundless curiosity. As a result we feel that we know him personally. We feel a sympathy towards him that we find it difficult to extend to many other personalities of the Middle Ages, when men were not much given to self-revelation in prose.

Gerald left us two works on Wales which give us a vivid impression of the country as it was as the twelfth century drew to its close. He accompanied Arch-

Geraldus Cambrensis' account of his journey through Wales with Archbishop Baldwin

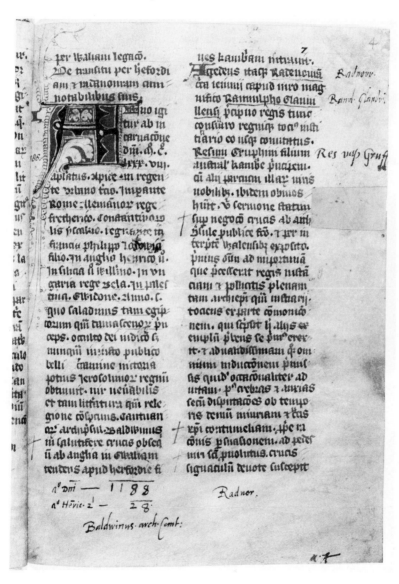

bishop Baldwin on his journey through Wales to preach the Third Crusade, and he also compiled a detailed description of the country. He paints an attractive picture of Welsh life, its warmth and simplicity. Houses, he says, were flimsy, built of woven osiers and replaced without trouble. The Welsh existed on a main diet of meat, oats, milk, butter and cheese. They were moderate eaters – they had to be since agricultural land was not as plentiful as in England. Hospitality was a duty and guests were entertained with music on the harp. At night, a simple bed of rushes was spread on the floor. Both sexes cut their hair in a circle level with their eyes. A hazel twig served as a toothbrush.

All Welshmen took a profound interest in matters of descent, a trait that has survived to this day. Their faults? They could be treacherous to outsiders. They could lose heart in pitched battles but soon recovered. And they had an unbreakable addiction to lawsuits. But they were also firm believers in prophecy, that a time would come once again when the Welsh would repossess their whole country. The whole spirit of the Welsh Revival is expressed by the celebrated story, recorded in the last paragraph of Gerald's *Description of Wales*, of the old Welshman at Pencader, in the days when Henry II was marching through the south. The King asked him if the rebels would continue to resist. Said the old man:

> This nation, O King, may now as in former times be harassed, and in a great measure weakened and destroyed by your and other powers, and it will often prevail by its own exertions; but it can never be totally subdued through the wrath of man, unless the wrath of God shall concur. Nor do I think that any other nation than this of Wales, or any other language, whatever hereafter may come to pass, shall, on the day of severe examination before the Supreme Judge, answer for this corner of the earth.

6

The Age of the Princes

The Welsh entered the thirteenth century with hope and confidence. The Norman menace had been faced and a Welsh Wales had survived. True, the usual succession disputes had occurred in Deheubarth and in Gwynedd, when the strong figures of Owain Gwynedd and the Lord Rhys had left the scene, but it did not seem possible that the Welsh states would disappear completely. A hundred and fifty years of struggle and counter-struggle had taught the Welsh a great deal about the technique of war. There are records of the Lord Rhys and his sons using siege engines against the Marcher castles and the Welsh were starting to build castles themselves. The old motte-and-bailey structures had long proved inadequate to the new conditions. The castles were now built of stone and were continually being elaborated according to the latest developments in castle building that penetrated from the Continent.

The Marcher lordships were also being consolidated. They had their own courts, where justice was done, 'according to the Law of the March', as Magna Carta put it. This Law was an amalgam of various laws and customs and, although the Lords Marcher were always quick to defend their peculiar system against any intrusions of royal justice, they were equally quick to borrow any useful new developments from the royal courts. They were generally content to follow the practice of Welsh law when it came to land tenure. They had accepted the Welsh system of land tenure when they had entered into Welsh lordships, and they were therefore bound to accept all the legal procedure that went with it. Thus the interesting Welsh practice of 'cynnwys', whereby an illegitimate son could have an equal share with legitimate heirs in their father's estate, was maintained in most of the Marcher lordships of north Wales.

We have records from some of these lordships, mainly from later dates, but there was no Bracton to summarise the code, no revised Laws of Hywel Dda for the Marches. Marcher lordships were usually divided into an 'Englishry' in the low-lying, richer agricultural areas and a 'Welshery' in the hilly country. Thus the 'Englishry' of the Lordship of Glamorgan lay in the fertile vale, the 'Welshery' up in what are now the mining valleys. In Gower the 'Englishry' occupied the easily-cultivated limestone country of the peninsula, the 'Welshery' – marked off by a line of commons – lay in the high country behind Swansea. This distinction has been maintained right up to the present day. The people of the Welshery thus felt under no disadvantage when pleading in the Marcher courts.

When the whole system was swept away in Henry VIII's Act of Union in 1536 there was much talk of the 'sinister usages and customs' of the Marcher courts and of 'the thraldome and cruelty used by the Lords Marcher'. But many people may have preferred the flexible and perhaps more easily understood methods of Marcher justice to the somewhat stern efficiency of the royal courts. In any case a great deal might depend on the character of the then Lord Marcher. A William de Braos might not be the ideal guardian of justice, whereas the upright figure of a William Marshall would command respect.

This was a period when a man who could unite several Marcher lordships by marriage or other means was bound to become a very powerful figure indeed and could play a dominant part in politics outside Wales, his power securely based on the unique privileges that came to him from his very position as a Lord Marcher. William de Braos, who began his career with the notorious massacre at Abergavenny, accumulated so many lordships that he dominated the internal politics of the March for nearly thirty years. His fall and exile under King John shook the whole of Wales. A more sympathetic baron was William Marshall. He was that unusual figure amongst the Lords Marcher, a self-made man. He was the penniless younger son of a comparatively minor baron, who began his career

The wooden effigy of a Marcher Lord from Abergavenny church

with the Counetable de Tancarville in Normandy, and he owed his early success to his amazing skill in tournaments.

These ritual mock-combats seem to have been invented in northern France by Geoffrey de Preuilly and immediately became popular throughout western Europe. The tournament fulfilled an important need for the baronial class. It gave the knights practise in the business of war, which was the only reason for his existence, under glamorous and often lucrative circumstances. Young William Marshall became a tournament champion, and then had the marvellous good chance of being appointed manager, as it were, of the tournament team organised to support Henry II's eldest son, known as the Young King. He was brilliantly successful. Henry II and Richard I promoted him. Finally he crowned his lucky career by winning the hand of the heiress of Richard de Clare. This eventually brought him all the de Clare holdings in Glamorgan, Gwent and Pembroke, as well as their huge claims in Ireland. William, at a stroke, became one of the greatest of the Marcher Lords.

But carefully watching the Marshalls, the Clares, the Braoses, the Mortimers, the Bohuns and the rest of them was always the King of England. English kings realised only too well how Marcher Lords could influence English politics, often to the royal disadvantage. Whenever possible they used the minorities of Marcher heirs to gain temporary control over their territories. Henry I had become a Marcher baron himself when he got complete control over Carmarthen. Richard I was too absorbed in his enterprises on the Continent to pursue a consistent policy in Wales. His successor, John, was more active, and was, at first, successful in his aims of dividing and so disintegrating both Marchers and princes. The chronicler of Strata Florida records for 1199: 'In that year, about the feast of Mary Magdalene, Maelgwn ap Rhys, for fear and also in hatred of Gruffydd, his brother, sold to the Saxons the lock and stay of all Wales, the castle of Cardigan, for a small, worthless price.' The Welsh execrated Maelgwn but the Crown had obtained a very useful starting point for further interference in Welsh affairs. Yet John, in the end, was unable to press home his advantage, and forty years later the Welsh seemed almost to have established an independent state.

The reason for this dramatic turn of events was, as usual in Wales, the emergence of a dominant personality on the Welsh side who knew how to turn all English difficulties to his advantage. In Gwynedd, Llywelyn ap Iorwerth had come to power in the classic way of Welsh princes bedevilled by the dividing rule of Welsh inheritance – he seized it from his uncle. He proved to be the greatest and most constructive Welsh statesman of the Middle Ages. In his long career he succeeded, by constant warfare, by tactful yielding under pressure and by masterly resilience the moment that pressure was relieved, in bringing under his control most of Pura Walia. When he died in 1240, full of honour and glory, he left a principality which had the possibility of expanding into a truly national state of Wales. His grandson, Llywelyn ap Gruffydd, extended its boundaries still further. There was a moment when an independent Wales seemed about to become a reality. The story of the rise, glory and fall of the Principality created by the two Llywelyns is the dramatic

A page from *Brut y Tywysogion, The Chronicle of the Princes*

and tragic theme of the history of Wales in the thirteenth century. The memory
of it can even affect Welsh politics today.

As the new century dawned, Llywelyn ap Iorwerth began to make a name for
himself as a young war leader at the head of a Gwynedd tuned for expansion.
The entries in *Brut y Tywysogion, The Chronicle of the Princes,* begin to multiply.
'A year after that [1201] Llywelyn ap Iorwerth, being a young man graced with
generosity and worthiness, gained possession of the cantref of Lleyn and Eifionedd,
after driving out Meredudd ap Cynan because of his treachery', or again, 'In that
year [1208], Gwenwynwyn was seized at Shrewsbury by the King. And Llywelyn
ap Iorwerth made for his territory [Powys] and gained possession of it and all

his castles and his townships.' Here we have the young Llywelyn intent on expansion and steadily establishing full control over Pura Walia. The moment was favourable. His home base of Gwynedd possessed, as we have seen, a defensive strength denied to his rivals. In the heart of their territory, the Princes of Gwynedd possessed an inner defence line that was very hard to break. Their principal seat was at Aberffraw on the island of Anglesey, and Anglesey was protected, not only by the sea but by the difficult currents of the Menai Strait. It was an island rich in corn. The Welsh called it Môn Mam Cymru – Anglesey, the Mother of Wales.

This secure granary was made doubly secure by the wild, mountain lands of Snowdonia across the Strait. Snowdonia is defended on the east by the deep trench of the Conwy valley, and all along the western side of this trench the range of the Carneddau rises to over 3000 feet, and presents an uncompromising wall. Yet behind that wall, running into the mountains from the western sea, are hidden valleys where the flocks could take refuge. Snowdonia and Anglesey between them held the secret of Gwynedd's astonishing recuperative power after every disaster.

The Welsh states of the south-west, Deheubarth, had fallen on evil days after the death of the Lord Rhys. There was no one to offer resistance to Llywelyn's ambition. Powys, on his south-eastern border, was also under strain. Powys, in fact, had always to appear more yielding in its policy to its big neighbour, England. It was right on the border and highly vulnerable. The great estates of the Marcher lords were equally vulnerable, for the reign of King John was one of continual tension. The king was at loggerheads with his barons and Llywelyn could play them off against each other. At one moment we find him marrying Joan, King John's illegitimate daughter; at the next he allies himself with the rebellious barons and gets his rights acknowledged in Magna Carta itself. After the death of John, the minority of Henry III gave him further opportunities.

It is true that Hubert de Burgh, young Henry III's Justicar, for many years strove to pin Llywelyn back into his Snowdonian limits, but Llywelyn had now become too strong for such tactics to succeed. By 1234 peace was made with Llywelyn, leaving him in control of a major section of Pura Walia including the royal castles of Cardigan and Builth. The peace remained unbroken until Llywelyn's death six years later. On his passing he was hailed in noble terms by the Cistercian annalist of the monastery of Aberconwy as 'that great Achilles the Second . . . he kept peace for men of religion, to the needy he gave food and raiment, he gave justice to all . . . and by meet bonds of fear and love bound all men to him'.

The words 'fear and love' are significant, for Llywelyn the Great deliberately set out on a policy of reconstructing the whole basis of Welsh political life, and not every Welshman was happy about it. Llywelyn lived in an age which saw the emergence of the centralised feudal state. Both France and England presented the spectacle of societies elaborating their administrative machinery, putting their taxation on a new and sounder footing and systematising their codes of justice. Any state that aspired to survive in the new world would have to modernise itself. Compared with countries like France and above all England, Llywelyn's principality was small and lacking in resources. Hostile English observers could wax satirical about its pretentions to international status: a clerk in the service of Archbishop Peckam, in the sad days of 1282, could write of the Welsh as a 'Trojan debris swept into the wooded savagery of Cambria under the guidance of the devil.' A better knowledge of the Wales of Llywelyn the Great would have shown him great changes at work, encouraged by the Prince. Under the two Llywelyns Pura Walia was also setting out on the same administrative road as its richer neighbours.

We see important offices of state coming into being, occupied by able men of the stamp of the famous Ednyfed Fychan, seneschal to Llywelyn the Great. He created a dynasty of administrators and was followed in his office by his sons Goronwy (d. 1268) and Tudur. The Prince had his chancellor and his chancery clerks and used his great and privy seals to authenticate his acts. His treasurer systematised taxation, and the lawyers turned with enthusiasm to the task of creating a common code out of the complex of law and custom that prevailed in the separate lands now coming under the sway of the Princes of Gwynedd. These codes always sought sanction from the great name of Hywel Dda, but they also reflected the needs of a developing thirteenth-century society.

The great Cistercian abbots with a view of affairs independent of Canterbury and the friars who entered Wales at this time with a fresh religious enthusiasm, all supported the new developments in Gwynedd. The bards gave strong encouragement in ringing verse. Dafydd Benfras hailed Llywelyn Fawr as 'the great chieftain of fair Wales' and sang of him as 'our common ruler'. In all this, we cannot yet talk of nationalism or of patriotism in the modern sense. The poets never use the word 'cenedl' in the sense of a 'nation'. Loyalty to individual principalities is still strong and is sincerely held; it was to cause trouble to the Llywelyns as they strove to make an unity out of Gwynedd, Powys and Deheubarth. But the bards did express the feeling of hatred of a common foe and their pride in their race and tradition. They looked to the Princes to support them.

Gwynedd was always the core of the power of the princes, but the expansion of their territory gave them ability to do many things beyond the power of previous Welsh rulers. We find Llywelyn ap Iorwerth and Llywelyn ap Gruffydd developing castle buildings on a considerable scale. The remains of Castell y Bere or of Ewloe, Dolbadarn and Dolwyddelan even show a distinctive Welsh style. The Princes gave charters to the small towns growing in their domains. They supported the abbeys and the friaries. There were significant changes in agriculture as well. We sense a new Wales coming into being, and, at that moment, it was basically an independent Wales. The great question was, would this new Wales – or this first approach to it – be able to develop its full potential without interference from without or protests from within? Llywelyn Fawr was fully alive

Opposite The castles of the Princes: *top left* Dolwyddelan, the birthplace o Llewelyn ap Iorworth: *top right* Castell y Bere under Cader Idris; *centre left* Ewloe Castle, built by Llewelyn ap Gryffydd; *centre right* Dinas Bron, at Llangollen, a seat of the Princes of Powys; *below* Dolbadarn Castle in the heart of Snowdonia

to the dangers that always threatened his work. Looming over it was the King of England. He was not likely to take kindly to a semi-independent Wales on his very doorstep. Llywelyn the Great from time to time sought friendly relations with the Marcher lords, which could be a useful counterbalance to the demands of the King. He married all his daughters to important Marcher barons while his son David married Isabella, the de Braos heiress.

The importance attached by Llywelyn to this last alliance can be illustrated by the tragic story of his wife Joan, King John's illegitimate daughter, and William de Braos. William had been taken captive during the disastrous Kerry campaign of the Justicar, Hubert de Burgh, in 1228. During his captivity he had arranged the marriage of his daughter with Llywelyn's son David and agreed to give the important castle of Builth as Isabella's marriage portion. But he also profited by his stay to carry on an intrigue with Llywelyn's wife Joan. When William returned for an Easter visit, Llywelyn discovered the intrigue and promptly seized William. Eight hundred men gathered on 2 May 1230 and as the Abbot of Vaudrey reported 'at a certain manor called Crokein he was made "crogyn"' (that is hung on a tree). Public opinion, not only in Pura Walia but in the Marches as well, was firmly on Llywelyn's side. It is pleasant to record after this that he eventually forgave his wife and she was buried with honour near Llanfaes, in Anglesey, where Llywelyn established a house of Franciscan friars to pray for her soul. The marriage of David and Isabella also proceeded, for Llywelyn was a political realist. The castle of Builth was a prize for which anything might have been forgiven. The King of England was not pleased.

For over all this hung the vexing yet vital question of the exact terms of Llywelyn's homage to the king. In the highly-organised feudal society of the thirteenth century, homage was a reality which had to be reckoned with. It was the social cement that held society together. The King was always acknowledged as being at the head of the pyramid and by the thirteenth century Welsh rulers also accepted the principle that homage should be paid to the King of England. Hywel Dda had done so, far back in the tenth century, and both Owain Gwynedd and the Lord Rhys had done homage to Henry II. But what should be the nature of that homage? Llywelyn ap Gruffydd, for example, claimed that this status in relation to the King of England was the same as that enjoyed by the King of Scotland. The barons of Wales had to pay their homage direct to Llywelyn, and the prince would then answer for them to the king. In Wales, the prince would thus be the acknowledged head of the feudal pyramid with all the power this gave him to develop the structure of his state on centralised feudal lines. The policy of the Llywelyns could not succeed in the long run unless they gained this power, and furthermore, their status had to be acknowledged by the king. The king took a different view. To him, the ruler of Wales was only *primus inter pares*. The great barons of Wales should also do their homage to him. This gave him a right of continual interference in Welsh affairs. When the princes were strong they could enforce a grudging acknowledgement of their position from the king. When they were weak, the king granted treaties firmly maintaining his view of homage. In

Welsh costume in the Age of the Princes, from a contemporary manuscript

the end, this vital question of the nature of homage brought Llywelyn ap Gruffydd to his tragic death.

Llywelyn the Great – Llywelyn ap Iorwerth – had sought to solve it before his death. He had two sons, Gruffydd by a Welsh lady and the younger, David, by his wife Joan, the natural daughter of King John, whom he had married about 1205. Welsh law laid down that both sons should have inherited – a law which had been the cause of so many of those disputed successions which had brought ruin to Wales in the past. In his own lifetime Llywelyn had seen how the land of Deheubarth had disintegrated under the squabbling of the heirs of the Lord Rhys. Llywelyn made a bold and half successful attempt to put this dangerous Welsh law aside in favour of the English system. He first, in 1220, got the consent of Henry III – or his advisors – to the succession of David as his sole heir. Then, shortly before his death, he called all the princes of Wales together at Strata Florida in 1238 and made them swear allegiance to David.

Llywelyn's plan succeeded on the first count. He secured an uninterrupted succession for David. On the second count, he failed. When David came to do homage at Gloucester in 1240 for his principality, Henry III allowed him to succeed but refused to let him have the direct homage of his barons. David struggled hard to avoid this term of the treaty – he even turned to the Pope. Mathew Paris records in his *Chronica Majora* under the year 1244, with a slightly acid tone: 'David intending to free his neck from the yoke of fealty to the lord King, took flight to the wings of papal protection, pretending that he held a part of Wales from the Pope directly.' [David may have tried further to maintain his independent status by altering the style of his title. He was the first to call himself 'Prince of Wales'. His father had simply called himself 'Prince of Aberffraw and Lord of Snowdon'. True, only one document has survived in which David uses the title and whatever the Pope may have thought of it, Henry III never acknowledged it. Indeed, the Pope eventually withdrew all support for David, and Henry III drove him back into Gwynedd's central core in a campaign in 1245 which brought the King possession of the Perfeddwlad, the country between Chester and the Conwy. He built a strong castle at Deganwy on the eastern bank of the Conwy estuary. The glories of Llywelyn the Great seemed lost in the past when David died in 1246. Once again the old principle had been asserted that Wales's opportunities depended on England's weaknesses. Henry III was no longer a minor as he was when Llywelyn the Great established his power. The King was vigorous and commanded a large army. The Welsh had no option but to retreat and hope for better days – in other words, for trouble in England.

David died childless and his two nephews, Owain and Llywelyn, inherited. The work of Llywelyn the Great seemed undone. Their father had been that Gruffydd who had been set aside by Llywelyn in favour of David. David had kept him in captivity but had been compelled to hand him over to Henry III, who confined him, in fairly honourable circumstances, in the Tower of London. The unhappy Gruffydd made a daring attempt to escape on St David's Day in 1244 but the rope broke under his weight – he appears to have been somewhat portly – and he was killed. But the escape attempt had made him a hero in Wales and the succession of his sons was welcomed, especially as the second son, Llywelyn, had been a notable supporter of his uncle David in his difficulties. The two young men only obtained their rights in Gwynedd by the harsh treaty of Woodstock involving the surrender of territory and the admission, once again, that Henry had the direct homage of the barons of Wales.

Their dual partnership could not last. Llywelyn was able and ambitious. He imprisoned Owain and became sole ruler of Gwynedd in 1255. He looked around him and sensed opportunities for a new and more adventurous policy. The political climate was becoming more unfavourable to Henry in England as Simon de Montfort began the movement of opposition to the royal policies which was to end in the violence of the Barons' War. There was serious discontent amongst the Welshmen who had recently come under royal rule in the Perfeddwlad. The great Marcher lords were becoming inevitably involved in the discontent in England. Llywelyn felt that the moment had come to strike.

In 1256 he launched his attack, with considerable military innovations for Welsh armies. He had armed horsemen to supplement his spear-carrying infantry; he had a plentiful supply of siege-engines and protected his coastline from Irish interference by a small fleet. His success was spectacular. In the years that followed, Henry made repeated attempts to stop him, but the growing political troubles that beset the king made his intervention increasingly ineffective. In 1258 Llywelyn assumed the title of Prince of Wales. The title seemed to have reality as Llywelyn took over the old lands of the Lord Rhys in south Wales, captured Builth and pushed deep into the lands of the Mortimers in mid-Wales and the de Braos estates of the south-east. By 1263 he had recovered the castles at Disserth and Deganwy. He was supreme in Brecon. The Marcher lords were shaken and demoralised.

His greatest opportunity came when Simon de Montfort led the barons in open opposition to the king and won the battle of Evesham in 1264. Simon de Montfort had sought the aid of Llywelyn, and even his defeat and the royalist triumph at Lewes in the following year did not shake Llywelyn's position. England needed peace and, as a result, gave Llywelyn almost all he asked for in the treaty of Montgomery, signed in 1267, twenty years after the treaty of Woodstock.

The two treaties present a staggering contrast. Montgomery seems to wipe away handsomely all the humiliation of Woodstock. Llywelyn's title of Prince of Wales was formally recognised together with his overlordship of the princes and barons of Wales. His territory stretched from the headwaters of the Taff to the most northerly tip of Anglesey. He controlled the Bohun inheritance in Brecon and the Pope himself recognised his position by allowing commissioners to go to Wales to try all citations to the court of Canterbury. The surrounding Marcher lordships remained, but all Pura Walia and even some Marcher territory were in Llywelyn's hands. Not even Llywelyn the Great had won such a triumph. But how solid was it? There were serious flaws below the splendid surface, that in ten short years would bring the whole structure tumbling dramatically to the ground. The scale of Llywelyn's success had brought back to the Marcher lords an appreciation of the threat presented to them by Llywelyn's new power. There was a younger generation of Lords Marcher, led by the fierce and vigorous Roger Mortimer, the lord of Wigmore, who had fought on the royal side at Lewes and had supported the Lord Edward as heir to the throne. Typical of them also was young Gilbert de Clare, Earl of Gloucester and Lord of Glamorgan, who was so alarmed by Llywelyn's presence on his borders and by the Welsh prince's attempts to claim overlordship over Senghenydd that he faced the expense of building the enormous concentric castle of Caerphilly, seven miles north of Cardiff, whose remains, surrounded by its vast moat, still astonish the modern visitor.

Left The carved face of Llywelyn, Prince of Wales, from Deganwy
Right The great seal of Gilbert de Clare

And behind these younger Lords Marcher was the rising figure of the Lord Edward himself, soon to become king, who had already proved his skill in warfare and who had now gone on a crusade from which he would return with a new determination and with an European outlook and reputation. It behoved Llywelyn to follow his grandfather's example and become flexible and not push his luck. Yet, on the face of it, this is just what he did not do. He firmly maintained every right granted him by the treaty of Montgomery, even though it was soon apparent that the climate in which it was signed was rapidly changing. When royal officials objected to the castle and market he was establishing at Dolforwyn on a hill over-looking the Severn not far from Montgomery, Llywelyn sent a stern reminder of his strict legal position: 'the rights of his principality are entirely separate from the rights of the King's realm although he holds his principality under the King's power . . . and the King has heard and in part seen that Llywelyn's ancestors and himself had the power within their boundaries to build and construct castles . . . without prohibition by anyone'. True enough, but hardly tactful.

Llywelyn had also become engaged to Eleanor, the daughter of Earl Simon de Montfort. After her father's fall she had gone into exile but Llywelyn still pro-posed to marry her. Again a source of irritation to the English king. Then in 1274 came the revolt of Llywelyn's troublesome younger brother, David; Owain played no part. David had been restored to Llywelyn's favour and given lands and status, but now he suddenly conspired with Gruffydd ap Gwenwynwyn of southern Powys to overthrow Llywelyn. Llywelyn discovered the treachery and seized southern Powys, while David and Gruffydd fled to Shrewsbury, from which point of vantage they conducted raids into Llywelyn's territory. It was at this critical moment that Edward returned to England as King Edward I.

Edward was now in the prime of life. He was a tried soldier and the friend of some of the most important crowned heads in Europe. He was also an organiser and a legalist, a ruler inspired by high notions of his position and of the honour he might bring to the realm, but also hard and inflexible. As soon as he returned, he took up the Welsh problem. His view was that of a man conscious of his rights. Llywelyn should first of all do homage, and then Edward would be willing to discuss all the other difficulties between them – the violations of the Montgomery treaty, the conspiracy of David and Gruffydd ap Gwenwynwyn, Llywelyn's mar-riage and his delay in paying his tribute money. It would be possible to come to an agreement on all the disputed points as had been done in the past. But homage would have to be done first.

Llywelyn put the priorities the other way – correction of grievances before doing homage. At this distance of time it is difficult to enter completely into the mind of a man of the thirteenth century and easy to blame Llywelyn. He himself, in a letter to the Pope, declared that he was acting on the advice of all his barons and counsellors. But it is clear that, at the back of Llywelyn's hesitation, must have lain his doubts about the nature of the homage Edward would demand of him, a fear that he might lose that direct control over his own baronage that lay at the very heart of the reconstruction of his Principality on centralised, feudal lines. This was a principle on which he dared not yield.

His hesitations were fatal. Edward repeated his summons and he sent the Arch-deacon of Canterbury as a trained diplomat to try and persuade Llywelyn. Llywelyn insisted that the place of homage be now moved to Oswestry or Mont-gomery. He feared for his safety. Edward finally determined to end the dispute by force. Sitting with his prelates and magnates in full parliament in November 1276, he rejected Llywelyn's excuses and decided to 'go against him as a rebel and a disturber of the peace'. And go against him he did, with devastating effect. Llywelyn's principality, so impressive to outside appearances, crumbled almost at a touch. Edward was a master of war and his army (and the campaign they fought) has been described as 'the best controlled, as it was the best led, that had been gathered in Britain since the Norman Conquest'.

Edward's strategy was soundly based and effective. He organised immediately a campaign in south and west Wales, which were clearly the weak points of Llywelyn's defences. Three military commands were created based on the English and Marcher counties nearest to the scene of operations; in the north, based on Lancashire and Cheshire; in the midlands, under the enterprising Roger Mortimer, drawing upon the resources of Stafford, Shrewsbury and Hereford; in west Wales, using Marcher lordships. These subordinate commands were so effective that by the spring they had regained the whole of the south Wales territories once occupied by Llywelyn. Edward himself arrived in June to conduct in person the final advance against Llywelyn's stronghold of Gwynedd. That advance was steady, methodical and overpowering.

An army of woodcutters cleared the way along the coast. By August Edward had reached Rhuddlan, at the point where the Clwyd is still tidal and could act as a port. Edward had mobilised an effective fleet from the tough seamen of the Cinque Ports. While he moved forward irresistibly to the line of the Conwy, he sent his fleet with a strong force to occupy Anglesey. The Welsh defences were outflanked, and in September the English harvested the rich crops of the island on which the Welsh were relying for their supplies. It was a thrust to the heart. Llywelyn's forces had hoped to repeat the traditional strategy of retiring to the wilds of Snowdonia until the winter rains came to their rescue. The Welsh had relied on these rains as confidently as the Russians relied on their winter snow against Napoleon and Hitler. But now there would be no Anglesey supplies to allow them to wait safely in Snowdonia for the winter weather. Llywelyn was forced to come to terms.

For a man who once held the whole of Pura Walia in his hand they must have seemed hard and bitter. By the treaty of Aberconwy the Prince of Wales kept his title, but was confined to his original principality of Gwynedd. David received land in the valley of the Clwyd, the princes of Powys returned and provision was made for Rhys ap Meredudd in Deheubarth. But the Marcher barons came back in force in Brecon and mid-Wales. Above all, the King gained the most from the surrender of Llywelyn. The royal power was now advanced to the banks of the Conwy and was firmly established on the west coast and in the valley of the upper Wye. Edward had become, in one stroke as it were, the greatest of the Lords Marcher.

The king proceeded first to make certain of his conquests by beginning an important programme of castle building. Aberystwyth, Builth, Flint and Rhuddlan were all under construction by the spring of 1277. Others were to follow. The administrative reorganisation of Edward's new possessions went on side by side. The king seems to have followed the precedent of the Lords Marcher and did not entirely sweep away the old Welsh law. But inevitably some English procedures were introduced which Edward's new subjects would find irksome and time-consuming. A new strictness would also be evident in such matters as tax collecting, and strangers would be occupying offices previously held by Welshmen. Llywelyn himself, it appears, tried to accept the settlement, although with natural misgivings, and the King of England might have hoped that he had settled the Welsh problem. He felt that he had not treated the Prince of Wales discourteously. He had waived some of the harsher money terms of the treaty of Aberconwy. He had restored Eleanor de Montfort to Llywelyn. He himself presided over their marriage in Worcester Cathedral where Llywelyn, according to the annalist of the Abbey of Osney, gained 'with a heart that lept for joy, his beloved spouse, for whose loving embraces he had so long yearned'.

There were other hearts in north Wales, however, which were being stirred to quite different emotions, Llywelyn's brother David foremost amongst them. He resented what he regarded as the inadequate provision made for him in the treaty of Aberconwy. He felt he had plenty of support from other Welshmen, now placed for the first time under the English. For six uneasy years they had tried to live in the restrictive conditions of the new administration, and they were near breaking point. In 1282 their discontent exploded into rebellion. David seized the castle of Hawarden on Palm Sunday and soon the whole countryside was aflame. David roused the south and the royal castles of Aberystwyth, Llandovery and Carreg Cennin were attacked. The Welsh princes of south and west Wales joined in. All the evidence points to the fact that Llywelyn was as surprised as Edward by the rising. But he could not face the shame of standing aside. Inevitably he was dragged in and had to take the lead in the insurrection.

In the first fury of rebellion things seemed to go well for the Welsh. Gilbert de Clare, who had command of the royal forces in the south, met with disaster at Llandeilo Fawr. Edward had not expected the rising and was furious with what he felt was the treachery of the Welsh, above all with David, the man to whom he had shown especial favour. He recovered his balance with impressive swiftness. The requisite forces were quickly organised and sent moving towards Wales. Edward's strategy was equally effective and followed in general the same pattern as in his first Welsh war. The breaking of resistance in the south was left to the subordinate forces under William de Valence, Earl of Pembroke, who succeeded the incompetent de Clare. By the autumn the task had been thoroughly done.

Meanwhile Edward himself had begun the reconquest of the north. Here again a major part was played by the fleet. Edward decided to begin with an effective occupation of Anglesey. Once the island was held, he would begin clearing the valleys of the Clwyd and the Conwy, for experience had shown that it would be dangerous to leave them in the hands of the Welsh. They would give the enemy the chance to cut in behind any army advancing up the coast road. Then the King would launch a two-pronged attack across the Conwy and from Anglesey.

According to the plan, Luke de Tany was landed in Anglesey. He mastered the island and built a bridge of boats near Bangor, but he was under strict instructions not to cross until the King was ready opposite Conwy. Edward set about clearing the Clwyd and Conwy valleys. By the middle of October the whole area was in Edward's hands, and he was ready for the final blow when he was much displeased by the arrival of Archbishop Peckham at his headquarters, who came in the hope of arranging a meeting to bring Llywelyn to reason. The well-meaning Archbishop had already sent on a distinguished Franciscan theologian, John of Wales, to meet Llywelyn in Snowdonia with suggested terms, and later the Archbishop went himself. Edward grew somewhat impatient during the long-winded negotiations, in which Llywelyn and David were offered compensation in English estates. The Princes rejected such terms which they felt would dishonour them. They may have been moved to reject them by the news from Anglesey. On 6 November Luke de Tany lost patience and disobeyed orders by crossing the bridge, only to meet disaster on the other side. He himself was drowned in the Menai Strait. Edward's resolution hardened and he prepared himself for a stern winter campaign.

But in the meantime disaster had also come to the Welsh – so complete and stunning that it broke the heart of their resistance. Encouraged by the defeat of de Tany, Llywelyn had slipped away to the south in the hope of reviving resistance there and again taking the pressure off the north. But his men were surprised and defeated at a ford on the river Irfon near Builth. Llywelyn, alone and away from his bodyguard, was run through by a squire who did not know who he was. Llywelyn's body was buried by the monks of Abbey Cwm Hir; his head was struck off and placed on a lance over a gate of the Tower of London.

The memorial to Llywelyn the Last of Cilmeri, near Builth Wells

David tried to continue the struggle. Edward closed in on Snowdonia and by January had captured Dolwyddelan. David slipped southward into the still wilder country in the heart of Cader Idris at Castell y Bere. In April 1283 even Castell y Bere was gone and David was a hunted man in the hills. He was captured and handed over to the English, as a chronicler sadly noted, 'by men of his own tongue'. Edward had no mercy for David, whom he regarded as an ungrateful traitor. At the parliament which met at Shrewsbury in October 1283, the unfortunate man was condemned to a terrible traitor's death. He was dragged to be hanged at the tails of horses, he was cut down and his body was quartered and the pieces sent to the four corners of the kingdom. His head was stuck on a lance and placed on the gate of the Tower of London, side by side with that of his far nobler brother. The dream of a Welsh independent state had come to a sudden and tragic end and there seemed no one worthy to revive it. Llywelyn's luckless wife, Eleanor, had died giving birth to a daughter, Gwenllian. The child was packed off to the distant obscurity of a nunnery at Sempringham. With one swift stroke the pride and hope of an independent Wales had been decisively crushed. No wonder the poet Gruffydd ap yr Ynad Coch poured out a cry of despair in that wintry December:

> O God, that the sea might engulf the land!
> Why are we left to long-drawn weariness?

7

Between Two Worlds

Edward I was now faced with the task of attempting a final settlement of Welsh affairs. He had first of all to try and create such a strong defensive system of castles and their garrisons throughout the new Welsh territory that the Welsh themselves would be intimidated into obedience, or if they risked rebellion, all the means to crush it swiftly would be at hand. The old castles, in areas previously surrendered to the Crown, were refurbished and expanded. Edward's castle building, particularly in Gwynedd, was on an impressive scale, and the group of fortresses with which he now ringed Snowdonia must rank as the finest system of mutually-supporting castles created in medieval Europe. Rhuddlan and Flint guarded the coastal approaches, Conwy the vital river-crossing into Snowdonia. Caernarfon and, later, Beaumaris, held both ends of the Menai Strait while Criccieth and Harlech sealed off Snowdonia in the west. They cost, for those days, the enormous sum of £80,000, and must have greatly contributed to the financial difficulties that later beset the king.

These Edwardian castles impress not only as fortifications but as genuine architectural masterpieces. They were created at a period when the medieval art of castle-building had reached its finest development, just before the advent of that great leveller, gunpowder. They embody all the latest ideas, including the concentric plan. Edward had had the luck to meet a master-builder and an organiser of genius when he stopped with his cousin, Philip of Savoy, on his return from his Crusade. Master James of Savoy seems to have been responsible for most of

The walled town of Caernarfon linked with the castle, as it appeared in the eighteenth century

the King's Works, as they were called. He could design with imperial grandeur, as witness the multi-angular towers of Caernarfon, with their echoes of the great and similar towers that ringed Byzantium. We admire them today, but the newly-conquered Welsh could hardly be expected to rejoice as they saw their own prison-walls rising above the still waters of the Menai Strait or on the high, craggy rock of Harlech. There were violent rebellions that tested Edward's new castle system to the utmost, including the revolt led by Madog ap Llywelyn in 1295, which, at one moment, almost captured the king, who had to race for safety back to his new castle of Conwy. But once again, Edward's military organisation proved to be very efficient and the castles, even when half-completed, proved their worth.

Side by side with the castle-building went the reorganisation of the whole of conquered Pura Walia. In the Perfeddwlad Edward rewarded three of his most faithful followers by creating what amounted to new Marcher lordships. Henry de Lacy received the honour of Denbigh, Reginald of Grey the lands around Ruthin, and the Earl Warenne Bromfield and Yale. This Edward had done while the campaign was still in progress, but in March 1284 he issued the long and elaborate Statute of Wales under which the country was governed for the next two hundred and fifty years. Basically, Edward extended the principle of the English shire system into Wales. Gwynedd was carved into the three new shires of Anglesey, Caernarfon and Merioneth. Cardigan and Carmarthen were re-shaped and the outlines appeared of the future Flint. The old Welsh 'commote' was retained as a basic administrative unit under the title of the hundred. Criminal law became English but the civil law remained basically Welsh. In truth the Edwardian settlement, in many respects, simply developed tendencies which were already being encouraged under the Llywelyns, and was perhaps more careful of Welsh susceptibilities than it used to be fashionable to admit. The country was ruled by the Justice of north Wales with his headquarters at Caernarfon, the Justice of south Wales based on Carmarthen and a Justice at Chester with responsibility for Cheshire, Flint and certain Welsh borderlands.

Edward also actively pushed ahead with the formation of new towns, most of them linked with the new castles and surrounded by walls, as at Caernarfon and Conwy. He was familiar with the 'bastides' planted by St Louis in Languedoc and which he himself had encouraged in his French possessions of Gascony. In addition to trade, the Welsh 'bastides' were also garrison towns in which the Welsh, for many years, were certainly not welcome. The castle-town concept however was not new to Wales and most of the towns of south Wales had started in that way in the previous century.

Finally Edward crowned his settlement in Wales by setting up his new shires into a principality. In 1301, over twenty years after the Statute of Wales, he invested his eldest son Edward with the honour at Lincoln and added to it the earldom of Chester. The new Prince of Wales thus became a man of power, far exceeding that of the average Lord Marcher. The late date of the creation of the title rather disposes of the most celebrated of the stories which gathered around the conquest and which is still firmly attached in the popular mind to Caernarfon Castle and to the modern Investiture ceremony. Dr David Powel, in his *History of Wales* written under Queen Elizabeth I relates how, after the Statute of Rhuddlan, the Welsh nobles refused to obey any other 'than a prince of their own nation, of their own language, and whose life and conversation was spotless and unblameable'. Edward promised them a prince who could not speak a word of English, who was born in Wales and whose life was free from all stain, and promptly presented them with his infant son Edward, who had recently been born in the new castle of Caernarfon on 25 April, 1284. The king, however, was certainly at Rhuddlan at this time and the young Edward was brought there on his way to London. He was not formally made Prince of Wales until 1301, although he had become heir to the throne in 1284 on the death of his elder brother Alfonso. Somehow it is hard to picture the Welsh nobles enthusiastically hailing an Alfonso as Prince of Wales!

They had now to come to terms with the Edwardian settlement and many found it difficult. In July 1284, a few months after he had issued the Statute of Wales, Edward held a great tournament at Nefyn which was long-remembered for its almost Arthurian splendour. The king may have had a reason for this beyond that of simply celebrating his victory. Medieval kings were accustomed to translate principles of government into practical symbols which could be easily understood by their new subjects. Edward had already tried to symbolise his earlier settlement by ceremonies which he hoped would give emotional sanction to the new regime. He had caused the reputed grave of King Arthur and Queen Guinivere in Glastonbury Abbey to be re-opened at Easter 1278, the year following his first Welsh war. Adam of Dowerham, a monk of Glastonbury, was probably present and gives a vivid account of how the graves were opened at dusk and two caskets discovered, one of which contained the bones of Arthur 'of great size, and those of Queen Guinivere, which were of marvellous beauty'. They were carefully wrapped in precious silks and reburied near the high altar. In all this Edward was clearly symbolising his right to be a true ruler of a united Britain. He was reminding the world and the Welsh that Geoffrey of Monmouth had glorified Arthur as the only rightful king over the whole island. And here was Arthur himself buried with honour not on Welsh but on English soil!

But there were many Welshmen who watched such ceremonies as the Nefyn tournament with anything but satisfaction. The revolts of Madog ap Llywelyn in 1294 and of Llywelyn Bren in south Wales in 1311 indicate the fires banked below the surface of general acquiescence. The administration of the new principality would inevitably seem intolerably English to men who remembered the days when Welshmen were in the seats of power. For the 'barons of Wales', those men of the princely class or the descendants of princes, now began a period of steady decline. The crown always looked cautiously at them as possible leaders of revolts, and with some justice. Their ranks were thinned out after each rebellion. The descendants of the Lord Rhys, with few exceptions, had lost their lands by 1300. The rulers of southern Powys had a more curious destiny. Gruffydd ap Gwenwynwyn of Powys had been the ally of Edward in his last campaign. He now regarded himself more of a Marcher Lord than the heir to an ancient principality. His sons carried the process even further, dropped their Welsh names and adopted the surname de la Pole. The inheritance finally passed to his grand-daughter, Hawise, who married John Charlton, a Shropshire squire, and southern Powys remained in the hands of their descendants. Even by 1336 it was still out of the hands of the crown. Gruffydd ap Gwenwynwyn thus had the final triumph over his old enemy Llywelyn.

Llywelyn himself left only the little Gwenllian who died unmarried. The claim to the inheritance of the Llywelyns ultimately passed to the descendants of Llywelyn's youngest and somewhat supine brother Rhodri, who had opted out of any struggle for the succession and had accepted estates in England where he lived safe but obscure. In his grandson however, the famous Owain Llawgoch, the fire and ardour of the great House of Gwynedd reappeared for the last time. He took service with the French some time after 1350 and became one of the greatest 'condottiere' of his time. Owain, himself, took his claim seriously and his employer, Charles V of France, obviously regarded him as an important card to play in his struggle against the English. Sir Owen de Galles was particularly popular in Paris and actually set about organising an invasion of Wales, which however ended abortively.

The English were naturally particularly sensitive about Owain's career. He may have been a gallant hero to the French but they were determined to prevent him, by fair means or foul, from eventually returning to Wales. In 1378 they succeeded in insinuating an agent, John Lambe, into his service, and Lambe pleased Owain so well that he made him his squire. One morning, while Owain was sitting watching his force besieging Mortaigne-sur-Mer in Poitou, Lambe suddenly turned on Owain and stabbed him to death. The assassin fled into Mortaigne and eventually received £20 as a reward for his foul deed. So died, under the knife of a spy, the last direct descendant of the great house of Gwynedd, of Merfyn Frych and Rhodri Mawr.

But as the descendants of the princes and the barons of Wales went into eclipse, another class was waiting in the wings and willing to take their places. Even before the fall of Gwynedd there were many Welshmen who saw the policy of the Llywelyns not as a noble assertion of Welsh independence but as a threat to freedom and a heavy financial burden. In Deheubarth and in Powys Gwenwynwyn the members of the old princely families of these parts resented the homage and the taxes imposed on them by the Princes of Gwynedd. The Welshmen of the Marches had long been in opposition and had had no hesitation in joining the royal armies in Edward's Welsh wars. The King's Welshmen formed a special guard. All these men almost welcomed the Edwardian settlement. The invasions that eventually ended the promise of a strong, centralised feudal state in Pura Walia were not exactly black and white affairs of patriotic Welshmen defending Welsh liberty against English oppression. This is not a picture that can be true, for medieval people's motives were not those of the nineteenth or twentieth centuries. Loyalties were local, personal and complex in the Middle Ages. We are not therefore surprised to find that there was one important class of men who were almost created by the Llywelyns but who yet found no difficulty at all in transferring themselves in a very quick time to service under the Crown.

These were the 'uchelwyr' noblemen – the lawyers, the civil servants, the administrators, of whom the arch-prototype is Ednyfed Fychan, the seneschal of Llywelyn the Great. His descendants seemed to be everywhere in the new government structure developed under Edward I and Edward II, and there were many others like them. These were the men who, in the social changes that altered the structure of land-holding in the fourteenth and fifteenth centuries, were to build up large estates and eventually to emerge in Tudor times as the 'new' gentry, on whom depended so much of the success of Tudor government. In fact, the family of Ednyfed Fychan supplied the founder of the Tudor dynasty as well.

The 'uchelwyr' were naturally working under the control of the men in the highest offices of the country who, for many more years ahead, would be English, but they remained Welsh in language and above all in their culture. To their homes came the bards, and the Welsh poetic inheritance remained safe in their hands. It was even at this time, when on the surface of things so much seemed to be lost, that the greatest poet Wales ever produced, Dafydd ap Gwilym, appeared on the scene. If he had written in a language more universally understood than Welsh, there would be no question of his European stature.

Dafydd came from the 'uchelwyr' class himself and was probably born in north Cardiganshire. He travelled freely through the Wales of his day, a jaunty figure, handling with masterly skill a new seductive metre, the 'cywydd'. The highly-complicated, sonorous, aristocratic verse that was the cult of the Welsh court had now given way to something far more popular. The form of the 'cywydd', and the themes which it treated, owed a great deal to continental influences. Like his contemporary Chaucer in England, Dafydd was familiar with such immensely popular European poems as the *Romant de la Rose*. But he struck a note that is also clearly his own. He regards the English with disdain and towns are places to avoid. He can laugh at himself, and turn aristocratic compliments and formal praises to noble ladies with the best of them. But the next moment he is singing of the white gull scudding through the waves, of sunlight filtering down into green glades where he lies in delight with more than willing women. He is nothing if not personal, a man made for the pleasures of the moment. Hear how, in Gwyn Williams' fine translation, he lures his love to the bracken with irresistible verve.

> Beauty, come to the hillside,
> Our bed be high on the hill,
> Four ages under fresh birches,
> The mattress of green leaves
> Valanced with brilliant ferns,
> A coverlet, against beating rain,
> Of trees that check the shower.

That voice hardly comes from a nation in despair.

There was another field besides that of the administration in which a Welshman could build a career in the king's service. He might not be welcomed in the new towns but he was encouraged to join the king's armies in Scotland and in France. At the beginning of the thirteenth century the long-bow appeared as a major battle-winning weapon and it was developed in Gwent and the south-east borderlands of Wales. The cross-bow may have been more accurate and had greater range, but the long-bow was a mass-produced weapon with ample penetrative power which, in the hands of an expert, could fire three times as fast. Against slowly-advancing armoured knights, as at Crécy and Agincourt, the effect must have been the same as machine-gun fire in World War I. The Welsh archers usually came from the Marches, and there were 3500 of them at Crécy. The north Walians were spearmen and probably stood with the archer as defensive support.

The first contingent of Welsh soldiers to fight on the Continent were the 5000 men enlisted for Edward's Flemish campaign in 1297. They were certainly brave in battle but they had a notable lack of discipline off the battlefield. The Ghent chronicler, Lodewyk van Veltham, visited them in their camp and was astonished at what he saw: 'There you saw the peculiar habits of the Welsh. In the very depth of winter they were running about bare-legged . . . Their weapons were bows, arrows and swords. They also had javelins. They wore linen clothing. They were great drinkers. They endamaged the Flemings very much. Their pay was too small and so it came about that they took what did not belong to them.' Their fighting methods came in for some criticism, too. The Welsh did not seem to understand the gentlemanly conduct expected on the battlefield by such knightly paragons as John the Good, or Froissart. They actually thought that the purpose of war was to kill your opponent, no matter to what class he belonged. Both sides condemned the Welsh soldier who jumped on the back of the Emperor's horse and tried to slit his throat, and Froissart expresses his grave displeasure at the Welsh footmen at Crécy who ran out amongst the fallen French chivalry and knifed them, blue blood notwithstanding; whereupon Edward III 'was after dyspleased for he had rather they had been taken prisoners'. And, no doubt, his Welshmen cost Edward a tidy fortune in ransom.

As the long French wars continued, the Welsh became seasoned and valued soldiers, although they never quite lost their reputation for enjoying life off the battlefield. The French used the term 'compagnon gallois' for born companions. But Wales also produced notable captains of the wars, like Owain Llawgoch on the French side or Sir Hywel y Fwyall who served with the Black Prince. Sir Hywel of the Axe (Fwyall) wielded the battle axe with such effect at Poitiers that he was said to have captured the French king himself. As a tribute, the Black Prince ordered the formidable axe to be placed in the royal hall where food was served daily before it. Sir Hywel retired as constable of Criccieth, one of the few Welshmen entrusted with the care of a royal fortress in the Principality.

Welshmen like Sir Hywel may have originally gone to the wars not out of any burning feeling of loyalty to the new dynasty but with a desire to make their fortune, yet curiously enough Wales did feel loyalty to Edward of Caernarfon,

Beaumaris

Harlech

OPPOSITE ABOVE Caernarfon BELOW Criccieth

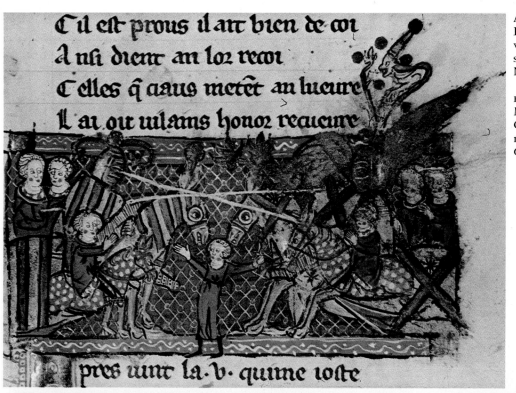

Cil est prous il art bien de coi

Ansi dient an lor recoi

Celles q̃ aẽus metẽt an lueure

Lai ou uilains honor recienre

pres uint la · v · quinte ioste

A medieval tournament. Edward I celebrated his victory with a particular splendid tournament at Nefyn, near Lleyn

BELOW The siege of Mortaigne, at which Owain Llawgoch was murdered. From the *Chronique d'Angleterre*

A Welsh spearman

their first English Prince of Wales, and it was to the Despencer lands of south Wales that Edward instinctively turned for help in the last tragic year of his reign, when hunted by his estranged wife Isabella, and her relentless paramour Mortimer. The whole lurid tragedy was closely linked with the politics of the Welsh Marches. Roger Mortimer was on the Queen's side, as lover and leader of the rebellious barons. The King's favourite, the younger Despencer, had married Eleanor, who had inherited the vast de Clare estates in Glamorgan when her brother had been slain at Bannockburn. Two great Marcher lords were once again clashing in a rivalry that was affecting the whole political structure of England. When all support fell away from them, Edward and the young Despencer naturally fled westwards into south Wales and Caerphilly, taking with them the royal Treasure and personal records. After some anguished wandering through Glamorgan, Edward and Despencer were captured near Llantrisant, perhaps in the dingle that tradition still names as Pant-y-Brad, the Vale of Treachery. Edward was taken back to England and eventually to shameful death at Berkeley Castle.

Yet behind these displays of loyalty to a fallen king, of service in royal armies in France and of willingness to enter the administration of the Crown, there were signs of deep-seated dissatisfaction. The fourteenth century is a puzzling one in Welsh history. Historians have called it the Age of Antipathy and Sympathy. On one side we see certain classes of Welshmen feeling that the conquest had brought them out into a wider world, giving them opportunities that neither Marcher Wales or Pura Walia could have offered. On the other there were still the memories of what might have been, and a deep-rooted hatred of the new English officialdom. In addition, Wales was not immune from the stresses that were running as well through society in England and on the continent as the century progressed.

The Black Death did not spare Wales. It entered the country in March or April 1349, and the effects were quite as horrific as they were in England. We have a description of its impact in a poem by Ieuan Gethin, all the more moving in that it describes the horror caused by the plague with the understanding of a poet and the symptoms with the precision of a trained observer. 'We see death coming into our midst like a black smoke, a plague which cuts off the young, a rootless phantom which has no mercy for fair countenance. Woe is me of the shilling in the arm-pit; it is seething, terrible, wherever it may come, a head that gives pain and causes a loud cry, a burden carried under the arms, a painful angry knob, a white lump.' By the end of March, the Lord of Abergavenny was dead and the nightmare was spreading rapidly through the Marches. It seems to have swept into the border counties of Hereford, Shropshire and Cheshire and then re-entered north Wales. The lead-miners of Holywell were so decimated that the workings had to be abandoned for a time. The Ruthin records show 77 of the inhabitants dead within six weeks. The plague seems to have reached south-west Wales by sea to Carmarthen. Again it began its irresistible advance up the west coast and soon decimated Cardigan. There is a lack of written records, but there can be no question that, eventually, not a corner of Wales escaped. It is also difficult to be precise about the exact effects of the Black Death on the Welsh social structure but in the Marches the manorial system was certainly as disrupted as it was in England.

In the Principality, too, the effect must have been profound and helped to speed up the sweeping changes in the system of land tenure which were already taking place. But, until a great deal more work has been done on this subject, it is difficult to pinpoint the exact contribution of the Black Death to the general malaise and discontent that seemed to run through all ranks of Welsh society as the century drew to its close. England had had its Peasants' Revolt in 1381. The Welsh explosion, when it came, was far more violent, it involved all ranks of society and almost reversed the Edwardian Conquest. Its roots were complex and some of them are still mysteriously hidden, but to the social causes must be added the racial tensions

The coat of arms of Owain Glyn Dŵr (Owen Glendower)

and the pride of the Welsh in their past, so sadly contrasted with their subordinate position in the government of the country. The materials for the explosion had thus been slowly accumulating as the century progressed. The disintegration of the manorial system in the Marches, the change to a money economy in the Principality, the 'new men' beginning the building of their estates, the new Edwardian boroughs, the strain on the unfree who, though less than one-tenth of the population, still supplied two-thirds of the royal revenue. And the Welsh had, in the English ruling class, the perfect target and scapegoat for all their own troubles and problems. It only wanted a leader to come forward and the Great Rebellion would begin. In 1400 he appeared in the person of Owain Glyn Dŵr.

Glyn Dŵr fulfilled all the requirements almost by accident. The Welsh did not want a John Ball or a Wat Tyler. The chosen leader would have to satisfy deeper national needs than just the aspirations of one class. The blood of the princely houses, however diluted, must flow in his veins. The bards, even though they might now be composing their 'cywyddau' for the 'uchelwyr', had always retained a strong prophetic theme, which had been unchanged through the centuries. Someone would eventually come who would restore the lost glories of the Cymry – a new Cadwallon, a new Arthur. On him would fall the noble task of driving the Saxons not only out of Wales but out of the whole of long-lost Britain. It was an impossible dream but probably all the more compelling for that.

Owain was descended on his father's side from the princes of northern Powys, on his mother's from those of Deheubarth. He had ancestral lands in the valley of the Dee, from which he took his name, but his seat was at Sycharth further south. Owain was thus a man of the Marches, for his estates bordered on those of Lord Grey of Ruthin. He also had close connections with the 'uchelwyr' class, for an important branch of the successful Tudor family were his first cousins, and the Tudors themselves were descended from the ubiquitous Ednyfed Fychan.

There were thus no revolutionary antecedents in Owain's family or indeed in his early career. He had learnt his law at the Inns of Court – in those days regarded as the place where members of the upper classes completed their education. In 1386 he was appointed a witness before a celebrated court of chivalry and his fellow witness was none other than the poet Geoffrey Chaucer. As a young man he had served in the Scottish campaign of 1385, and the bards who sang his praises paint a vivid picture of him, with a flamingo feather in his helmet, chasing the Scots before him like goats. By 1399 he was a successful man with the very adequate income, for the period, of £200 a year, settled in his comfortable manor of Sycharth. But in that year Richard II was deposed after being seized at Llanddulas in north Wales on his way back from Ireland. Henry, Duke of Lancaster, had met him at Flint Castle and had taken him back to England to deposition and death, just as nearly eighty years before, another king had been dragged out of Wales to the same fate. Richard II, like Edward II before him, had gained the support of the Welsh. The Tudor brothers were zealous in his cause. When Henry usurped Richard's throne he could look for little sympathy in Wales.

It was in this political climate that a dispute occurred over land ownership between Owain Glyn Dŵr and Lord Grey of Ruthin. Owain appealed to the King but Grey was a Henry supporter, and although there is no evidence that Owain had any personal connection with the fallen Richard, Welshmen were probably suspect at the new court. Owain turned then to Parliament. Although there is no actual record of it on the parliamentary roll there is no reason to doubt the story that Owain's case was thrown out with insult, Owain and his supporters being designated 'scurris nudipedibus'. Owain was now a man of middle-age who had won honour in the royal service and occupied an important position in the Welsh borderland. The insult was more than he could stand.

In September 1400 he met some of his supporters on his estate at Glyndyfrdwy in the valley of the Dee. With him was a figure called his 'wizard' in the English reports, but who must have been his household bard. Owain was straight away proclaimed Prince of Wales and immediately descended on the town of Ruthin. The rebellion had begun, and it progressed at a startling speed. Welsh students at Oxford and Cambridge hastened home to join it. The English parliament rushed anti-Welsh legislation on to the statute book but this only added fuel to the flames. Owain's cousins, the brothers Gwilym and Rhys ap Tudur, were with him from the start. They captured Conwy castle by surprise while the garrison were at church. Owain, himself, was now strong enough to move south to win an impressive victory on the slopes of Plynlimon. Soon the whole of Wales was in an uproar. The state of English politics worked in his favour. King Henry's usurpation of the crown had raised enemies against him and England was on the verge of civil war. Once again, England's difficulty was Wales's opportunity.

Owain had the stroke of luck he needed when, in 1402, he captured not only Lord Grey (who gave him a large ransom) but the even more important Edmund Mortimer of the great Marcher house. Mortimer's young nephew, the Earl of March, had a far stronger claim to the English throne than Henry, for he could trace his descent from the Duke of Clarence, Edward III's second son. Henry's claim came through, John of Gaunt, who was only the third son. Henry was thus in no hurry to get Mortimer ransomed. Mortimer, in his turn, listened to Owain. He became his son-in-law and, through Mortimer, Owain came into intimate contact with the baronial opposition. Owain then took part in the first of the great conspiracies that came near to displacing Henry from the throne. He allied himself with Henry Percy, the heir to the Earl of Northumberland (and Shakespeare's Hotspur). In 1403 Hotspur marched south to join Owain but Henry caught him before the junction could be effected, and Hotspur was defeated and killed at Shrewsbury.

Hotspur's defeat did not stop Owain. He still had his contacts with the Earl of Northumberland and, in 1405, Percy, Earl of Northumberland, Mortimer and Owain signed a tripartite Indenture that divided England and Wales into three. This gave to Owain an astonishing section of the country, a Wales which would have run from the Severn to the Mersey, including many of the border counties. It must be doubted if Owain ever thought of this as a practical proposition, but the division gave to Wales the Six Ashes on the Bridgenorth road and had not Merlin himself prophesied that here the Great Eagle would rally the armies of Wales for the Day of Deliverance? Owain knew how to keep his image bright in Wales as the appointed Liberator. This ambitious prospect naturally foundered, but meanwhile Glyn Dŵr had obtained a firm base for his operations. In 1404, he captured the royal castles of Harlech and Aberystwyth. He could now set up a court, construct an administration and give reality to his claim that he, alone, was the true governor of Wales. The countryside, with the exception of some remnants of Marcher lordships in Pembrokeshire and south-east Wales, was solidly behind him.

These were the years of Owain's glory, which his countrymen will always remember. In them he established his claim to be far more than a successful rebel. If the fates were kind, Owain would be able to construct that Welsh independent state that had eluded the Llywelyns and which would, moreover, have commanded the willing allegiance of every Welshman. He summoned his famous parliaments at Harlech and Machynlleth in which he consulted with representative figures from

Owain Glyn Dŵr's parliament house at Machynlleth

all over Wales. He was crowned Prince of Wales before the envoys of France, Scotland and Castile. He had his great and privy seals and, as his coat of arms, he took those of Gwynedd, a reminder that he was building on foundations laid by the great men of the past. More important still, he had started to win the support of the intelligentsia – the administrators from that 'uchelwyr' class who had done so well under the kings of England for the last hundred years. Not all of them; for there were plenty of cautious office-holders who preferred waiting to see which way the cat would jump, but enough to make his administration look impressive. John Trevor, Bishop of St Asaph, was now with Owain, together with Lewis Byford, Bishop of Bangor. Perhaps the most important recruit was the great lawyer, Dr Gruffydd Young, who Owain appointed as his Chancellor. These were all men of stature, with contacts on the Continent. With their support Owain's schemes now took on an impressive amplitude. He planned to set up two universities, in north and south Wales, to give him the trained administrators his new state would need. St David's was to become a metropolitan see, freed for ever from the foreign domination of Canterbury, and the policy was enthusiastically endorsed by a Synod of the Welsh clergy gathered at Pennal in 1406.

Owain seemed about to establish that independent Wales, so long prophesied and yet so difficult to achieve. Even his enemies now looked upon him with a certain admiration and awe, which finds an echo, so many years later, in Shakespeare's description of Glyn Dŵr (Glendower):

> In faith, he is a worthy gentleman,
> Exceedingly well-read and profited
> In strange concealments, valiant as a lion
> And wondrous affable, and as bountiful
> As mines in India.

But he is also a wizard, who 'can call up spirits from the vasty deep' and control the weather – King Arthur and Merlin combined.

Glyn Dŵr, however, was a realist. He knew well enough that everything must ultimately depend on military success and he needed allies – above all aid from France. Here was his most promising source of money and men-at-arms and for a moment it seemed as if he might get them in plenty. He drew up a treaty with the Regents who then governed France in the name of the mad king, Charles VI, which promised him aid in return for Owain's recognition of Benedict XII at Avignon, the schismatic Pope backed by France. In 1405 a French force did land at Milford Haven and Owain marched with it to Worcester where together the Welsh and French confronted Henry's army. Confront it was all they did – for eight days, during which neither side felt like leaving their strong positions to attack the other. Then the French slipped away in the night and Owain had to follow them. Never again would he be able to pose such a dangerous threat to English power. If the French had sent a stronger force, Henry might have been defeated and who could have foretold the consequences? But the French failed to understand their opportunity. Louis of Orleans became the influential man at

Right The Privy Seal of Owain Glyn Dŵr

Left Commission of the ambassadors of Owain Glyn Dŵr to the King of France

King Henry V of England

the French court and he directed the French effort into Aquitaine. The decisive moment passed. Owain still looked firmly seated in Wales but he was strategically now on the defensive and rebellions on the defensive are eventually doomed.

The rebellion took many more years to run its full course, but the end was inevitable. Henry IV had surmounted the crisis of his reign and had begun to get the better of the opposition at home. His son, Prince Henry, was beginning to demonstrate those military talents which were later to bring him European fame as the victor of Agincourt. His father could now reinforce him with men and money. Prince Henry was able to strengthen the castles which still held out in the midst of the rebel sea. By 1408 he was strong enough to march on Owain's main bases of Harlech and Aberystwyth.

It was now that the big guns proved their worth. Owain had always been short of artillery but Prince Hal could call on the Royal Arsenal. The great guns were shipped down from Yorkshire, where they were no longer needed against the northern barons. They were sent to Bristol and then brought by sea to the Cardigan coast. Stone shot, sulphur and saltpetre were gathered in quantities at the base of Hereford. The fortresses did not fall at the first shot. Aberystwyth held out for a long time but the guns made the end inescapable. It was the same with Harlech. Worse still, Owain's family fell into English hands and Mortimer died. By 1410 Owain himself had to take to the hills, no longer the Prince of Wales who sat in parliament at Machynlleth planning a confident future but an outlaw, a man on the run. The Tudor brothers were captured and in 1412 taken to Chester where Rhys was promptly executed. 1412 is also the last year in which we hear mention of Owain. Then silence falls. When Prince Henry succeeded to the throne he twice offered him pardon, but there was no reply. No one knows what happened to him. Some say he took refuge with his daughter's relatives-in-law, the Scudamores, in the remote Golden Valley of Herefordshire. It would be pleasant to think of the old rebel, at his sunset, finding a country peace. Wherever he may have gone, Wales could never forget him. Surely he had but gone into a magic retirement in some secret cave, from which he would return like a second King Arthur, when Wales had need of him! The support that ultimately went to Henry Tudor owes a great deal to the feeling aroused in Wales by Glyn Dŵr.

One morning, so the sixteenth-century story goes, Owain was walking on the hills near Valle Crucis when he met the Abbot. 'You are up betimes, Master Abbot,' said Owain. 'Nay sire,' replied the Abbot, 'it is you who have risen too early – by a hundred years.'

Tudor Triumph

T he wreckage left by the revolt of Owain Glyn Dŵr cluttered Welsh life throughout the fifteenth century. The bill for the material damage alone was enormous. In some of its aspects, Owain's rising had the furious passion of a Welsh Wat Tyler's revolt, and his peasant supporters burnt the property of English townsmen with a special gusto. The rebellion ranged wide and deep into the Marcher lordships as well as in the Principality. The castle of Swansea, for example, had to face major repairs for 'building anew and mending the walls of the bailey, broken and thrown to the ground . . . because of the coming of Owen Glyndourdy and other traitors threatening and rising in these parts.' Similar laments fill the records of most of the towns of Wales. The English armies burnt Owain's pleasant manor at Sycharth and wrecked the abbey of Strata Florida. Owain's men burnt Abbey Cwm Hir. Both sides adopted a 'scorched earth' policy and Wales bore the scars of the rising for many years to come. It has been suggested that the material damage has been exaggerated. Tudor writers, like Sir John Wynn of Gwydir, talked of the grass growing in the streets of Llanrwst for years after the rising, while Glyn Dŵr 'like a second Assyrian, the rod of God's anger did deeds of un-heard of tyranny with fire and sword'. But the Wynns, the Stradlings, the George Owens, were writing under Elizabeth and were taking care to contrast the blessings of Tudor peace with the miseries that had gone before. Yet the physical damage, in all conscience, must have been serious in a small country like Wales, where the total population could not have exceeded a quarter of a million.

The political damage may have been even more serious. For the first time, stern penal laws were placed on the statute book against Welshmen as Welshmen. No Englishman was to be convicted in Wales on the evidence of a Welshman. 'No rhymer, minstrel or vagabond' (in other words, a bard) 'was to maintain himself by making cymorthas or gatherings upon the common people'. No Welshman not loyal to the king could bear arms in town or in church or on the highway; no Welshman could hold office under the crown or serve on juries; intermarriage between the English and Welsh was forbidden. If it occurred, the English partner and the children would have to assume the disabilities of the Welsh spouse. Most of these provisions proved impossible to carry out completely and seem to have been tactfully allowed to lapse after the death of Henry IV, but the fact that they were enacted at all exacerbated grievances between Welsh and English, and kept writers on both sides nursing a deep sense of injury. The authors of the *Libell of English Pollecye* could declare as late as 1435:

> 'Beware of Walys, Christe Ihesu must us keepe,
> That it make not our childer's childe to weepe . . .'

Poets like Lewis Glyn Cothi and Guto'r Glyn were equally bitter on the Welsh side.

The anti-Welsh feeling in the towns took a long time to subside, while, for the Welsh, the words 'Burgess' and 'sais' (Englishman) became terms of insult. Yet life has to continue even when two races are insulting and distrusting each other. Again we come to that curious swing between antipathy and sympathy which has marked so much of Anglo-Welsh relations. While the Welsh poets were still polishing their insults, Welsh fighting men were entering the armies of England within a few years of the end of the revolt. Once more we come across a distinguished roll-call of soldiers from Wales, and many a gallant Fluellin fought with Henry V and in the long years of war that followed. David Gam of Brecon died at Agincourt. Sir Richard Gethin of Builth fought at Cravnant in 1433 and distinguished himself at the siege of Orleans. Sir Griffith Vaughan, Sir William ap Thomas and Sir William Herbert all made names for themselves, but perhaps the outstanding professional soldier was Mathew Gough, or Goch, a native of Maelor Saelor Saesneg, who fought all through the last period of the French wars and made a powerful impression on the French, who knew him as 'Matego'. He was in the battle of Formigny, when Normandy was lost, and met his death defending London Bridge against Jack Cade and his rioters in 1450. Most of the men of this nature came from the 'uchelwyr' class, and we cannot trace any connection between them and Glyn Dŵr's circle. Indeed, David Gam was regarded as a bitter enemy. Such men may have returned with considerable rewards from their war services, but their families were well established already. Sir William ap Thomas, the Blue Knight of Gwent, was able to build the splendid Yellow Tower at Raglan, so some of the wealth from the loot of France must have flowed back to Wales.

Was the Glyn Dŵr rising, therefore, all in vain, 'an expense of spirit in a waste of shame'? At the time it might have seemed so, but terrible though the experience had been, Welshmen were well aware that Owain had changed the course of their history. He had rekindled the flame of their nationality. Glyn Dŵr may have departed into the mists, but thereafter the Welsh were never to lose the feeling that they were a separate people – even when the law bound them ever closer to England. Modern Wales, it is claimed, really begins in 1400.

Fifty years later, in mid-fifteenth century, the clouds seemed to be gathering over Wales again. But this time they came from across her borders. Wales was still a country divided into two – the royal Principality and the Marcher lordships, but now the administration of Wales was going to be profoundly changed as a result of the long, complex agony that Tudor historians christened the Wars of the Roses, or, in the words of Shakespeare, 'the intestine shock, And furious close of civil butchery'. Deep currents of discontent were now flowing under the surface of English society. The humiliating failure in France seemed to tarnish the glory of the hero king, Henry V. The war had brought changes in trade, agriculture and social habits to which men found it difficult to adjust. There was an intellectual malaise in the air, almost as if intelligent people sensed that the old certainties in medieval religion and culture were beginning to show signs of strain. The times needed a strong king and that is just what they did not get. Instead of a Henry I, an Edward I or a Henry V, an incompetent sat on the throne of England.

Henry VI had succeeded his father at the age of two. Long minorities were always dangerous in the Middle Ages, when the character of the king had a profound influence on the state. He was not only the fountain-head of honour and preferment and the natural leader in war. He was also the head, the lynch-pin of the administrative machine. If he was incompetent, the machine faltered and the country fell apart. Henry VI grew up to be well educated, cultured and a lover of art. He was also excessively pious. Later Lancastrian propaganda tried to make him out to be almost a saint. If he was one, he was surely the most incompetent saint in the calendar. He had one final and terrifying drawback – he was subject to strange fits of melancholia that came close to madness. For long periods he would be silent and incapable of conducting any business at all. A grim prospect

The Yellow Tower of Raglan Castle, built by Sir William ap Thomas, 'The Blue Knight of Gwent'

indeed for a country facing an uncertain future.

There was an ever-growing feeling in the country that, somehow, the fumbling Henry should be replaced, but in an intensely monarchical structure, how can a king be legitimately deposed? It would be almost a sacrilegious act to push him off his throne.

> Not all the water in the rough, rude sea
> Can wash the balm off from an annointed king

Whoever replaced the ruler had to have an almost equally strong claim to the crown. In his veins should run some of that mystical tincture of the blood royal – the more of it the better. As the sceptre wavered in the fumbling hands of Henry VI, there was one man in the kingdom who had the right credentials to push forward and take control. Richard, Duke of York, could point out with justice that he was descended from the Duke of Clarence, the second son of Edward III, while Henry descended from the third son, John of Gaunt. In any case, the House of Lancaster had come by the throne through the usurpation of Henry IV, who had violently deposed the 'annointed king', Richard II.

The Wars of the Roses are thus a struggle for the control of the central power in the state, made all the more bitter by the scale of the prize at stake and by the fact that the claims of the contestants were so evenly matched. The Lancastrian supporters were the party in power and determined to stay there. Henry VI may have been useless as a leader, but behind him stood his formidable wife, Margaret of Anjou, who was determined to fight like a tigress to safeguard the rights of her son, Edward, Prince of Wales. Richard of York may have been a ruthless, unattractive boor, but once he had been removed from the scene early in the struggle after the battle of Wakefield, the Yorkist leadership passed to his son, Edward, Earl of March, a brilliant soldier and an able politician. He emerged from the opening stage of the Wars of the Roses as the first Yorkist King, Edward IV.

Wales was bound to be drawn into the turmoil as the two sides prepared for action. Both looked to Wales for support, for here the Lords Marcher had command over what were virtually private armies. They were bound to play a vital part in the struggle, but it would be their last appearance on the political stage. When the bloodbath was over the Crown emerged as the greatest Marcher lord of them all.

In Wales, the Yorkist strength lay in the east, the border counties and Gwent. Richard of York was, himself, a powerful Marcher lord through his possession of the Mortimer lands, while his great supporter, Richard Neville, Earl of Warwick, was all-powerful in Glamorgan. The Nevilles also held Abergavenny. The Lancastrian strength lay further west, above all in the royal Principality, and in the earldom of Pembroke. The lesser lords and the gentry hurriedly grouped themselves around their powerful patrons.

Those great propagandists, the bards, also followed suit. They still cherished the dream of a new Arthur, who would emerge out of the welter to revive the glory of the Cymry. The name of the deliverer varied according to the lordship in which the bard resided and the lord from whom he got his patronage. Huw Cae Llwyd and Guto'r Glyn became Yorkist admirers, while Lewis Glyn Cothi sang the praises of the Lancastrians. The Battle of the Bards could be as fierce as the clash of armies and, as a result, the drama of the Wars of the Roses – the personalities and the battles that stirred and influenced the Welsh – are somewhat different from those which affected England. For example, there were two big men in Wales on the Yorkist side when the troubles began. One was Edward, Earl of March, who would be the future King Edward IV. The other was William Herbert – 'Black William' to the bards. Both were young, vigorous and handsome, and naturally became close friends. An interesting man, this 'Black William': he came of comparatively lowly stock and had once been actually engaged in commerce. He was a sort of fore-runner of the enterprising Tudor 'new men'. The Welsh appreciated his ease of manner, his strength and his administrative talent. When he was killed, along with some of the leading Welsh gentry, at the battle of Banbury, the disaster was regarded as a Welsh Flodden.

The key man in Wales on the Lancastrian side was Jasper Tudor, who was the Earl of Pembroke when the wars began. With him we come to one of the great romantic stories in Welsh history – the rise of the House of Tudor.

The Wars of the Roses were to have two results of profound importance to Wales. The first was predictable from the nature of the fighting. Every battle ended with an almost ritualistic bloodbath in which the victors paid off old scores and killed their high-born prisoners. The Crown emerged as the main beneficiary from these orgies of aristocratic self-destruction. The second result was totally unpredictable, although it was closely related to the post-battle slaughter. When it was all over, the only surviving claimant to the crown proved to be a man of Welsh descent, Henry Tudor. To the astonishment of all concerned, a Welsh dynasty now sat on the throne of England. The story of the Tudors is so full of improbable chances that it comes perilously near illustrating the Cleopatra's Nose theory of history!

The Tudors were not exactly an obscure family back in their native Wales. They could trace their descent from Ednyfed Fychan, the seneschal of Llywelyn the Great. A Sir Tudor had cut a dashing figure at the pleasure-loving court of Edward III. Although some of the Tudor clan had blotted their copybook by taking part in the Glyn Dŵr rising, Sir Tudor's grandson Owain had been accepted into the household of Henry V. Perhaps the memory of his dashing grandfather eclipsed the memory of the Tudor rebels.

At any rate, this handsome young Welshman was at hand when Henry V unexpectedly died, leaving his beautiful young wife, Catherine of France, a widow with an infant son. She must have felt desperately lonely. She turned to this attractive Welshman of her own age, who may also have felt a stranger in a strange land, but was gifted with irresistible charm. Surely, never has sexual attraction had such an influence on the history of Britain! Although there is no actual record, it seems certain that Catherine and Owain got married in secret. It sounds like something out of a romance in a woman's magazine. The couple had three sons and one daughter, and lived happily together without any adverse comment from official quarters. When their association became public on the death of Catherine, there was some fuss about it. Owain did a spell in Newgate. In the event, the mild and forgiving Henry VI condoned his mother's offence – if offence it was – and Owain retired quietly to his native Wales, where he held the post of Keeper of the King's Parks in parts of Denbighshire. As Professor Chrimes puts it: 'At last, Owain ap Maredydd ap Tudor became unquestionably Owen Tudor, Esquire.'

His two elder sons did even better. Henry VI was tender towards the half-brothers to whom he had so unexpectedly found himself related. Edmund, the eldest, was created Earl of Richmond, and at the same time his younger brother, Jasper, was made Earl of Pembroke. In 1455, Edmund married an important heiress, Lady Margaret Beaufort. She was descended from John of Gaunt, Edward III's third son, through his mistress, Catherine Swynford. The liaison had been legitimised and the Beaufort line made respectable. Through the blood-letting of the Wars of the Roses Margaret would survive to eventually become the heiress of the Lancastrian claim to the throne. It would be through her that Henry VII would inherit his claim.

The marriage of Edmund and Margaret was short-lived. Edmund, who had gone to order affairs in Wales when the wars began, died in Carmarthen. His

The tomb of Edmund Tudor, removed from Carmarthen Priory to St David's Cathedral

pregnant young wife had perforce to place herself under the protection of her
relative, Lord Herbert. Through the whirligig of civil war, he was now Earl of
Pembroke, not the fugitive Jasper. Henry was born in Pembroke Castle. He was
a small boy in Wales, but can he be regarded as a full-blooded Welshman? He
also had English and French blood in his veins. Although he pensioned his old
nurse with a Welsh name when he came to the throne, we cannot be certain that
he spoke the language. No matter. He bore the name Tudor, and that guaranteed
him the unfailing loyalty of the Welsh.

He would certainly have need of it, for young Henry Tudor was growing up
in a violent and dangerous age. Every twist and turn of the civil wars would thrust
the lad forward into increasingly perilous prominence. From the start he received
continuous lessons in the art of political survival. No wonder that he grew up
into a ruler who could keep his own counsel, a cool and wise judge of his fellow
men. He had one unexpected yet precious asset: behind him stood his uncle Jasper
– no great soldier, it is true, but a consummate politician of infinite resource, and
what was even more important in this world of constantly-changing fortunes,
of unquenchable optimism. Again and again Jasper was to slip out of his enemy's
clutches. He would keep the Lancastrian cause alive in the hills of Wales long
after it had died elsewhere. If there was one single man responsible for the astonishing success of the House of Tudor, it was surely uncle Jasper.

Young Henry Tudor was only five when the opening moves of the Wars of
the Roses brought him face to face with the grim realities of civil strife. The Yorkists
took the first tricks. York, himself, almost took the throne. The indomitable
Margaret gathered her armies out of the north and Jasper roused Wales. The
Lancastrian cause revived. York was removed violently from the scene at the battle
of Wakefield, but that only left the way clear for his far more able and attractive
eldest son, Edward, Earl of March, who showed that he was a born soldier when
he crushed Jasper and his Welsh supporters at Mortimer's Cross on the Welsh
border. Jasper, always nimble on his feet, slipped back into the Welsh hills, but

there was one Tudor who was not so lucky. Old Owen Tudor was captured and sent to be executed at the market cross in Hereford. The gallant old amorist had been prepared to do his bit for the Lancastrians, to whom he owed so much. He had buckled on his armour and marched with the best of them to Mortimer's Cross. Even now, in Hereford, he remained an optimist. He could not believe that anyone would wish to execute him. All he had done was to console a lovely and lonely woman. It was only when they ripped off his doublet that he realised that the axe would really descend. He then made his exit with the dignity of a Great Lover. He turned to his executioner and said, 'this head shall lie on the stock that was wont to lie in Queen Catherine's lap.'

That head once caressed by a queen was set up on the top of the market cross and, says the chronicler, a mad woman came out and combed the hair and washed the face free of blood and set a hundred candles burning around that head that was wont to lie on a queen's lap. The act of a mad woman? Rather a tribute to the power of love even in the grim feudal world.

So the little boy, Henry, back in Wales, received an early lesson in the danger of being a Tudor of the male line. Mortimer's Cross was followed by the overwhelming victory of Towton. Edward, Earl of March, then took the final step. He had himself crowned as Edward IV. Margaret and her precious son fled overseas. Jasper flitted like a ghost among the Welsh mountains. Only Harlech Castle remained as a symbol of Lancastrian resistance. Stout old Dafydd ap Eynon declared: 'I held a castle in France until all the old ladies in Wales heard about it. I will hold this castle in Wales until all the old ladies in France hear about it.' But at last even Harlech fell – to the cannon of William Herbert, who became Earl of Pembroke in place of Jasper. Little Henry Tudor would now be brought up at Raglan, not Pembroke, in the care of the man who had taken his uncle's

Opposite Pembroke Castle, the birthplace of Henry Tudor

Below Raglan Castle, where young Henry Tudor was brought up

title and driven him into exile. No wonder that in his later years, Henry VII told Philippe de Commines that he had spent his early life either as a prisoner or a fugitive. He was growing up in a hard school. The Yorkist cause had triumphed and, on the face of it, there seemed no reason to suppose that any Lancastrian would ever again wear the English crown.

The Yorkists seemed to have everything going for them. Young Edward IV was proving to be a vigorous, competent king, in sharp contrast to poor Henry VI, who now disappeared into the obscurity of the Tower of London. Edward's rule was almost a preview of later Tudor policy. He even set about tackling the problem of the perpetual lawlessness of the Principality through a specially-created council for Wales and the Marches – a policy that the Tudors were only too glad to borrow.

Edward, however, made one strange mistake in the first part of his reign, a mistake which would never have occurred to Henry VII. He married not for reasons of state but for love. Worse still, his bride, the beautiful Elizabeth Wood-ville, was the widow of a Lancastrian supporter. Edward promoted the Woodville clan to high positions in the state. Warwick saw his power base with the king being eroded. Nicknamed 'the Kingmaker', Richard Neville, Earl of Warwick, had been one of Edward's firmest supporters. The years that followed the king's marriage were years of intrigue, of cynical double dealing, which came to a climax when Edward forced Warwick into exile. Warwick replied by taking the almost unbelievable step of allying himself with his worst enemy, Margaret of Anjou. The year 1471 saw the bloody end to the whole disreputable business, with Warwick being killed in the battle of Barnet and Margaret and her son, Prince Edward, landing too late with their army. Edward IV fell upon them at Tewkesbury. Prince Edward was killed in the rout almost before his mother's eyes. A few days later the hapless Henry VI was quietly liquidated. The last member of the Lancastrian line left in direct succession was the Lady Margaret Beaufort, the mother of Henry Tudor and subsequently the wife of Lord Stafford and then of the Earl of Derby. In such times, a woman was hardly likely to step forward as a claimant to the throne. Margaret wisely contented herself with supporting the career of her son. He must now take up the challenge. Not that there was much hope of him supplanting the now firmly-established Edward IV. Jasper Tudor, ever the optimist, whisked young Henry hurriedly off to exile in Brittany in the hope of better days.

If the House of York had behaved with ordinary loyalty and decorum, those days would never have arrived. Edward IV was a successful and popular ruler. His eldest son, Edward, Prince of Wales, was a bright and promising lad. The future looked assured, but once again, the luck of the Tudors came into secret operation. Edward IV died suddenly after a few days illness at a comparatively early age – he was not quite forty-one. His son and heir was only twelve. Richard of Gloucester, the late king's brother, became Protector of a realm that now faced the prospect of another royal minority. The temptation was too great. Richard usurped the throne. That usurpation destroyed the House of York at a time when ordinary prudence would have made it solid and safe for the future. Once again, a strange and unexpected bonus for the House of Tudor. The Yorkists were destroying each other.

There is no need to accept the Shakespearean picture of Richard as a crook-backed, designing villain – an Iago of politics. He was a good soldier and had served his brother loyally, but he now had the excuse that, in these stormy times, the country needed a strong hand at the helm. Once Richard had taken the fateful step of seizing the throne, there could be no turning back. In spite of the modern cult that has gathered around him, few serious modern historians doubt that Richard eventually got rid of the inconvenient young prince and his brother. It was a deed in the ruthless spirit of the Renaissance and the Borgias. Unfortunately for Richard, it also deeply shocked his contemporaries. Once again, that 'divinity that hedged a king' had been violated. The thoughts of many previously loyal citizens instinctively turned to the Lancastrian heir.

The whole nub of the affair was the growing certainty in the country that the new king had murdered his nephews. Why else should men who had everything to gain from a continuance of Yorkist rule turn to a young exile who was comparatively unknown and who had not lived in Britain since he was fourteen? Jasper Tudor, with his sensitive political nose, scented the change in the wind. Henry should show himself in England and put forward his claim. His first attempt, in 1483, was premature. It ended in the execution of the Duke of Buckingham, who had once been one of Richard's principal supporters. Had he been sickened by the murder of the princes? By 1485, the omens had become more favourable. Richard had lost his wife and his frail son and heir. He seemed to be a lonely, suspicious and beleaguered man. There were great men prepared to desert him. Treachery was in the air.

This time, Jasper wisely decided that Henry would land in Wales. Here the Tudor name would work its old magic. The bards were already hailing the young man from Brittany as the new Arthur, and, on 3 August 1485, the new Arthur duly embarked with his little armada at the mouth of the Seine. One observer described Henry's 2000 men as 'the worst rabble one could find'. Henry didn't depend on them. His venture was going to succeed or fail on the support of the Welsh and the secret pledges of certain great men. The support of the Welsh, at least, was totally assured. The greatest man in south Wales, Sir Rhys ap Thomas, would come over to him as soon as he had safely landed. Henry put foot on shore near Dale at the mouth of Milford Haven, and immediately began that march along the west coast of Wales that has accumulated as many legends as Napoleon's march on Paris after the return from Elba. The story goes that, as he approached Machynlleth in mid-Wales, Henry contacted the celebrated bard Dafydd Lloyd of Mathavarn to demand an assurance of victory. Dafydd had been one of the loudest voices calling for a new Arthur. He consulted his wife who advised him to prophesy resounding success. 'If he wins he will not forget you. If he loses you can forget him.' In the days that followed, there were many people on the road to Bosworth who were ready to act on Dafydd's wife's advice. Henry joined

Rhys ap Thomas on the Long Mountain near Welshpool. Here support came in from north Wales as well, and Henry's motley army, with its strong Welsh contingent, pushed on deeper into the heart of England, accompanied by bellowing herds of black cattle for supplies.

Henry met Richard's forces at Bosworth. The whole story of the battle is mysterious. It obviously turned on the pre-arranged desertion of the man under the great magnate, Lord Stanley, who was also a major landowner in North Wales. Richard, realising that he had been betrayed, hurled himself bravely into the midst of the fighting and was killed. The chroniclers say that the circlet worn by Richard rolled under a thorn bush. It was picked up and Henry crowned himself on the battlefield. He had won the throne by the sword. His great merit was that he stayed there.

For the Welsh the verdict of Bosworth was decisive. The whole nation felt that the age-long struggle with the English had ended in glorious victory. The prophecies had been fulfilled and Welshmen could hold up their heads again. Henry had marched to victory under the Red Banner of Cadwaladr. It was in Wales that he had been first welcomed and Welsh soldiers had played a major part in the battle. There would be some disillusion in the future, but all through the Tudor period Wales still basked in the afterglow of Henry's astonishing adventure. There was no further need to call for a new Owain Glyn Dŵr. The successor of Arthur was now installed in Windsor, surrounded by his Yeomen of the Guard, many of whom were Welshmen.

The king was not unmindful of how much he owed to Welsh support. He rewarded his followers generously. His uncle Jasper, the true architect of the royal good fortune, became Duke of Bedford and Justicar of south Wales, and later Lord of Glamorgan. Rhys ap Thomas was knighted and appointed Constable of Brecknock, Chamberlain of Carmarthen and Cardigan and Steward of the lordship of Builth. William Gruffydd became Chamberlain of north Wales. Welshmen entered into local positions of power on a big scale. Henry supported four Welshmen as bishops. Welsh sheriffs appeared in north Wales. Curiously enough no-one bothered formally to repeal the old anti-Welsh laws, some of which remained on the statute book until the reign of James I. Clearly there was no need to worry about them since Bosworth had made them a dead letter. But there were other delicate attentions to Welsh pride. Henry named his eldest son Arthur – the first fruit of his politic and successful marriage with Elizabeth of York, which symbolically united the red rose and the white. And he engaged expert genealogists to establish the Welshness of his descent.

Welshmen were made welcome at his court, and there was something like a Welsh job rush to London from Wales, such as occurred from Scotland later on with the accession of James I. So many Welshmen came to seek their fortunes that the somewhat atrabilious poet, John Skelton, circulated the story that St Peter, tired with the clamour for better jobs from the Welshmen in heaven, arranged for an angel to shout 'caws pobi' (toasted cheese) outside; whereupon the Welshmen rushed out in a body and St Peter slammed the Golden Gates behind them.

Henry VII, King of England and Wales

But for many an ambitious young Welshman Henry VII had left the Golden Gates to success wide open. Dafydd Seisyllt of Alltyrynys entered the royal body-guard. His grandson, with his name suitably anglicised, was William Cecil, Lord Burghley, Queen Elizabeth's great statesman.

Henry's own character had something of the 'Welshman on the make' about it. He had, after all, come to the throne after years of conspiracy and exile and he was determined to hold on to it. He early realised that a solvent king was a successful king, and when he died the crown, for the first time in centuries, had a big money reserve. The common picture of Henry is greatly influenced by the life of him written, a hundred years or more after his death, by Francis Bacon. Bacon admired Henry's statecraft; 'what he minded he compassed', and argued that Henry Tudor was 'the best sort of wonder, a wonder for wise men'. The king's care for money struck a slightly jarring note, for royalty was expected to make a noble show in those days. It was part of the technique of governing.

But what of his policy in Wales? Indeed, did he have a thoroughly thought-out policy at all? The Wales that Henry had been called on to govern by right of conquest was an administrative mess. It could be inconveniently divided into three parts, each of which had its separate administrative structure and even separate laws. First came the Principality – the lands conquered by Edward I and always granted to his eldest son. Then came the King's own holdings, most of them for-feited or gained from the Lords Marcher. Finally there were the remaining Lords Marcher holdings. The Greys, for example, still held the lordship of Powys and the Duke of Buckingham the lordships of Brecon and Hay. When a Buckingham was brought to the block, later on in 1521, the ranks of the once-powerful Lords Marcher looked thin indeed. With the death of the childless Jasper Tudor, all his vast lands in Wales also reverted to the Crown. But, even when in Crown hands, the Marcher lands – and the Principality, too, for that matter – remained one of the most lawless parts of the realm.

Social disorder was the major, the most pressing problem, that Henry was called upon to solve in Wales. He tackled it by trying to make existing institutions func-tion more efficiently and not by remodelling them completely. That was to be the task of the next reign. But he did re-animate the Council in the Principality and the Marches of Wales. Like the Star Chamber in London, which Henry was finding so useful in suppressing over-mighty subjects in England, the Council in Wales had been sketched out, as it were, by Edward IV. Henry developed it. He was anxious to have a court which would avoid the inconvenience to poor Welsh suitors of having to travel to London. He was also anxious to establish his son. and heir in a position where he would gain administrative experience. Arthur was now fifteen and had just married Catherine of Aragon. He proceeded to the Marches and set up his court at Bewdley, heading the Council, but within six months he was dead. A sad blow to the hopes of the king.

But the Council continued and ultimately made its centre at Ludlow. Through-out Tudor times and even under the Stuarts, Ludlow could be regarded as the capital of Wales, as far as it had one. Certainly, it was the spot to which ambitious lawyers tended to gravitate in default of London. Henry's Council worked hard, but as long as the separate legal structures existed in Wales, the Council's work was bound to be frustrating.

In all this, Henry, consciously or unconsciously, was simply giving an open field for the advance of the 'uchelwyr' – the gentry. They were taking over the secondary administration in the Principality. They had been his strong supporters in the march to Bosworth. From their ranks would come the 'new men' on whom the Tudors based their administration, the loyal gentry on which they could always rely. The bards may have dreamt of a Wales in which every office would have been held by Welshmen, and some of them were already lamenting that Henry was not behaving like another Cadwaladr. The hard-headed gentry knew better. They were firmly convinced that Henry's victory had not only opened the path

Ludlow Castle, when it was the legal centre of Wales

of glory to them but the wide road to cash and social advancement as well.

Henry died in 1509. George Owen, the Elizabethan historian of Pembrokeshire, gives a patriotic account of the king's deathbed, in which he says of Henry that 'he gave in charge, as it is thought, to his son, Prince Henry, that he should have a special care for his own nation, the Welshmen'. There is no evidence that Henry VIII felt that he had to take a special care for Wales. His father was bound to realise how much he owed to Welsh support, but Henry had come to the throne in his own right and looked on Wales not as something special but as part of the general problem of government. In any case, after the repeated Tudor marriages, first of Edmund with Margaret Beaufort and then of Henry VII with Elizabeth of York, the blood of the family of Ednyfed Fychan was getting pretty diluted. No matter. That drop of Welsh blood would ensure the basic devotion of the Welsh to the House of Tudor, come what may. What eventually came under Henry VIII was a drastic solution of the Welsh problem that is still the cause of furious debate today – the complete union, both political and legal, of Wales with England.

Side by side with the Acts of Union came an equally thorough Reformation of the church. On the face of it, both events look like a violent and complete reconstruction of the whole life of Wales, ruthlessly imposed from without. Many later critics have looked back on this Tudor settlement of Welsh affairs with regret and dismay, even as the source of many of the ills they lament in modern Welsh society. When all the consequences had worked through the social fabric, Wales would be left a land of anglicised gentry, 'discarding', so it is claimed, 'all sense of responsibility for native Welsh society'. The religious life of the church would be so atrophied that it would eventually need the excesses of a Methodist revival to resurrect it. 'Mute, suffering Wales,' lamented the late Victorian historian, Sir Owen Edwards, 'apathetic while the world around was awakening to a bright morning, suspected by rulers who thought that its very patriotism was tinged with a smouldering rebellion, betrayed by the reformers whose selfishness and insolence had brought the spirit of the Reformation in a degraded form to its mountains.' Eloquent words, that depict a sad sea-change in that once high-spirited, Catholic Wales that Henry VII is supposed to have commended with special care to his son!

Yet there is one aspect of these events which continues to puzzle us and demands an explanation. No one doubts that the Tudor legislation wrought remarkable changes in Welsh society, but how violently were they resented – if they were resented at all? There is a suspicious quiet about the whole affair. If the Acts of Union did such damage to the life of Wales and its language, where was the new Owain Glyn Dŵr to lead the protest? If the Reformation in Wales was 'the unwelcome Reformation', where was the Welsh Pilgrimage of Grace, on the lines of the rising that shook the north of England with the Dissolution of the Monasteries? We will only reach a fair understanding of the Tudor approach to the Welsh dilemma if we try to see it through the eyes of contemporaries. King Henry VIII and his advisors were not legislating for posterity. They were trying to tackle a pressing problem in the best ways available at the time. In the eyes of most contemporary Welshmen – or at least, the Welshmen of influence in society – they succeeded.

The great Acts of Parliament that reconstructed the legal and political life of Wales and the Reformation of the Welsh Church were all the products of the middle and old age of Henry VIII. In his vigorous youth, Henry was determined to cut a dashing figure on the European stage. The tedious business of administration was left to Cardinal Wolsey. Affairs in Wales remained as Henry's father had left them and the same principles of policy applied.

The King was supreme in Wales. The old lands of the Principality had been at the ultimate disposal of the crown since 1284. Henry now held directly most of the Marcher lordships. The only great estates out of his clutches were those of the Earl of Derby in north-east Wales and the holdings of the Earl of Worcester in the south and west, including Raglan and Gower. The mighty of the Marches

The Dissolution of the Monasteries: (TOP) the ruins of Tintern in Gwent and the fortified priory of Ewenny in Glamorgan

The shrine of St Winefred at Holywell. The well was closed in the Reformation

The rood–screen at the lonely church of Llanano survived the zeal of the reformers

Thomas Cromwell, the powerful minister of Henry VIII

had indeed fallen. If the King decided to tackle the reorganisation of Wales, there would be no one to resist him.

The moment of decision for Wales came with the advent to power of the formidable and able minister, Thomas Cromwell. Henry had reached breaking point with Rome in the urgent matter of his divorce. Cardinal Wolsey had failed to obtain it and had fallen, Sir Thomas More had opposed it and gone to the block. True, Henry was being driven to desperate measures by his middle-aged infatuation with the beautiful and designing Anne Boleyn, but he was also haunted by another obsession. He was now approaching his forties and there was still no male heir. The nightmare loomed again of a female on the throne in the future or of a long minority; an ironic fate for the descendant of that supreme and potent amorist, Owen Tudor. In the background lay the ferment of the Lutheran Reformation on the continent which deepened and sharpened the intellectual argument surrounding the divorce. To the swift solution of these complex matters Thomas Cromwell brought the incisive mind of a brilliant administrator. Professor Elton has produced powerful arguments to mark Cromwell as the real creator of the modern state in England, the builder of its bureaucracy. It was inevitable that he would turn his reforming zeal on to the problem of Wales.

He gave a foretaste of his intentions when he appointed one of his nominees to the Council of the Marches, in 1534. Roland Lee was a very ruthless fellow indeed. He had been made bishop of Lichfield and Coventry, but did not worry overmuch about Holy Orders. His policy was to be merciless, to strike terror into wrongdoers the whole length of the border. His enemies reported to Cromwell: 'You have lately holpen an earthly beast, a mole and an enemy to all good learning into the office of his damnation.' Lee cared not a jot about such criticisms. He had brought the calm of fear into the unruly borderland. But although Lee's methods might succeed on the surface, they did not solve the real problem – the impossibly complicated process of justice in the Marcher lordships. A solution to the problem had been long delayed mainly because there had been no real determination to tackle it from the centre. With Cromwell, that determination was there in strength.

In the eight short years during which he held power, he imposed upon the old, untidy medieval administration of the country a centralised order. He made England a modern, sovereign state on the new Renaissance model. Everything, the Church included, became subordinated to the underlying power of the King. Cromwell was therefore bound to set about tidying up the administration of the outlying possessions of the Crown – Ireland, the Channel Islands and Calais and he could not leave out Wales, the land closest to the seat of government. Its perpetual lawlessness, the chaos of its legal arrangements, must have been a sore trial to his tidy administrator's mind. He set about drastically remodelling it.

Cromwell outlined his plans for the new administration of Wales in the first of the Acts of Union in 1536. It is worth looking at the Preamble, for it clearly defined the purpose of the act and also contained phrases that can still rankle in the minds of modern Welshmen. 'Albeit the Dominion, Principality and Country of Wales, justly and ever hath been, incorporated and annexed, united and subject to and under the Imperial Crown of the Realm as a very member of the same, wherefore the King's most royal Majesty is very head, king, lord and ruler; yet notwithstanding, because in the same country divers rights, usages, laws and customs be far discrepant from the laws and customs of the realm and also because the people do daily use a speech nothing like or consonant with the mother tongue used within this realm, some rude and ignorant people have made distinction between the King's subjects of this realm and his subjects of Wales . . . His Majesty ordains . . . that Wales shall for ever, from henceforth, be united and annexed to and with his realm of England.'

That bland phrase about Welsh not being 'consonant to the mother tongue used within this realm' has irritated Welshmen down the ages. The Act went on to create the machinery whereby Wales would become an integral part of England, working within the same legal, political and administrative structure. The shire system, already established in the Principality by Edward I, was now extended over the whole country. Some lordships were attached to existing shires like Cardigan and Carmarthen. New shires were formed out of old Marcher and royal lord-ships in Monmouth, Brecon, Radnor, Montgomery and Denbigh. English was to be the language of the courts and a knowledge of English was to be the test of fitness for public office. The second Act of Union, passed after Cromwell's death, filled in the details and departed from Cromwell's plan for complete identification with England. Wales was now to have its own system of higher courts, the Courts of the King's Sessions in Wales, independent of the high courts in Westminster. The country was divided into four circuits, with the exception of Monmouthshire, which was attached to the Oxford circuit for convenience of travel. In other respects, Monmouthshire remained in Wales. The law to be administered in all courts, high and low, was to be the Common Law of England. The act of 1542 also provided for the continuance of the Council of Wales and the Marches, with its special responsibility for the overseeing of law and order.

For contemporary Welshmen the really important part of the acts was the prov-ision they made for all Welshmen to have equality before the law. Welshmen no longer needed letters of denizenship to participate in municipal life in the boroughs. Wales was also to have its own knights of the shire in Parliament. More important still, eight justices of the peace were to be appointed to each Welsh shire. This was in accord with the Tudor policy, already well established in Eng-land, of associating the gentry, the men of substance, with the practical details of government at local level. This policy proved equally effective in Wales and gave stability to the whole administrative structure. The justices of the peace became the men who really controlled the everyday life of Wales and their support became doubly important during the other great revolutionary change introduced by Cromwell, the Reformation of the Church in Wales.

The Union and the Reformation are hard to disentangle in Welsh politics. One seems to complement the other, yet it should be remembered that the great changes in church government were already in full swing before the first Act of Union. Between 1529 and 1534, all the major acts had been passed establishing royal supremacy over the Church. Nothing is more remarkable than the lack of any real, violent protest in Wales among all classes as hammer-blow after hammer-blow smashed the old religious structure. There were some individual protests, some background murmuring, as it were, but there was no Pilgrimage of Grace. Wales alone, among the Celtic areas of Britain, did not feel it incumbent to defend the Old Religion in arms. The truth of all this may lie in the old axiom: 'Men will defend so lightly only what they so lightly hold.'

Monasticism, for example, had long lost its hold on the people. The glories of the Welsh Cistercians lay two hundred years in the past. Even a once-great house like Tintern had only thirteen monks. There were no vast scandals to unearth when the first commissioner went on tour, although it does seem a little strange that the Abbot of Valle Crucis could be arrested for highway robbery in 1535 or that a monk of Strata Florida was caught using his cell for a quiet piece of coin forgery! The monasteries had outlived their usefulness and there was no real protest when they were dissolved. The gentry were only too pleased to be able to purchase the land. Even fervent Catholics like Sir Edward Carne, one of the leading men of Glamorgan, who afterwards became Queen Mary's ambassador to Rome, did not hesitate to traffic extensively in monastery property. And her great Catholic magnate, the Earl of Worcester, got most of the rich lands of Tintern, and at bargain prices at that!

The Welsh did not feel deeply over the question of papal supremacy. The Pope was a distant figure who impinged little on their everyday lives, and whose financial exactions they were glad to get rid of. The doctrinal changes that the Reformation brought in its train were a little more bewildering. Wales was a small, poor and backward country on the outer edge of civilised Europe as far as the early reformers were concerned. The intellectual side of the Reformation had made little impact. The language barrier had something to do with it. The invention of printing had been one of the major reasons for the rapid spread of the reform doctrines, but there were, as yet, no printed books in Welsh. There were indeed some brilliant young Welshmen who had become enthusiasts for the Reformation – men like Richard Davies and William Salesbury, who would make their mark in the future, but the most prominent protagonist of the early Henrican Reformation in Wales was William Barlow, who came from the anglicised area of south Pembrokeshire. The little ports of this part of the country had long contacts with Bristol. They could be receptive to advanced ideas which would have no foothold in other parts of Wales.

Barlow owed his rise to the favour of Cromwell and, intriguingly enough, to the support of Anne Boleyn – Henry had given her the lordship of Pembroke. Barlow was hardly a tactful man and set to work as Bishop of St David's with a furious zeal that made him plenty of enemies among his own clergy. He transferred the official cathedral of the see from the old centre of St David's, with its long tradition of pilgrimage, to Carmarthen. The noble bishop's palace in St David's was abandoned as Barlow made Abergwili, just outside Carmarthen, his official administrative centre. It was a convenient point from which to control his far-flung diocese, but outraged the traditionalists. When Barlow was transferred to Bath and Wells in 1548, there was a sigh of relief throughout the south-west. His tactless methods had conspicuously failed to proselytise the area for the New Religion. His successor, Robert Ferrar, was to suffer martyrdom under Queen Mary. There was sympathy for him but no help. Protestantism was not yet a cause for which many Welshmen would risk their lives.

Towards the close of his reign Henry put a brake on violent doctrinal change. The Welsh clergy were only too pleased to pause and draw breath, but as soon as death had claimed the most formidable of the Tudors in January, 1547, the pace quickened again. The young king, Edward VI, was in the hands of the advanced reformers. They began a major assault on the last bastions of the Old Religion. There was a wholesale appropriation of the funds of collegiate churches, the monies for chantries and charity endowments. The reforming zeal spread to the destruction of images and rood screens and the confiscation of church plate. Next it was the turn of the Welsh shrines of popular pilgrimage. Away went the

The remains of the Chapter House of Margam Abbey

wonder-working image of the Virgin of Cardigan and her miraculous taper. The wooden image of Derfel the Mighty was sent to Smithfield to be burnt. St Winefred's Well at Holywell was closed. The reformers feared popular reaction, and gave instructions that the famous shrine of the Virgin at Pen-Rhys, high on the mountain top behind the Rhondda, should be destroyed at night. They need not have worried. Again there were murmurings, individual protests, but no rising. No doubt the ordinary people resented the despoiling of their local churches, where greedy hands had removed everything of value, leaving the building a bleak, cheerless place to the worshipper. Poets lamented the unhappy fate of their old-fashioned, easy-going parish priests, forced by the reformers to reject the doctrine of transubstantiation to 'bury His body and summons men to the mere eating of bread crumbs.'

But no historic movement can be set down in plain black and white. If the Reformation had merely been a matter of looting church property it would never have got off the ground, even in remote Wales. It had been fuelled by the intellectual ferment of the Renaissance and driven to success by the propaganda of the

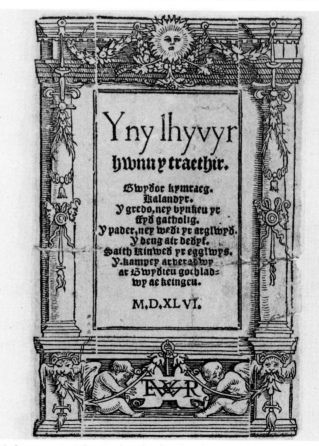

Above Yn Y Llyfr Hwn – In This Book – the first book printed in the Welsh language

Top The Strata Marcella indulgence slip

printing press. There were now Welsh scholars among the Reformers, who were few in number but all the more passionately determined to bring their country into line with the new 'humanism'. It was high time that the powerful modern technique of the printed word should be applied to the Welsh language, above all in the service of religion.

William Salesbury had been fired by the New Learning while at Oxford. He was a remarkable scholar and the master of an amazing number of languages, from Hebrew and Greek to German. He devoted himself to the work of marrying the Welsh tongue to the printed word with boundless zeal. Between 1547 and 1553 he poured out an impressive list of books, from a dictionary to a translation of the epistles and gospels from Cranmer's recently issued Book of Common Prayer. The first to appear was his English-Welsh dictionary, but it may not have been the first book actually printed in Welsh. That honour is disputed by Sir John Price of Brecon who published, in the same year, 1547, a small volume known, from its first words, as *Yn Y Llyfr Hwn* (In This Book). It contained a translation of the Creed, the Lord's Prayer, and the Ten Commandments, although the author, either by accident or happy design, omitted the eighth commandment!

A further small irony. Although these were the first printed books in Welsh, they did not contain the first words concerning Wales in printed form. Years before, printed slips had been sold in Carmarthen bearing indulgences from sins – the very practice that had sparked off Luther's first defiance of the Pope!

How far had the devoted labours of men like William Salesbury and his friend, Richard Davies, affected the nation? How deeply had Reformation ideas penetrated the minds of the average Welshman? The test came when the sickly young Edward VI died prematurely in May, 1553, and the Catholic Mary came to the throne. Again England was to do a dramatic turnabout and Wales dutifully followed. Lady Jane Grey had been proclaimed in one or two places in north Wales but there was no support for her. Mary was a Tudor in the direct line of succession. That was enough.

The new queen came to the throne determined to undo the work of the Reformers. The papal supremacy was restored and the doctrinal changes declared null and void. Wales accepted it all once again without protest, but was it from a deep devotion to the old Catholic religion or because Mary was Henry VII's granddaughter? There were only three Protestant martyrs in Wales and they did not come from the Welsh-speaking areas. Robert Ferrar, once Bishop of St David's, was brought back to his old diocese to die with noble courage at Carmarthen. William Nichol was burnt at Haverfordwest and a fisherman, Rawlings White, went to the stake at Cardiff. Perhaps we should not use the fewness of the number of martyrs in Wales as an indication of the extent of Protestant sympathies. There may have been Welshmen among those who suffered in the south-east of England, where the authorities were more determined to use the stake to deter other heretics. Some Welsh churchmen took the fiery hint and fled overseas. They included Richard Davies, while William Salesbury retired to live obscurely in the country.

The well-connected Protestant sympathisers in the upper ranks of society seem to have been left alone. They were too powerful to be touched, but the clergy were in a different position, especially when it came to the vexed question of clerical marriage.

The gentry were the key men in Tudor administration. They were happy enough to agree with the doctrinal changes. They were not too distressed about the difficulties of the clergy, but on one thing they were adamant. Even the most fervent Catholics among them would not restore the church lands and property which had come into their hands. On this point, the Marian restoration faltered. It collapsed completely when Mary died, a bitterly disappointed and childless woman, in 1558. The reign of Edward VI had been too short to establish extreme Protestantism. Mary's reign had been equally short – a mere five years – and had given her no time fully to restore the Old Religion. The new, young queen was Elizabeth I. She was to reign for a glorious forty-five years, ample time to soothe the wounds inflicted over those tumultuous decades of change; time to reach that most desirable of political havens – an acceptable and workable religious compromise.

As the reign of Elizabeth began, it is possible to get a clearer picture of the way things were going in Wales after the momentous upheavals of the recent past. Once again, her church settlement was accepted without serious trouble. The Acts of Supremacy and of Uniformity, passed in 1559, restored the Queen as head of the Church and enforced the use of the prayer book of 1552. A few distinguished Welsh Catholics felt that they could not accept the change. Sir Edward Carne, who was now ambassador to the Holy See, preferred to stay in Rome rather than return. Gruffydd Roberts, one of the greatest of the Welsh 'humanists', left Bangor with another great scholar, Morys Clynnog, to go into exile in Milan. These men, and others like them, were to play a distinguished part in the later attempts by the Douai and the Jesuit missionaries to restore England and Wales to the old faith. But although these daring seminary priests did have some impact on the old Catholic remnants in the north and south, the country as a whole remained indifferent. It showed the same indifference to the more extreme forms of Protestantism as well. Later in the reign, John Penry, one of those involved in the Martin Marprelate affair, made an eloquent appeal for a preaching ministry in Welsh, but his was a lone voice. He went to the gallows in 1593 and the Puritan movement did not come to grips with Wales until fifty years after his death. The vast majority of the clergy and gentry sought the Middle Way. Below them, the ordinary people went on with their old practices, unaware of many of the controversies that raged furiously above their heads. The lower clergy, come what may, would have to remain Welsh-speaking if there was to be any religious communication with their congregations at all.

The people in Wales who had emerged most successfully from the early turmoils of the Tudor period were undoubtedly the gentry. They were the keystone in the system of government, the firm cement of its society. They were not a hom-

Sir John Wynn of Gwydir and Gwydir Castle, near Llanrwyt in the Conwy valley

ogenous class. There was a wide social gap between a great lord like William Herbert, Earl of Pembroke and George Owen, the Baron of Cemaes. Wider still
between men of the middle type of gentry and the poor squire in the wilds of
Merioneth. But they all shared one thing – they were the people of power in
their own locality, the men to whom the central government looked to run the
country. They also shared a general desire to aggrandise their estate, to 'get on'.
The Mansels and the Stradlings in Glamorgan, the Wynns and the Bulkeleys in
north Wales, built up their fortune on monastery lands. They were also eager
to acquire the respectability of a long, impressive pedigree. Sir John Wynn of
Gwydir was engagingly frank on this point. 'A great temporal blessing it is and
a great heart's ease to a man to find he is well descended, and a greater grief it
is for upstarts and gents of their first head, to look back into their descents, being
base of such sort.' For proof of their being 'well descended', the aspiring gentry
had still to turn to those guardians of tradition and experts in genealogy, the members of the bardic order.

The poets had always been central to the old Welsh social structure in a way
that had no parallel in contemporary English society, and which had its roots far
back in the old Celtic world. Their duty was to praise their patrons, and guard

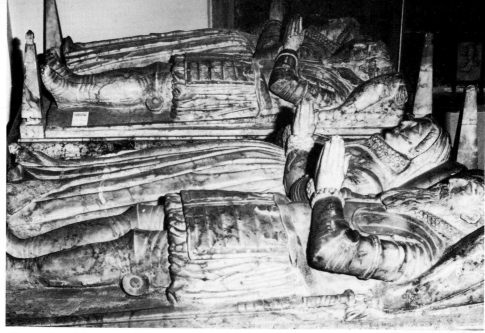

The tombs of the Mansell family in Margam Abbey church

tradition. No man could set up as a bard without undergoing a long discipline under established masters, and he had to become familiar with the complex metres of old Welsh poetry.

There was no denying however, that, as Elizabeth's reign progressed, the bardic order seemed to be steadily losing ground. The problem was not so much the withdrawal of patronage by the gentry – although there were signs of that, too – but the harsh fact that the whole corpus of the bardic tradition, rich and splendid as it was, began to seem out of phase with the new Humanism, the new intellectual world that had developed in Europe with the Renaissance. The bards formed a closed order who jealously guarded their privileges.

But times were changing, there was now grave danger in this exclusivity of the bards. They were not only the genealogists and poetic practitioners. They were also the guardians of the language, the men who set the standards. What would happen to Welsh in the modern world – the world of the new Humanism and Renaissance learning, the world where the new national states were taking a new pride in their native languages and using them to circulate new, exciting ideas – if it did not adapt itself to the winds of change blowing through the whole fabric of European society?

Those early reformers – William Salesbury, Richard Davies and their friends – had been determined to profit by the learning of the bards. Salesbury especially, with his deep love of the native literature, his wide learning and, we must add, his close contact with one of the finest practitioners of the bardic craft, Gruffydd Hiraethog, was the real hero of the first humanist attempt to bring Welsh bravely into the modern world. He may have been somewhat pedantic and had his grammatical quirks, but there was no disputing his infectious zeal and industry. His friend and ally, Richard Davies, returned from exile with the advent of Elizabeth.

He became bishop of St Asaph's and then of St David's. He gathered scholars and literary enthusiasts around him at his palace at Abergwili. At last it would be possible to realise the great dream of the reformers, the translation of the complete Bible into Welsh, 'so that every Welshman could draw the truth of the Scriptures from the fountain-head in his own language'.

As in the story of the English Bible, many hands would be set to work before the complete volume was in the hands of the public or on the lectern in the churches. William Salesbury must be given the honour of being the pioneer. He had made a start in 1551 with his translations from Cranmer's prayer book, 'Kynnliver llith a ban' (All the lessons and articles). The Catholic reaction under Mary had put a stop to any further work, but now Elizabeth was on the throne and Bishop Davies had become a man of influence. He was undoubtedly the leading spirit behind the passing of the act of 1563, authorising a translation of the complete Bible into Welsh. He and Salesbury went to work immediately, and the New

The Bible in Welsh, 1588

Testament and a version of the Prayer Book appeared in 1567. Salesbury was the leader and Davies the gifted and inspiring collaborator. Now others took up the work, including Dr John Davies, Lallwyd and Bishop Richard Parry. Above all, Bishop Richard Morgan, doing his work in the lonely vicarage of Llanrhaedr-ym-Mochnant, lost in the Berwyn Mountains. The complete translation was published in the year of the Armada, 1588. It is a remarkable achievement. The earlier translations were shorn of their peculiarities and the language emerged elegant, clear, imbued with the spirit of the old poetry and yet intelligible to the average, educated man. It set the standard in prose and speech for Welsh which has remained ever since. If ever one single book saved a language, that book is the Bible in Welsh.

As the long reign of the last of the Tudors drew to its close, it is possible to draw up some sort of a 'State of the Nation' report, and to see how Wales had fared under a dynasty that most Welshmen continued to regard as peculiarly their own, to be served with unswerving loyalty come what might. The hundred and eighteen years that stretch between Bosworth and the death of Elizabeth saw immense changes. We begin still in the Middle Ages and we end among men that we can recognise as belonging to our own world. Wales, when Henry VII landed in 1485, was a desperately poor country. When Elizabeth died the country was immeasurably better off materially. Compared with neighbouring England it was obviously not rich, but under the Tudors we can see a modest prosperity penetrating Wales. We can trace it in the increased population of the small towns, in the development of coal and lead mining, in the trade carried on through the little ports and in the houses being built for the gentry and in the very dress worn by the tenant farmers. Highden, in his rhymed Polycronycon, had described the tough, bare-legged Welsh peasantry in the mid-fifteenth century, clad only in their single woollen mantles and britches:

> Bothe in wynde and rayne
> In this clothynge they be bolde,
> Though the weder be ryghte colde.

The average Elizabethan farmer was far better clad. He and his peasants all had shoes, knitted stockings, jackets and felt hats. Ready money was coming back into the economy of the rural areas with the growth of the cattle trade into the markets of lowland England. Not that order had magically descended on social life with the Tudors. Riots, and cases of big men taking the law into their own hands, were frequent. Elections and boundary disputes could lead to fine displays of old-time head-bashing. Elizabeth's favourite, Leicester, clashed furiously with the north Wales gentry when the Queen granted him the Lordship of Denbigh and the older rangership of the royal forest of Snowdon. The fall of a later favourite, the glittering Earl of Essex, had repercussions in Wales, for his main support came from his lands on the Welsh border. His chief agent in the plot was Sir Gelly Meyrick, the Welshman who perished with Essex on the scaffold. The Essex affair seems to be the last flicker of the old feudal order and of the loyalties of the Marchers.

But the general picture is one of growing order. Welshmen took to fighting their battles with enthusiasm in the law courts, and in this they were not alone. Litigation was a popular national pastime in Elizabethan England as well, the Star Chamber being particularly favoured. The Welsh gave equally strong support to the Council in the Marches, which reached the height of its effectiveness and prestige under the presidency of Sir Henry Sidney in the period of the Armada. Ludlow became the legal and administrative capital of a country which had always lacked a natural capital within its borders, equally convenient to north and south. The pull of England was powerful, but the Tudor gentry were not yet anglicised. They had not severed their connection with their cultural background. When all is said and done, the Acts of Union had not been as drastic as they seemed. Certainly they did not outrage the Welshman of the time. The substitution of English law for Welsh law only confirmed a tendency which had been going on for some time. The language clauses, which put Welsh into an inferior position in legal and administrative affairs, were not a deliberate attempt to discourage the speaking of Welsh but were intended to help the process of unifying the country. Wales was not an Irish 'pale', where the use of the native speech in everyday life was severely punished. We have no evidence that anyone objected when Welsh was used in court proceedings. In practice the administration could not have been carried on without it. Even among the gentry there was no deliberate attempt to abandon the old language. The overwhelming presence of England – the seat of power, the place of opportunity, was the real danger to the tongue of Dafydd ap Gwilym and Owain Glyn Dŵr.

The public image of Wales in England – to use a convenient modern expression – was high throughout the Tudor period, in sharp contrast to the suspicion of most things Welsh in the century before Bosworth and the almost total oblivion that descended on the Principality in the late seventeenth and eighteenth centuries. The Welsh characters in Shakespeare are all sympathetic, from the noble Glendower to the gallant Fluellen. The character of Prospero in *The Tempest* was probably based on the remarkable London Welshman, Dr John Dee – mathemati-

The Renaissance gateway of Beaupre Castle in the Vale of Glamorgan

John Dee, mathematician, astrologer and cartographer, who Queen Elizabeth called her 'philosopher'.

cian, astrologer and cosmographer, who Queen Elizabeth called her 'philosopher'. Dee was at the centre of the circle around Sir Humphrey Gilbert which was vital to the Elizabethan expansion overseas, and it may have been through Dee that the strange Welsh story of the pre-Columbian discovery of America by the twelfth century Welsh Prince Madoc was used to buttress English claims against Spain in the New World. The early history of the Celtic Church was equally useful to the apologists of the Elizabethan church settlement in their controversies with Rome.

There is one final comment to be made about those Acts of Union. They did not change or eliminate in any way the right of the monarch to create his eldest son Prince of Wales. A Tudor Prince of Wales, even working from Ludlow, might have formed a point around which national feeling might have crystalised. Unfortunately all such speculations were in vain. Henry VII, the descendant of Owen Tudor, proved totally incapable of providing a family of strong male heirs. His only legitimate son, Edward, was already a sickly boy when he came to the throne and he died too soon. Mary and Elizabeth were childless. There had been no chance of a Prince of Wales for over fifty years. Wales could echo the cry of regret that Elizabeth is supposed to have uttered when she received the news of the birth of James I: 'The Queen of Scots is lighter of a fair son, and I am a barren stock.' In 1603, the 'fair son', James VI of Scotland, succeeded to the Tudor heritage as James I of England – and, let it be remembered, of Wales as well.

9
Stuart Tragedy

The almost mystical loyalty that Wales had shown to the Tudors was now gently transferred to their successors, the Stuarts. There was every reason why this should be so. Upper-class Welshmen, and even the smaller gentry, had benefited materially from the close connection with England. Here now lay their fountain of honour, their hopes of a career on the wider stage of the big world. Squire William Vaughan, of Llangyndeyrn in Carmarthenshire, felt that he had right on his side when he made his oft-quoted declaration: 'I rejoice that the memorial of Offa's Ditch is extinguished with love and charity; that our green leeks, somewhat offensive to your dainty nostrils, are now tempered with your fragrant roses . . . God give us grace to dwell together without enmity, without destruction.'

James, himself, encouraged Welsh loyalty. His accession had symbolised, even more than Henry VII's victory at Bosworth, the growing unity among the disparate nations of these islands. Sir William Maurice, the prolix but intensely loyal MP for Caernarfonshire, bombarded the new monarch with support for the suggestion that the newly-united country should be called Great Britain. The very name of Welsh suited ill with this mood, for it came from the Anglo-Saxon word meaning a foreigner. How could the original inhabitants be foreigners in a Great Britain? Sir William Maurice, and many others like him, preferred to style themselves 'Cambro-Britons', and this curious usage persisted until the eighteenth century.

James enjoyed the homage of his Cambro-Britons. They were as welcome at his court as they were at those of the Tudors. His son Henry, from whom so much was expected before his early death, became Prince of Wales. Ben Jonson produced his celebrated masque, 'For the Honour of Wales' before an appreciative court. James naturally turned first to his fellow Scots but he also agreed with Ben Jonson's eloquent panegyric of Wales: 'Where hath the crown at all these better servitors, more liberal of their lives and fortunes?'

Welshmen had successful careers under the early Stuarts. The great Herbert family, the earls of Pembroke, continued to bask in the royal favour, until they rather tarnished their record of loyalty at the outbreak of the Civil War. Sir Robert Mansel, of Margam and Oxwich in Glamorgan, became Vice Admiral of England in 1617. Another Glamorgan man, Sir Thomas Button, won fame as one of the explorers of the North-West Passage in the wake of Hudson, and afterwards became 'Admiral of the King's Ships on the Coast of Ireland'. James Howell, the author of the celebrated collection of letters published in 1645 under the title *Epistolae Ho-elianae*, was with Charles when, as Prince of Wales, he made his notorious visit to Spain to court the Infanta. Two of James I's twelve judges, John Trevor and William Jones, were Welshmen. There were Welshmen, too, who prospered exceedingly in the commercial world of London, including the Myddleton brothers. Hugh Myddleton made money out of the developing lead-mines of Cardigan and was the creator of the New River scheme which, for the first time, brought a regular supply of water to London. In the law and the world of learning, Welshmen made their mark. Sir Ebule Thelwall partially refounded Jesus College, Oxford, which became the favourite for Welshmen coming to the university.

In Wales, too, the later days of Elizabeth and the beginning of Stuart rule saw the foundation of grammar schools on the English model. Latin formed the basis of the curriculum, and Welsh, naturally, never featured. The decline of the old language proceeded apace among the gentry and the successful commercial classes. The great bards fell silent and literary standards in Welsh deteriorated. In Stuart days, there was no poet of the standard of the Elizabethan, William Llŷn. But the long peace that held the country from the accession of Elizabeth to the outbreak of the Civil War did increase the material well-being of Wales. The population increased, although no reliable figures are available until the first census nearly two hundred years after the accession of James I. At an estimate, the population of Wales had stood around 233,600 in 1545 and had risen to around 341,500 by 1670. Industry benefited by this increase and so did coastal trade, but the growth of industry must not be exaggerated. Wales remained, until the Industrial Revolution in the eighteenth century, a predominantly rural economy where land was still the greatest source of wealth, and compared to England, much of that land was poorish mountain pasture. There were richer areas in places like the Vale of Glamorgan and Monmouthshire, and here lay some of the most lucrative big estates, in the possession of families like the Herberts and the Mansels. In the hill country, things were different. Here what wealth there was came from the flocks and the vast herds of black cattle that were now driven, across a countryside long at peace, to the markets of London and the lowlands. The average Welsh squire lived in his modest stone house, surrounded by his retainers in whom he felt an almost patriarchal interest. He stayed loyal to the crown and remained unworried by the religious and political stresses and strains that were beginning to disturb the more prosperous sections of society in England.

In church matters, Stuarts had succeeded Tudors with scarce a ripple in Wales. The Catholic attempts at reconversion of the Principality could hardly be claimed as a success. There were captured priests who bravely died a martyr's death in Wales, but when a complete return of communicants to the established church was made in 1603, it gave a figure of 200,000 communicants to a mere 800 declared Catholics. Nor were the Puritans more successful. Independent communities of dissenters grew around Wrexham in north-east Wales and in Monmouthshire, but again they did not bulk large against the general number of established church

Henry Herbert, 2nd Earl of Pembroke

Charles I, a portrait by Daniel Mytens

supporters. The bishops and local clergy under Elizabeth and James were not unmindful of their duties and many of them were still Welsh-speaking. There were praiseworthy attempts to improve the standards of recruitment to the clerical ranks. Vicar Pritchard of Llandovery wrote homely homilies in verse which were later published under the title of *Canwyll y Cymru* (The Welshman's Candle), and they had an immense influence on the ordinary folk of Wales. Vicar Pritchard was no Puritan but a churchman who was a strong supporter of the king. The publication of a special cheap edition of the Welsh translation of the Bible, 'Y beibl bach coron', with money subscribed by prominent London Welshmen, was an important event which began the real movement of placing the Bible in every Welsh home. But behind every effort at improvement lay the hard fact of the poverty of the Welsh Church. The Reformation settlement never left it enough money for its real needs.

There was one Welsh churchman, however, who was never prevented by any lack of resources from rising to the highest position in the land. This was the celebrated John Williams of Conwy, the godson of Sir John Wynn. He had a brilliant career after leaving Cambridge. James I made him Lord Keeper before he was forty. This virtually made him Lord Chancellor. He was a man of hot temper and vast ambition, but generous and gifted with a capacity for statesmanlike moderation. Inevitably he clashed with Archbishop Laud.

Laud had been Bishop of St David's at one stage in his rise to power. He was a man of great learning, transparent honesty of purpose, a saint in some respects but, like many a saint, utterly lacking in tact. His vision of a church, ordered by the superior wisdom of authority and purified and made beautiful by ritual, chimed in perfectly with Charles's own vision of the state governed through the Divine Right of Kings. Charles appointed him Archbishop of Canterbury with relief, in place of his father's old nominee, George Abbott, who had favoured a policy of tolerance towards the Puritan party in the church. His was a church of compromise, which did not insist on minutiae of ritual. Unfortunately Abbott is remembered as the only Archbishop of Canterbury who committed a murder during his tenure of office. He accidentally shot a game-keeper while out hunting. A church controlled by such a man was anathema to Laud and Charles.

They set about bringing back order to clerical affairs in a constant stream of new instructions and regulations, which steadily mounted over the years, and which gave rise to an irritation which mounted equally steadily in the church left behind by Archbishop Abbott. They upset the old, easy-going incumbents. What, for example, was the Vicar of Llanidloes in mid-Wales to do about Laud's instructions on the importance of church vestments and on decorum in church when he had cheerfully allowed his parishioners to go shooting birds in the nave and rip up the surplices for towels? On the other hand, the more Puritan-minded clergy were equally offended by the prohibition of the growing practice of preaching outside the church on other days than Sunday. In the isolated parts of rural Wales, this was often the only way for a conscientious pastor to get in touch with his parishioners. William Wroth of Llanfaches was ruthlessly hauled before the High

John Williams, Archbishop of York

Commission for the practice. Walter Craddock, a curate at St Mary's Church, Cardiff – described by the Commission as 'a bold, ignorant young fellow' – threw up his curacy and set off on a personal preaching tour through South Wales, outside the church. Such men as Craddock would become the founding fathers of the Old Dissent in Wales.

John Williams, super-subtle and a man who had grown up in the Abbott tradition, was bound to become the leading spokesman for the anti-Laudian party. As Bishop of Lincoln he had repeatedly intervened to calm matters in the squabbles that arose in his diocese over the vexed question of the nature and the placing of the communion table in church. He produced a soothing pamphlet on the subject with the somewhat less-than-enthusiastic title: *The Holy Table: Name and Thing*. Laud was outraged. The contest between the two men increased. Williams overstepped the mark when he took a hand in the quarrel between the King and Parliament and laid himself open to the charge of betraying state secrets. Was there a touch of the opportunist Lloyd George about the Bishop of Lincoln? Laud seized his chance and flung the slippery bishop into the Tower on the only too probable charge of perjury.

But Williams in the Tower proved to be as great a nuisance as he was outside. He stuck stubbornly to his own moderate point of view, and bombarded Charles with good advice. Had the King been wise enough to listen to a Williams instead of to a Laud, the crisis with Parliament might have run a different course. As things turned out, however, it was Laud who was impeached and eventually went to the block, while the irrepressible Williams emerged to become Archbishop of York in 1641. Too late. In the very next year, Charles raised his standard at Nottingham, where it was immediately blown down by a gale. The Civil War had begun.

There was no doubt the way the majority of Welshmen would turn. They were for the King. Both James and Charles had found Wales one of the least cantankerous parts of their kingdom to manage. The tensions that were tearing apart the more advanced society in southern and eastern England had not shown themselves in any great degree in the Principality. Puritanism – one of the fiercest driving forces behind the Great Rebellion – had no deep roots here. The 'gathered' congregations of dissenters were few and scattered. There was no big, enterprising mercantile class striving to break the economic bondage of paternal government. There was nothing comparable to the City of London, the rich agricultural areas of East Anglia or the great fleets of merchantmen crowding the estuaries of the Thames and the Humber.

This does not mean that Wales had gone quietly along as a passenger when the Stuart ship of state had begun to run into storms. Welsh MPs had protested against James's use of monopolies, and had become restive under the increasing demands for ship money under Charles I. Wales had willingly accepted the first call for this tax, for Spanish pirates were rampant along the coastline and rebellious Catholic Ireland was just across the water. The coastal counties could see the need for a better navy, but as the King started making ship money a regular levy, the counties took leave to default. However, once the royal standard was raised at Nottingham, these small difficulties were forgotten. All those long years of favour from the Tudors and James paid off handsomely.

The royal strategy at the opening of the war was simple. As soon as Charles had gathered a strong enough force he proposed to drive straight at the heart of the rebellion, the powerhouse of Parliament, London. To raise this army, Charles left Nottingham and moved westward. Immediately the importance of Wales in the royal planning became clear. Here, behind the barrier of the Severn, he had a sure supply base and a powerful area of recruitment. Wales would be 'the nursery of the King's infantry'. But that infantry would need training. The long peace of the Tudors had left England – and Wales with it – the most unmilitary nation in Europe. The navy was another matter; not all the levies of ship money had gone into the courtiers' pockets. But the army – or rather the militia, for there was no permanent, standing army – remained a ramshackle affair and had never taken its training seriously. Sir Edwin Cecil lamented: 'This kingdom hath been too long in peace . . . the knowledge of war and almost the thought of war is extinguished.' The Welsh peasant from Radnorshire who was being sent to battle by his landlord, or the shepherd from Llŷn who was setting off to follow his local gentry to the King's side, had to learn in a hurry how to handle the two main infantry weapons of the period, the musket and the pike.

The pike was a formidable affair, at least fourteen feet long, and demanding great strength in handling. The toughest and fittest men were assigned to it. The pike was also regarded as the most distinguished of the two principal infantry weapons, and Sir Roger Williams, the famous Welsh soldier under Elizabeth, devotes a special chapter to its praise and use in his celebrated military text-book, *A Discourse on War*. The smaller men became musketeers, although the musket was as cumbersome and complex to handle as the pike. Musketeers were assigned to the regiments of pikemen in the proportion of two to one, and many a battle was decided, not by musket fire, but by 'push of pike'.

With all that they had to learn, it is small wonder that the raw Welsh levies made a poor showing at their first battle at Edgehill, but as the King advanced on London, they redeemed their honour by storming the barricades at Brentford. Thereafter, they settled down to the business of war and became an indispensable part of the royal armies.

One wonders, by the way, how much the patient Welsh soldier understood about what was happening, and whether his loyalty to his squire would have been affected if he had. It does not seem that anyone went out of their way to explain matters to him. In the Parliamentary pamphlet entitled *The Welshman's Resolution* of 1642, the propagandist sneered at the uncertain English of the Welsh soldier who inquired 'wherefore her must fight and for what her must venture her tears plud, for twas not yet manifest in her mind for what her did fight'. It is extremely unlikely that any Welsh soldier noticed the gibe, for out of the thousands of pamphlets both sides fired at each other in the Battle of the Press, not one was in Welsh.

The Welsh gentry probably marched off to the wars as inexperienced as their men. Few of them, on the royalist side, had gained experience in the continental wars, and none distinguished themselves in the highest commands. There were brave men a-plenty at a slightly lower level, including dauntless Sir John Owen of Clenennan, who was severely wounded in the storming of Bristol. But the aristocratic appointees were less effective. In fact, Lord Herbert of Raglan was singled out for incompetence by no less an authority than Lord Clarendon, in his famous *History of the Great Rebellion*. Herbert, maintained Clarendon, had allowed himself to be ignominiously defeated at Higham in 1643, with a great loss of gallant Welsh gentry, and thus cost his royal master his chance of an early end to the war. Herbert's father, the Marquess of Worcester, made up for his son's shortcomings. He was a Catholic and the greatest land-owner in south-east Wales. From his great castle at Raglan, he poured out his vast wealth without stint in

Milford Haven

the royal cause, and loyally ruined himself in the process. To Raglan Charles sent the thirteen-year-old Prince of Wales, at the beginning of the troubles, and the young prince gave early proof of his future charm and tact when he spoke to the local gentry.

'Gentlemen,' he said, 'I had heard formerly of the great minds, the true affections and meanings of the ancient Britaines – but my kind entertainment hath made me confide in your love, which I shall always remember.' Not all the ancient 'Britaines' were so prodigal of love and affection for the royal cause, and, significantly, they were concentrated in non-Welsh-speaking areas or in places close to the English border. In north Wales, Wrexham was a centre of Puritan influence, coming from nearby strongly-Puritan Cheshire. In addition, the Myddletons of Chirk, with their long connections with the City of London, stood firmly for Parliament, and could look for support to the Cheshire Roundheads. The Royalists would thus not go completely unchallenged in the north. Away in the south-west lay another centre of Parliamentary power. The small ports of southern Pembrokeshire – that 'Little England beyond Wales' – had trading connections with Bristol and were far more open to English influences. John Poyer, the mayor of Pembroke, had early warned Parliament of the importance of the magnificent inlet of Milford Haven as a landing place for the royal troops from Ireland. The immediate declaration of south Pembrokeshire to the Parliamentary side effectively blocked this route for the King, but, to counter-balance this blow, the astute Archbishop John Williams hastened back to his native Conwy and fortified the town and castle at his own expense. Charles was thus assured of the north Wales route for his Irish reinforcements.

There was one surprising recruit to the Parliamentary party among the Welsh aristocrats and he was probably motivated not by conviction but by personal pique.

The John Speed map of Pembrokeshire

The Earl of Pembroke held Cardiff Castle and was a great landowner in the Vale of Glamorgan. The Earl of Essex, who also had great estates scattered through south Wales, opted for Parliament, too. He was a man of far nobler character than Pembroke and was Parliament's first choice as their commander-in-chief.

Sir John Meyrick became one of Essex's leading lieutenants. It was far easier for able and humble, non-aristocratic Welshmen to rise high in the Parliamentary armies than in the royalist ranks. Like the armies of Revolutionary France and Napoleon, Parliament's forces offered a 'carrière ouvert aux talents'. Colonel John Jones from Merioneth certainly carved out a great career for himself. He became Cromwell's son-in-law and won a high reputation in the Irish campaign. His birth-place, in the lonely farmhouse of Maes-y-Garnedd, set in the wildest valley of the Rhinog Mountains of North Wales, seems to reflect his own rugged strength of character. In south Wales, Colonel Philip Jones of Llangyfelach played a leading part, not only as a soldier but as an administrator. Colonel John Jones and Thomas Wogan, the MP for Cardigan, were the two Welshmen who signed the death-warrant of Charles I. Colonel Philip Jones was tactfully absent.

But nothing is cut and dried in a civil war. Strongly Royalist areas still had individuals who stood for Parliament. Men acted, not only from conviction but for personal advancement. There were Royalists who sat on the fence to see which way things would go, and Roundheads who deserted the cause for gain. And many

Colonel Philip Jones

a country squire must have remembered the old Welsh saying, 'When a kingdom is tossed in a blanket, happy is he who is out of it.' Many distinguished men sought refuge in the seclusion of Wales as the struggle developed. The great Anglican divine, Jeremy Taylor, took refuge at Golden Grove in Carmarthenshire and Arch-

St Donat's castle, in the Vale of Glamorgan, where Archbishop Ussher sought refuge

bishop Ussher of Armagh came to the safety of St Donat's in the Vale of Glamorgan. That pure poet, Henry Vaughan, after some service in the royal cause, retreated to his home in the lovely and undisturbed valley of the Usk, to contemplate, above the civil turmoils, that fair country 'far beyond the stars,' where 'above war and danger, sweet peace sits crowned with smiles'. In 1642, sweet peace was a long, dangerous and disturbed decade away.

So the two sides squared up to each other as the struggle began, and Wrexham and south Pembrokeshire had given warning that the King's hold on Wales was not going to be as secure as it had seemed. Inevitably, the great battles of the war – Edgehill, Newbury, Marston Moor and Naseby – would take place outside Wales, as Charles first struck at London and then, in turn, the strengthened Parliamentary armies pushed out north and west to smash the Royalists before they could fall back on their bases. But as long as south Pembrokeshire, Wrexham and Cheshire were in Roundhead hands, the Welsh base could always be threatened by daring raids and breakouts from these opposition strongholds. The Civil War in Wales is thus a reflection of the big events across the border.

The King's first campaign in 1642 had ended in stalemate. He had failed to take London and had retired to his bases in the west. He still felt that he had all the best cards in his hand and planned his 1643 campaign with care. Once more he made London his main objective, which would fall to a three-pronged advance. But first he had to clear the three great, outlying Parliamentary strongholds of Bristol, Gloucester and Hull. Prince Rupert successfully stormed Bristol and the Welsh troops under that stout Royalist, Sir John Owen of Clenennen, played a leading part, although Sir John was severely wounded. The fall of Bristol encouraged the Welsh Royalists remaining in Wales to launch a bold campaign on their own to liquidate the nest of Roundheads in their rear in south Pembrokeshire. Under Richard Vaughan, Lord Carbery, they captured Tenby and Haverfordwest and left the Parliamentarians only a small foothold in Pembroke town itself. The royal campaign for 1643 had got off to a good start.

Then came a check. Hull could not be captured. Worse still, Gloucester held out as well, and Gloucester was the key to the lower Severn valley and the main road into south-east Wales. It was equally vital to Parliament. Gloucester's resistance had serious repercussions for the use of Wales as a Royalist base. The hesitant Lord Herbert of Raglan had first laid siege to it, but, with his usual incompetence, he let himself be badly defeated at Higham in the Forest of Dean. The King then swept Herbert aside and took charge of the siege himself, with no greater success. All this gave time for Parliament to mount an attempt to rescue and relieve heroic Gloucester. In a famous march, the trained bands of London left their base, and after marching at speed through a hostile countryside, the Earl of Essex led them into the cheering city.

The Relief of Gloucester has been called the psychological turning-point of the war. With the city in his hands, the king would have had uninterrupted access to his supplies and recruiting ground in south Wales. Now a hostile Gloucester could threaten the isolation of south-east Wales. Worse still for the King, the town of Pembroke also continued to hold out, so Milford Haven was not free for the import of Irish troops and supplies. To complete the discomfiture of the Royalists, Essex managed to beat off the King's army when it tried to intercept him at Newbury, and he got his triumphant trained bands back to welcoming London.

As the year 1643 progressed, the King's cause seemed to recede. He cast around urgently for reinforcements and Ireland and his Irish troops became all the more vital to him, especially when Parliament also turned outside for allies and signed a pact with the Scots. At least the north Wales route to Ireland was still open, thanks to the foresight of Archbishop Williams. The north Wales Roundheads were well aware of the new importance of this passage for troops from Ireland. They determined to anticipate the arrival of these dangerous royal reinforcements and, under Sir Thomas Myddleton of Chirk, advanced themselves in November 1643 and seized Wrexham, Mold and Holywell. They were too late, for in the same month the 'Irish' army safely landed in Anglesey. Irish is hardly the correct description of the new forces. They were not the wild, tribal Catholics depicted by Protestant propaganda, but old veterans of the Irish wars. They looked formidable on paper, but their morale was not high. Charles, however, gave them one of Prince Rupert's abler lieutenants, Lord Byron, as commander. Myddleton hurriedly fell back before him and the Royalist cause seemed to take on a brighter hue. But, again, Charles's hopes were disappointed. Byron advanced deep into Cheshire but was caught and defeated at Nantwich by the top Parliamentarian commander, Sir Thomas Fairfax.

There was trouble for the Royalists in south Wales as well. The Parliamentary fleet had reinforced Pembroke, and under a young and vigorous commander, Rowland Laugharne, the Roundheads were able to break out and catch the supine royal commander, Lord Carbery, completely off balance. In quick time Laugharne mopped up the small garrisons into which Carbery had unwisely divided his forces. Tenby fell in March 1644, and Laugharne even occupied the Royalist stronghold of Carmarthen. The King was threatened with the loss of the whole of west Wales. He sacked Carbery and put in his place a tough, professional soldier, Sir Charles Gerard. Gerard advanced swiftly through south Wales and swept Laugharne out of his conquests in a series of brilliant moves. He recaptured Carmarthen, Cardigan and Newcastle Emlyn. Haverfordwest fell to him in late August. Laugharne was confined to Tenby and Pembroke.

Once again, we see the events on the wider battlefields of England influencing events in Wales. While Gerard was successfully campaigning in south-west Wales, dramatic moves were taking place in Yorkshire. Prince Rupert and the Earl of Newcastle were confronted by Fairfax and Cromwell at Marston Moor. When darkness fell on that fatal battlefield, the Royal cause in the north was smashed beyond recall. The addition of Scottish power to the Parliamentary armies had done the trick. The King had perforce to recall Gerard with his work incomplete. When Rupert came back to Wales after Marston Moor he found the Royal cause in disarray. A further disaster followed. The Parliamentarians under Myddleton had begun to move forward again in north Wales. Myddleton had raised the siege of Oswestry and captured Newtown. He then took possession of Montgomery Castle, a key fortress on the Welsh border, by what Royalists felt was the traitorous conduct of that cultivated philosopher and historian, Lord Herbert of Chirbury. In September, in the biggest battle fought in Wales in the first Civil War, Lord Byron was utterly defeated at Montgomery by Myddleton and Brereton. The King had lost all his power in north Wales and 1645 dawned dismally for his cause.

In the first part of that year, a last illusory ray of hope fluttered over the King's supporters. Essex's army was defeated and compelled to lay down its arms in Cornwall. Charles felt that if he now collected every military unit left to him, he might still win the final battle. He tried, for the last time, to safeguard his Welsh base before he moved out for the 'show-down'. Once again Gerard swept back Laugharne by marching down from Chester and ravaging his way through mid-Wales. He met Laugharne at Newcastle Emlyn, defeated him and penned him into his two sea-supplied bases of Pembroke and Tenby. Then, once again, Gerard was recalled. It was the eve of Naseby.

Left Sir Thomas Myddleton of Chirk   *Right* Colonel Rowland Laugharne

Parliament had reacted to Essex's disaster by creating the New Model Army under Sir Thomas Fairfax, a formidable, well-paid, well-officered fighting force, double the strength of the army that Charles was hoping to bring against it. In north Wales the Parliamentary command was firmly reorganised under Sir Thomas Myddleton. On the Royalist side, Archbishop John Williams, sensing the way things were going, was drifting towards neutrality. Again he was taking the sensible way of compromise in the hope of saving his fellow-countrymen from the worst consequences of defeat. Again, common sense was out of place in war. That uncompromising old soldier, Sir John Owen of Clenennan, promptly moved in and possessed himself of Conwy. So matters stood in Wales, when, on 14 June 1645, the New Model Army confronted Charles and Rupert at Naseby in the heart of England. The evening before, Cromwell had arrived to command the Parliamentary cavalry to the exultant shouts of 'Old Ironsides has come'. In the battle that followed, the New Model utterly smashed King Charles's last serious army. His Welsh infantry, surrounded and with their flanks driven in, fought stubbornly and then laid down their arms. The patient cannon-fodder had had enough. In the rout that followed, the triumphant victors over-ran the royal baggage train and plundered and slit the noses of the Welsh-speaking camp followers under the impression that they were the hated Irish.

Naseby was decisive, but even now Charles did not abandon hope. Wales could surely be relied upon, once again, to supply another army. He retired to Raglan, where you can still see the bowling green where the unfortunate monarch forgot his cares for a moment while he negotiated with his Welsh supporters. They were

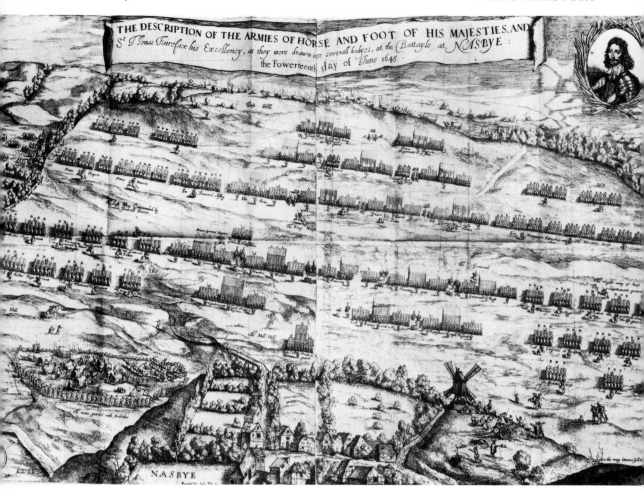

The battle of Naseby, a contemporary print

unresponsive. The 'Peaceable Army' of Glamorgan refused to march. The Welsh countryside had been alienated by the professionals in the armies of Rupert and Gerard, brutalised by the tradition of plunder learnt in continental wars. In vain Captain Thomas Dabridgecourt lamented to Prince Rupert: 'If your Highness shall be pleased to command me to the Turk, or Jew, or Gentile, I will go on my bare feet to serve you, but from the Welsh, good Lord deliver me!' The Welsh were now in the mood to return the cry for deliverance — from all the miseries of the war. King Charles went unhappily towards north Wales. His last small fighting force was annihilated before his eyes under the walls of Chester. Laugharne emerged from his Pembrokeshire bases and swept almost unopposed through south and west Wales, after defeating the Royalists at Colby Moor, outside Haverfordwest.

The war in Wales degenerated into a series of sieges. Finally, the Roundhead net closed in on Raglan. The Marquess of Worcester held out desperately against

Sir Thomas Fairfax, but all in vain. The skilful if diminutive Colonel Thomas
Morgan – a Welshman with an European reputation as a siege expert – drew his
lines ever closer and on 19 August 1646, the marquis had no option but surrender.
He stood in the great hall, surrounded by his household, and as he looked out
through the tall, graceful windows, he saw Fairfax and his officers pouring in to
the Outward court, 'as if a flood gate had been left open'. The great castle, with
its magnificent collection of paintings, its rare manuscripts, its rich furniture and
its curious and ingenious engines driven by water power, was given up to the
sack. It was the end of a way of life in Wales. In March 1647, the last Welsh
Royalist stronghold surrendered. As usual, it was Harlech.

The second Civil War did not last long. In Wales, it began in Pembrokeshire,
where there had been much mutual recrimination among the victors. Colonel
Poyer refused to surrender Pembroke Castle to the man Parliament had appointed
to relieve him. Royalists joined in and the revolt swept south Wales. Rowland
Laugharne himself threw in his lot with the rebels. But they were crushed by
a section of the New Model Army at St Fagan's outside Cardiff. Cromwell
appeared on the scene and besieged Pembroke. The castle surrendered after holding
out for forty-eight days. Poyer was shot. The rising in north Wales was quickly
stamped out. That old irreconcilable, Sir John Owen, tried to attack Caernarfon
but Mytton cornered him at Llandegai. He was condemned to be shot but was
reprieved, apparently by the intervention of Ireton. There was a small rising in
Anglesey under Lord Byron but it was quickly stamped out. Wales lay at the
mercy of Parliament or, rather, of the army. The second Civil War brought King
Charles to the block and his death warrant contained the names of Colonel John
Jones and Thomas Wogan.

The economy of Wales recovered fairly speedily after the fighting, for the
wounds of war heal rapidly in a basically agricultural country. There had been
looting and some destruction of property but nothing on the scale of the Glyn
Dŵr revolt. Raglan had been deliberately wrecked after surrender and other lesser
houses were burnt. The old castles, which had played an unexpectedly troublesome
part in the Age of Gunpowder, were 'slighted', with towers blown up and curtain
walls cast down to ensure that they would never go to war again. The gentry
were as cast down as the castles; they saw their world in ruins. The victors were
now faced with the task of reorganising and governing a country in which they
knew they were profoundly unpopular.

In a spirit of grim determination Parliament settled down to govern Wales.
On the whole, the new rulers meant well by their own lights. They were bringing
a new, more decent order to one of 'the dark corners of the land'. In the good
work of establishing the Rule of the Saints they would have preferred the co-
operation of the conquered. Cromwell sighed with frustration: 'I am as much
for government by consent as any man, but where shall we find that consent?'
Not, on the whole, from the Welsh. For the Rule of the Saints had one unfortunate
defect when it came to popularity – it was expensive. The Commonwealth established after the execution of Charles – 'thet black desaster', as James Howell called

it – depended for its ultimate authority, however much it might try to disguise the unpalatable fact, on a standing army. A standing army meant heavy taxation. From the beginning, it had been Parliamentary policy to make the Royalists pay for the war and as a result, those who had fought for the king were fined or had to compound for their estates if they were not forfeited. There was a vast reshuffle of property in land, out of which many Parliamentarians did very well, especially the two powerful Joneses! Under their shadow many new families established themselves, who even succeeded in retaining their newly-acquired wealth and social position after the Restoration. The sequestration of estates, the complex land deals, the monies from fines that frequently found their way into unexpected pockets – all this was the seamier side of the government of the Saints. When a 'kingdom is tossed in a blanket', there is bound to be a cash fall-out for opportunists. There was, however, a better side, or at least a more well-meaning aspect of Commonwealth policy in Wales.

Prominent among the many motives that had driven the Parliamentarians first to war and then to the extreme step of cutting off the head of their king was their deeply-held antipathy towards the Established Church. The triumphs of the battlefield were the sure proof that Puritanism had the approval of Heaven. The messenger who brought the news of Cromwell's victory at Dunbar announced it, quite naturally, with the words: 'The Lord hath appeared for us gloriously in Scotland.' It was now Parliament's duty to ensure that He appeared equally gloriously in Wales. In 1650 the purged and truncated House of Commons, popularly known as The Rump, passed the Act for the Better Propagation of the Gospel in Wales. Colonel Thomas Harrison and seventy commissioners were given the task of reconstructing the whole church structure and educational policy in the Principality. Harrison was a good, able soldier and a fair-minded man, but he and his colleagues faced formidable difficulties from the start. Puritanism had never been strong in Wales before the Civil War and not enough people of the right sort were available to act on the commission. It was bound to contain too great a proportion of Englishmen and men from the border counties, few of whom could speak Welsh. The language barrier was to operate through the period of the Commonwealth and set a limit to the Puritanisation of Wales.

There was a handful of old enthusiasts ready to go to work, men like Vavasour Powell, Morgan Llwyd and Walter Cradock, who had been among the pioneers of the 'gathered' churches in Wales. John Miles had founded the first Baptist chapel at Ilston in Gower in 1649, and he now spread the gospel further and built up a structure which was the nearest approach to a Welsh Presbyterian organisation. But these men were still a devoted few and their problem became acute when the commission got down to the work of examining and purging the parish clergy. Over two hundred and seventy of them were ejected from their livings. This left a yawning gap in the religious life of the people. The Commission endeavoured to fill this gap by the appointment of itinerant preachers and few of them were of the calibre of Vavasour Powell and Walter Cradock, who, themselves, travelled unsparingly through the remoter parts of the countryside. In spite of all their

The Orthodox true Minifter,   the Seducer and falfe Prophet.

Church versus Conventicle, from the tract 'A Glasse for the Times'

efforts, the dream of a Puritan Wales refused to become a reality. The hearts of the Welsh peasantry remained unmoved by the word of the Lord. Perhaps it was not spoken in Welsh.

The commissioners had far more success in the field of education. Here they were praiseworthy pioneers. They set up over sixty new schools to supplement the existing grammar schools, which they left undisturbed. Education was free, and in many cases the commission took the revolutionary step of opening the schools to girls. We have few details of the actual curriculum, but it clearly had no place for Welsh. But here, at least, the Puritans were breaking new ground, and they must have been disappointed in the Welsh reaction to their well-meaning and devoted efforts. In the beginning, Cromwell had agreed with the optimistic report of the possibilities of the conversion of Wales: 'God hath kindled a seed there indeed hardly to be paralleled since the ancient times'. The seed, however, stubbornly refused to germinate.

Nothing illustrates the aloofness of most of Wales from the revolutionary tumult of the times more than the small numbers of Welsh people who became involved in the numerous cults and minority movements during the Civil War and the years that immediately followed the death of the king. For a short time in our history authority had been removed from society in a single stroke. This was a moment when men of all sorts and conditions felt that they had to rethink the very basic assumptions of the state in which they lived. They did their rethinking inside the accepted religious assumptions of their time. Rationalism was a good hundred and fifty years in the future, and the seventeenth-century revolutionaries naturally expressed themselves in the rich language of the Bible. For all that, the content of their thought was still revolutionary.

As Gerald Winstanley, the leader of the Levellers, put it: 'The old world . . . is running up like a parchment in the fire.' God had now opened the eyes of the common people, 'and discovered unto them their Christian liberty'. Above all, their liberty to think for themselves. Some of their thinking may not have been logical – it was the work of simple men struggling to find a solution to their pressing problems. The Diggers and the Levellers were only too clear about the right, true aim of society. They anticipated twentieth-century socialism. The Seekers and the Ranters seemed, in some respects, to be edging towards the modern permissive society. The Fifth Monarchy Men expected the imminent establishment of the reign of Lord Jesus with justice for all men. It was a time for bold, exciting thinking. Conservative Wales looked on with suspicion. The dispossessed gentry were hardly likely to look with approval on the behaviour of William Ebury, once Vicar of St Mary's, Cardiff.

Together with his curate, Walter Cradock, he had been ejected by Laud from his vicarage in 1638. He naturally strongly supported the cause of Parliament and eventually became a chaplain in the New Model Army. He was an influential chaplain, too, who advocated extreme solutions to the army's problems. Let there be heavy taxation on 'rich citizens, racking landlords . . . and mighty, moneyed men'. Ebury was a Holy Revolutionary, and although, in the end, he declared that the people of God should not meddle in affairs of state, in his heyday he was regarded as a dangerous man by those in authority. There is no sign that his words exercised any influence on Welsh-speaking Wales.

Those who concentrated on the affairs of the soul rather than those of politics had slightly more effect. George Fox, the Quaker, came to Wales and had a vision on the slopes of Cader Idris which convinced him that God 'would raise up a people to himself in this area'. He made converts and laid the foundations of the Quaker connection with Wales. But, again, the numbers concerned were comparatively few. That earnestly hoped for general conversion did not occur. In the end the Lord only raised up a handful of the faithful. They may have been people of quality, and would be the forerunners for future change; but that change was still a long way off.

The last hope for the immediate establishment of the true and holy republic of the Saints faded when Cromwell made his dramatic entry into the House of Commons in 1653 and dismissed the Rump. As Lord Protector he brought back order into society but it was an order which now had no place for the dreams of the Diggers, the Ranters, or the Levellers. Dr John Owen, Cromwell's favourite chaplain – a man of Welsh blood, although he had had slight connection with the Principality during his long career which, at one point, took him to the Vice-Chancellorship of Oxford University – had published in 1652 a book with the appropriate title: *The Labouring Saints Dismission to Rest*. This was exactly what the Lord Protector's government proceeded to do. The dreams of the Saints were gently laid to rest. The Revolution was over. Vavasour Powell had Fifth Monarchy leanings and was outraged. He called Cromwell the most 'disobligingest, perjured villain'. The Lord Protector struggled to find general acceptance for his regime. He tried expedient after expedient. When parliaments proved restive, he fastened on the unfortunate experiment of the Major Generals. Wales came under the control of Major General James Berry. Again, like Harrison, he was a fair-minded man, anxious to do his best, but somehow the Good Cause never prospered in sullen Wales.

But the Protectorate was still there, and as the regime continued, more people felt that they had to come to terms with it. They grudgingly admitted that it had some merits. Blake's victories had cleared the seas of the pirates that had infested the Welsh coasts. Schools had been built and there was even a project for the establishment of a Welsh university. Wales, one die-hard Royalist said bitterly, was becoming a nation of trimmers and adopting the attitude of Squire Howell Gwyne of Carmarthenshire: 'Heigh god, heigh devil, I will be for the stronger side.' It was possible to believe that Wales would have settled for the status quo had not Cromwell died at the comparatively early age of fifty-nine. In the two years of troubled uncertainty that followed the Lord Protector's passing, Wales held its breath and waited.

10

Myth, Methodists and Machines

After the vivid colour of the Elizabethan age, the drama and tragedy of the first Stuarts and the stern discipline of the Commonwealth, the years that followed the restoration of Charles II seem drab and unexciting in Wales. It was as if the whole country had had enough of heroics, enthusiasm and controversy. Wales gave a sigh of relief when the king came back to 'enjoy his own again'. No more civil marriages, itinerant preachers, long exhortations to the Good Life accompanied by endless taxation. The conduits of Carmarthen town ran with wine, and an Anglesey rhymster predicted 'rhyddyd a llawenydd' – freedom and fun for ever more – for all concerned. For all, that is, except the old Commonwealth men. They were swiftly swept off the stage like an old board of directors after a ruthless city take-over. Vavasour Powell was flung into jail, where he wrote an 'apologia pro vita sua' under the moving title of *The Bird in the Cage, Chirping*. Others had less to chirp about. Colonel John Jones met the death of a regicide with impressive courage and dignity. Thomas Wogan fled overseas. Colonel Harrison joined John Jones on the scaffold. John Miles led the few faithful of his congregation to America where they founded the new town of Swansey in Massachusetts. As for the supple Colonel Philip Jones of Llangafelach, he tactfully disappeared for a brief interval and then, incredibly, re-emerged to become owner of Fonmon Castle and High Sheriff of Glamorgan in 1671. He knew where all the scandals were buried. Wales quietly entered its supine century.

For the next hundred years, Wales was on the sidelines as far as the rest of the country was concerned. A character in one of Sir John Vanbrugh's plays, called, as might be expected, Quaint, announces that he had a Welsh mother. 'A Welch Woman,' his friend inquires, 'Prau of what Country's than?' 'That, Sir, is a Country in the World's backside . . .' comes the enlightening reply. A country in the world's backside! So, indeed, must the Principality have now appeared to many an ambitious Welshman anxious to get on in politics. For power in Wales was now firmly in the grasp of a handful of great families who had managed to emerge on top, after the trials and tumults of the preceding age, which had overwhelmed the lesser gentry. They had the grandiose titles, the vast estates, and they used them to control local politics. Families like the Bulkeleys and the Williams Wynns in north Wales, the Harleys in Radnorshire, the Pryses in north Cardigan, or the Dukes of Beaufort in Glamorgan, came to regard parliamentary seats as their own personal property. The Vaughans of Golden Grove held the record

Chirk Castle, the seat of the Myddletons

– they supplied Carmarthen MPs for an unbroken and astonishing sixty-one years.

Principle hardly entered into the political scene in Wales. Gone was the romantic loyalty so freely given to the Tudors and inherited by the first Stuarts. From the Restoration onwards, Wales was to behave like the celebrated Vicar of Bray – and be all things to all kings. When James II, for example, in the course of his troubled reign, asked Wales to recruit a force of ten thousand men, the Principality readily agreed. When William of Orange landed, the projected Prince of Wales's regiment was cheerfully transferred to the other side, and eventually became the Royal Welch Fusiliers. Later, when the unattractive Hanoverians came to the throne, there was some sentimental attachment to the exiled Stuarts. The Circle of the White Rose in north Wales and the Society of Sea Sergeants in the south met to drink toasts to 'the king across the water', but when the testing time of their loyalty came with the Jacobite rising in 1745, most of the members kept on raising their glasses instead of their swords. The Prince had high hopes of Sir Watkyn Williams Wynn. As he marched south, he sent a letter to the leader of the White Rose circle: 'I am persuaded that you will not break my expectation.' Sir Watkyn, for some reason, failed to move. A few young Welshmen joined Bonnie Prince Charlie and fought at Culloden. The most remarkable of the Welsh Jacobites was Henry Lloyd, who went overseas after the failure of the rising, made a European reputation as a soldier and wrote a military text book which was studied in every military academy in the eighteenth century, and deeply impressed the young Napoleon.

THE SOUTH EAST VIEW OF POWES CASTLE, IN THE COUNTY OF MONTGOMERY.

This page Eighteenth-century social power: *above* the Orangery at Margam, West Glamorgan and, *below*, Powys Castle

Opposite Sir Watkin Williams Wynn, 1740, by Thomas Hudson

For the most part, Welsh politicians carefully avoided such dangerous excesses. They supported the ministry and the only struggle they were absorbed in was the battle between the 'ins and the outs'. The Denbigh election of 1741 was the most memorable of these Eatanswill-type of contests. The Myddletons of Chirk clashed with the Wynns of Wynnstay. The campaign lasted for two years, cost Wynn £20,000 and ended with Wynn safely in the seat and William Myddleton in Newgate. And all this pointless outpouring of energy simply proved that the Welsh establishment was still solidly behind the English one.

The Church in Wales was also solidly linked to the Hanoverian government pattern. It is all too easy to produce any number of examples to show how far and fatally this link affected the vigour and spiritual life of the Welsh Church. The bishops had seats in the House of Lords and their political support was necessary to the government. Prime Ministers like the Duke of Newcastle, a master of political manipulation, placed bishops first in the poorer sees, in the confident expectation that his appointees would behave themselves in the hope of being transferred to more lucrative benefices. Wales, unfortunately, had a profusion of poorer sees, and this led to some appointments which were curious indeed.

William Beaw had fought for the King in the Civil War and been a soldier of fortune in Europe. He took Holy Orders, with the laudable object of speeding up his career to wealth and preferment. In 1679 his friends told him that 'a little bishoprick', Llandaff, 'is fallen', and, as Beaw admits, 'upon the persuasion of all my friends, and in expectation of a sudden Remove, I was at last moved to accept of it'. Beaw was disappointed. He was stuck in Llandaff for the next twenty-six years. He made a gallant attempt to get made Bishop of Hereford, when he had private word that the holder of the office was 'old and feeble and sick and every hour dropping off'. But there were other rivals in the field. As Beaw sorrowfully admitted, 'a Brother of mine, who was upon the watch and too quick for me, made the first catch at the bishoprick and carried it.' Beaw had to stay at Llandaff, 'a desease which none of his predecessors were suffered to labour under so long'.

Some of the other state appointments were equally bizarre. Bishop Watson of St David's, was tried for simony. One bishop of St Asaph got himself transferred before he ever went near the place. Hoadley, a Georgian appointee to Bangor, was one of the most powerful and distinguished of the political bishops, but he never visited his see.

All this tended to separate the bishop from his subordinate clergy, who lived in comparative poverty and who, when candidates for preferment, might have to hunt out their bishop after long journeys, sometimes across the border. The Bishop of Gloucester was amused to be importuned by 'a little Welsh deacon who flew hither from his native mountains by accident, like a woodcock in a mist'. Amusing, no doubt, for the bishop, but hardly for 'the little Welsh deacon' and his distant flock.

There were, as always, exceptions to the general rule. George Bull, the saintly bishop of St David's appointed by Queen Anne, was acclaimed for his knowledge of the early fathers as one of the glories of Anglican scholarship. But the general tone of the Georgian church was cool and uninspiring. No bishop appointed between the accession of George I in 1714 and 1871 was capable of preaching in Welsh. The greatest Welsh poet of the period, Goronwy Owen, was left to break his heart as an obscure curate. The Anglican Church establishment was not basically interested in Welsh Wales.

Below the upper layer of great landowners, lesser gentry and the clergy lay the mass of the people of Wales. By the eighteenth century, the cultural separation

Llandaff Cathedral, near Cardiff

between the two layers was complete. The upper layer was Anglicised, looking for its standards of social behaviour, its literature, its speech and religion across the border to England and to western Europe. The lower layer was almost totally Welsh-speaking, but this layer, too, had undergone a profound change in the years that followed the Civil War. The old Welsh high culture, its poetry and music, had been an oral one. The bardic order had been its guardian. It was the bards who passed on the complex art of composing poetry according to the 'strict measures'. They were also the historians, the genealogists and the musicians. With the final collapse of patronage in the Civil Wars, this wholly orally transmitted culture disappeared.

Already the Elizabethan scholars and the antiquaries who followed them had managed to preserve a great deal of the literary and historical products of this culture in manuscript collections and, in some cases, in print, but the musical tradition collapsed completely. Welsh musicians had been famous in the Middle Ages. There had been Welsh players of the 'crwth', a complicated stringed instrument, at the courts of Edward II and Richard II, and the Welsh were skilled in part singing. The original Welsh harp was small and portable, and Welsh harpists also appeared at court. But by the beginning of the eighteenth century, the old-style harp had been replaced by a version of the Italian baroque harp and scarcely a soul was left who could tune a crwth, let alone play on one. It is a sad loss that the old musical tradition never reached the printed page, to be passed on to posterity. One lone manuscript remains, written by Robert Ap Hew, who was harpist to King James I. The symbols he used have defied interpretation. Many distinguished musicians have tried their hand at it, but this Welsh Linear B musical problem still awaits its Michael Ventris.

There was one other notable consequence of the sad collapse of the old culture. The ancient system of nomenclature disappeared. In its place came a dull uniformity. In medieval Wales, when social status depended so much on birth, names were of vital importance. A man had to count his ancestors back many generations. He was proud to remind his hearers that he was 'ap' – the son of – a distinguished father or grandfather, and so on back into the mists of time. After the Tudor Acts of Union, English lawyers had found this custom confusing. Maredudd ap Tudor ap Llywelyn ap Iorwerth ap Rhys could command respect in an assembly of bards, but might cause dismay and delay in a court of law. Henry VIII had advised great landowners to adopt the name of their estate and some of them did so. Lesser gentry adopted convenient English names. The process spread steadily down through the classes. Anglican clergy now handed out biblical or royal names to the poorer people. So the noble old Welsh names like Duddgu, Tegwaedd and Gwernhyfer, that had so delighted the great Welsh antiquarian Edward Lhuyd disappeared from the land and Wales became a nation of Thomases, Joneses, Williamses and the like. As sad a loss as the old music played by the 'crowders', with such fire and spirit, that was replaced by versions of tunes from English printed collections. 'Men of Harlech' is a rousing chorus, but no native-born man from Harlech ever marched to it.

Among the 'middling people' – the lawyers, the lesser gentry, the shopkeepers and the richer farmers – the old oral culture had been replaced by a printed book culture. The books may have been in Welsh, but they were printed in England. There was no printing press in Wales until Isaac Garter set up his pioneer establishment in 1711 at Newcastle Emlyn. The books varied from practical guides to pious tracts, but they served to separate the Welsh peasantry still further from their traditional leaders and culture. Were they thus a cowed, listless lot – as some writers would have us believe? Were they bent down to an ungrateful soil under the whiplash of absentee, English-speaking landlords, like the peasants depicted by La Bruyère under Louis XIV or the *sans-culottes* of pre-Revolutionary France? The few travellers through Wales in the period give a different picture. There was poverty, even grinding poverty, a-plenty, but this was still a high-spirited peasantry, behaving with Brueghel-like boisterousness on feast-days, delighting in the ballad-singers and in the interludes supplied by strolling players, like those of the celebrated Twm o'r Nant, the so-called 'Cambrian Shakespeare'. But the decay of the old oral culture had left them without leadership. There was a cultural as well as a social hollow in the heart of the Supine Century. Wales seemed to be hesitating between two worlds, waiting for some new departure but not exactly certain for what it waited. There were no bards left to prophesy the coming of a new Arthur or the return of Owain Glyn Dŵr. In any case, this would have seemed absurd in the Age of Reason. And when the departure occurred, it was not based on solid, rational considerations. No Welsh national revival ever was!

Perhaps we should talk not of one revival but of three. And revolution not revival would be the word for them. There were three such revolutions before the eighteenth century had run its course – a religious revolution, a cultural one and an industrial one. In the end, all three revolutions were running together. Between them they profoundly altered the old social scene. By 1850, we will be contemplating a Wales which would have been utterly unrecognisable, and even horrific, to the men of the old Wales – to the scholars of the Elizabethan Renaissance, the gentry who fought in the Civil War, the bards and the crowders, happily playing for the slightly boozy peasants dancing in the churchyards, and the rest of them. This will be the Wales of a stereotyped image which still haunts us today, even after it has long disappeared – the Wales of Nonconformist chapels, powerful preachers carried away by the 'hwyl', of pubs shut on Sundays, of miners' choirs, of fiery politicians denouncing the Establishment and of continually victorious rugby teams. A caricature Wales, agreed, but with some underlying truth about it. Old carefree 'Merrie' Wales was about to be dragged, with some reluctance, into a grimmer, more serious Future.

The religious revolution came first and the ground had been quietly prepared for it many years before the great emotional outburst of Methodism began around 1735. The Commonwealth had helped the growth of Nonconformist communities in Wales. They had come through the fires of persecution under Charles II and had developed quietly under the protection of the Toleration Act of 1689. They were not numerous, but the Baptists, the Unitarians and the other denominations contained men of quality, who felt the need of a firm intellectual foundation for their faith. The academies established by the dissenters throughout Wales gained so high a reputation that Anglicans sometimes sent their sons to them in preparation for the universities. The dissenters had inherited from the Commonwealth a critical attitude towards authority, but the average peasant was not attracted to their somewhat austere and educated discipline. Thus, when it came, the Methodist Revival entered untouched territory, and the Anglican church was now neither strong enough nor flexible enough to contain this astonishing outburst of 'enthusiasm'.

There were forerunners, for no new movement springs into the world entirely unheralded. The Society for the Promotion of Christian Knowledge, the S.P.C.K., had been active in Wales during the reign of Queen Anne, and had received strong support from the Pembrokeshire magnate, Sir John Philipps. But the real herald of the Revival was Griffith Jones, the vicar of Llanddowror, in Carmarthenshire. He organised a remarkable system of 'itinerant masters', who would go from parish to parish, spending three months in each parish at a time teaching the illiterate to read. Griffith Jones was primarily concerned with the religious conviction of the average man, not with his education, but he began making Wales literate, and, above all, literate in Welsh. He brought one further important element to the religious scene. He could preach eloquently to Welshmen in their native language. The spoken word, with its power of immediate impact, was the spark that touched off these dramatic conversions which were almost compulsory in the progress of Methodism. The three great leaders of the movement in Wales, Howell Harris, Daniel Rowland and William Williams – known as Pantycelyn to all Welshmen from his birthplace in a little farmhouse in a green valley of the Epynt hills – all had the same experience as St Paul on the road to Damascus. And they were all in close touch with Griffith Jones. They were young men in their twenties and Griffiths Jones was forty-eight when he began his work. They had the energy to build on the foundations he had laid.

The pillars of the Methodist revival in Wales: *left to right* William Williams (Pantycelyn), Daniel Rowland and Howell Harris

Howell Harris was converted at the age of twenty-two, on Palm Sunday in 1735, after listening to the preaching of the vicar of Talgarth. Daniel Rowland's conversion came a little later, in the hands of Griffith Jones himself. William Williams, Pantycelyn, the son of dissenters, heard Harris at Talgarth and was moved to take Holy Orders. All these young men were south Walians, and all of them had distinctive personalities and left a permanent mark on the movement they inspired.

Howell Harris was, in many ways, the most remarkable of them all. A handsome, masterful man, his enemies – and he had many – accused him of being driven by an out-sized power complex, but there can be no question of his gifts of leadership and his ability to supply some sort of intellectual basis which this emotional movement badly needed. The date of his conversion is important. Harris began his career before he had heard of John Wesley's Holy Club. Welsh Methodism thus had an independent origin from English and retained an independent structure, although Harris had early contact with Whitefield. He was also powerfully influenced by the Moravians and this explains the mystical element in his religion. While Wesley's movement kept firmly within the confines of the church, Harris tended to give his Methodism a more presbyterian cast. Very early on, he began to organise his converts into associations or 'sassiwns'. In the conflict that arose later between Wesley's Calvinism and Whitefield's Arminianism, Harris sided with Whitefield although he and Wesley remained on friendly personal terms. He also came under the influence of an imperious lady from Llŷn, Madam Griffith, to the scandal of some of the faithful. Then his thoughts turned to the foundation of a community on Moravian lines, and with the help of money supplied by Lady Huntington, established a college at Trevecka in Breconshire, one of the most fascinating religious experiments of the time. Harris died in 1773 alienated from the main Methodist movement, but where would it have been without him? His tireless energy, his magnetic personality and his organising power drove it forward irresistibly in the early days.

If Harris was the driving power of Welsh Methodism, Daniel Rowland was its voice. He did not travel on anything like those intensive missionary journeys undertaken by Harris but preferred to preach in his own parish at Llangeitho in Cardiganshire, where thousands used to gather to hear his sermons. We cannot judge, at this distance of time, how Daniel Rowland achieved his effects. There was no recording equipment in the eighteenth century! But clearly his voice, his pulpit presence and above all his command over moving words in Welsh were deeply impressive. Was he the first to use in the pulpit that mesmeric rise and fall of the voice, that almost hypnotic technique which later Welsh preachers knew as the 'hwyl'? William Williams, Pantycelyn, declared, in his elegy on Rowland's death, in 1790: 'When dark night covered Britain without a sign of dawn, Daniel sounded the clear trumpet of Sinai, shaking solid rocks with its powerful echo.' The great voice of Daniel Rowland inevitably died with him. The softer, sweeter voice of his chief assistant, William Williams, still sounds today. He was a hymn writer of genius, whose verses seemed, to those who sang them, to incorporate

The Trevecka community, Powys, founded by Howell Harris

the new Methodist experience of direct personal contact with the Divine Power.

Inevitably men like Rowland and William Williams came to disagree with Howell Harris when that erratic genius took to new experiments. Why, remarked Williams sardonically, did Harris want to build a monastery at Trevecka when Henry VIII had destroyed such buildings by the thousand? Conversion, not architecture, should be the proper business of a Methodist, and there were still huge areas of Wales untouched by the new fire. The honour of carrying the message into Anglesey, that stronghold of 'benighted Anglicanism', fell to a younger man, Peter Williams, again a south Walian, who had been converted at Carmarthen by Whitefield in 1743 and had become a curate to Griffith Jones. North Wales, however, was not yet ready for the message. Peter Williams was imprisoned for the night by Sir Watkyn Williams Wynn in the dog-kennels at Wynnstay!

The spread of Methodism in the north came later with the arrival of Thomas Charles, again a south Walian, who had been born a few miles from the fountainhead of Llanddowror. Charles settled at Bala and revived the Griffith Jones scheme for Sunday schools throughout north Wales. He gave the movement its platform in the magazine he founded, *Y Drysorfa*, and he clearly defined its doctrinal structure.

It fell to Thomas Charles, in 1811, to lead Welsh Methodism to take the decisive step − one taken with the greatest reluctance − of severing its connection with the Church of England and becoming a separate denomination. The break, in the long run, was to prove devastating for the Church of England in Wales.

The new Methodist Church took with it a great body of the old Established Church's membership; but that was not all. The older dissenting communities

'Enthusiasm' – jumpers at a Methodist meeting

had begun by rather despising the emotional methods of the Methodists. They were one with the gentry in condemning the frenzied scenes, the jumping about in ecstacy that sometimes occurred at Methodist meetings. But they found the ground prepared by the Methodists congenial ground for their own expansion. The Established Church was now 'yr hen eglwys Lloegr' – the church for the English and the gentry. The mass of the Welsh-speaking Welsh had gone elsewhere.

The chapels multiplied through the land, scattering Biblical names over the countryside. Hence the numerous Bethels, Hermans, Hebrons and all the little 'causes', each with its memories of the stalwarts who founded it, the 'saints' who had sustained it through its early days. The chapel, not the church, now held the loyalty of the people. Architecturally it could not compare with the older building, although some of the early chapels that survive have a moving simplicity. Too often the inscription 'ail-adaeladwyd' (rebuilt) appears over the door, showing that the chapel had moved away from its pristine simplicity and now flaunted classical pillars and even spires in some cases, as the land grew richer and the faithful more prosperous. Chapel and Church were to confront each other all through the nineteenth century.

Now that so many years have passed and so many changes have occurred in recent times to the society created in Wales by the Methodist Revival, it is possible to see it apart from the partisan feelings it aroused for over a century and a half.

There can be no question that the Methodists laid the foundation for a more democratic way of life in Wales, although, paradoxically, this was the last thing that the leaders of the Revival aimed at doing. They were concerned with the things of the spirit and not of the material world. Nevertheless, they participated in the material world. They were conservative in politics, strong supporters – when they were allowed to be – of the accepted social order. Howell Harris, for example, took a commission in the county militia, and when war broke out against Catholic France in 1759 he accompanied the twenty-four recruits he had raised to garrison duties at Yarmouth. His heavy musket is still preserved at Trevecka. But, inevitably, people who had run their own Sunday schools, who had built their own chapels and stood apart from the gentry, were bound to feel more democratic. Through its pulpit oratory and the study of the Bible, the Revival gave the average Welshman a new respect for himself and his ancient language.

There were grievous losses as well. Wales, after the Revival, was a sterner, grimmer place. Edward Jones, the harpist, bitterly lamented the passing of the old way of life. 'The sudden decline of the Minstrelsy and Customs of Wales,' he wrote, 'is in a great degree to be attributed to the fanatic imposters or illiterate plebeian preachers . . .' The dancers, the fiddlers, the carefree interlude players, all faded before the stern Methodist admonition to Welshmen that their first duty was to save their souls from Hell. On the walls of the porch of the little church of Llanfair Discoed in Gwent is the inscription:

> WhoEver heir on Sunday
> Will practice Playing At Ball
> it May Be before Monday
> The Devil Will Have you All.

Before such disapproval, the boisterous games in the churchyard would disappear. The teetotal Welsh Sunday was already on its way!

The Methodists had found one way of filling the yawning gap left in Welsh life by the decay of the old oral culture, and they had profoundly stirred the lower ranks of society. But their methods could not appeal to many intellectual and cultivated Welshmen who also yearned for a new order, a break in that bland indifference to Wales and things Welsh which was the hallmark of the Supine Century. They felt that the true path of national revival lay in restoring to eighteenth-century Wales its pride in the glories of the Welsh past, in its literature and its history. The recapture of the past was to be the driving force in the regeneration of the present.

Even in the darkest days of the Supine Century the memorials of the past were not entirely lost. Great antiquaries like Edward Lhuyd, enthusiasts like the remarkable Morris brothers from Anglesey and scholars like Edward Evans, had ensured that the rare manuscripts scattered through the libraries of the gentry were collected and preserved. Lexicographers, like John Walters of Llandough in the Vale of Glamorgan, had produced modern dictionaries that had restored people's pride in a language once dismissed as the 'Gibberish of Taffydom'.

Penillion singing to the harp. The frontispiece of Edward Jones's *Bardic Museum* (1802)

London Welshmen came forward to play a leading and even a decisive part in what Dr Prys Morgan, the leading authority on the subject, has described as the Welsh eighteenth-century Renaissance. Ever since the job-rush under the Tudors, much of the cash and inspiration for movements of change in Wales had come from the Welshmen who had 'made good' in the metropolis. In 1751 they had founded the society of the Cymmrodorion, which still flourishes today, devoted to the encouragement of Welsh literature and of all things Welsh. Later on came the more radical society of the Gwyneddogion. Out of the fruitful partnership between London money and Welsh scholarship these societies provided came a series of vitally-important publications of the manuscript records of Welsh literature and history, culminating in the monumental *Myvyrian Archaiology of Wales*, printed at his own expense and to his ultimate financial embarrassment, by a successful London leather merchant from Denbighshire.

These Welsh associations in London were important points of contact between the English literary and scholarly world and developments in Wales. They were also convivial get-togethers, staged not in chapels but in taverns like the one kept in Southwark by the genial and radical Jac Glan y Gors. Certainly a curious contrast to John Wesley's Holy Club!

The cultural revivalists looked back not only to the ancient literature of Wales but to its history also, and the further back the better. They remembered that, after all, they were the original inhabitants of the island, the true Ancient Britons. They gloried in the thought. And as they peered excitedly into the mists of history, they were bound to encounter the most ancient Britons of them all, the Druids. Inevitably the Druids took them over. These Druids of the eighteenth-century imagination had no possible connection with the real priests of the Celtic heyday, and it was John Aubrey, and William Stukeley who followed him, who started this new type of Druid on their conquering career through the literature of the Romantic Revival. For Aubrey and Stukeley had associated the Druids, quite erroneously, with Stonehenge. White-robed Druids, guardians of the esoteric lore of the Celtic past, moving with noble dignity under the great stone trilithons – the combination was irresistible! It wasn't long before the Welsh were placing the Druids in the forefront of their history, alongside Arthur himself. Henry Rowland of Llanidan in Anglesey published a handsome volume on his native island in which he firmly associated the Druids with the megalithic cromlechs. But on no one did the druidic spell fall with more powerful effect than on one remarkable man who was at the very centre of the eighteenth-century Renaissance, Edward Williams, known to history by his bardic name of Iolo Morganwg.

Iolo was born at Fleminston, in the Vale of Glamorgan in 1747 and earned his living, in his early days, as a stonemason. He came into contact with the lexicographer, John Walters, and developed a remarkable knowledge of Welsh manuscript sources as well as great poetic gifts. He became an important source of inspiration to the London Gwyneddogion and was regarded by English literary figures like Southey as an authority on all things Welsh. There can be no question that Iolo had genius, but it was a slightly flawed genius. In his over-riding passion for reviving the glories of the Welsh past, he had no hesitation in adding to them on his own account. He forged poems by Dafydd ap Gwilym and medieval chronicles so brilliantly that he deceived scholars up to our own day. But it was forgery in a heroic cause. His soaring imagination led him to revive what he claimed was the original governing body of the bards, the Gorsedd of the Bards of the Isle of Britain, the heirs to the Druids. 'I am giving you,' he said somewhat grandiloquently to the Welsh nation, 'the Patriarchal religion and theology, the Divine Revelation given to mankind, and those have been maintained in Wales until our own day.'

The first meeting of the Gorsedd took place on, of all places, Primrose Hill in London, and there is no record that the Wales of the Methodists and the fox-hunting squires was unduly impressed. Iolo and his friends didn't mind. They were dreaming of creating a new nation from below, and Iolo sensed, with the instinct of genius, the need of every nation for symbolic ritual, for some sort of ceremony

Left The eighteenth-century dream of the Druid, 'the wisest of men', complete with a sprig of oak leaves

Right Edward Williams, 'Iolo Morganwg'

that would crystallise its sense of nationality. The older monarchies had ceremony enough and to spare for all occasions. The new-born states of America and revolutionary France set about creating ritual as soon as possible. In our own day, communist Russia has its ritualistic glorification of the state on May Day in Red Square.

Wales in the mid-eighteenth century had no ceremonies of its own, although some decades later that much misunderstood monarch, George IV, toyed with the idea of creating an Order of St David to match the English Order of the Garter and the Scottish Order of the Thistle. This order was naturally for the upper classes only, and the scheme was immediately cancelled by George's successor, William IV, on the ground of expense. Iolo's Gorsedd, however, survives. The bards in their white robes still move in dignified procession on to the platform at the National Eisteddfod – the only national ceremonial order in the world based upon cultural merit.

A newly-revived nation has need not only of ritual but of heroes. The Druids and Owain Glyn Dŵr were welcomed back with enthusiasm into the national pantheon, but a special welcome was reserved for the mysterious figure of Prince Madoc, claimed to have been the son of Owain Gwynedd. Madoc is supposed to have sailed boldly westwards in 1170 over uncharted seas until he discovered a land, which could only have been America. He came back to Wales to report his discovery and set off again on a return voyage. Prince Madoc and his companions then disappeared from history as mysteriously as they had entered it. In the days of Queen Elizabeth I, strange reports purported to come from North America of a tribe of Red Indians who spoke a language curiously like Welsh. Clearly, they could only be the descendants of Prince Madoc!

The Madoc story had first found its way into print in the high noon of Elizabethan exploration, suspiciously at the very time when England was disputing the exclusive Spanish claims to the New World. The London Welsh societies now embraced it with such fervour that they sent out an explorer, charged with contacting these Welsh-speaking red men at all costs. The favourite candidates for the honour of being the heirs of Madoc were the Mandan Indians, who lived in remote country on a bend of the Missouri river. John Evans, a young man from Waenfawr in Snowdonia, set off up the Missouri to reach them. It was a journey of incredible hardship, for the territory was still claimed by Spain and Evans had to travel under Spanish auspices.

Alas, when at length he contacted the Mandans, he received a severe shock. The Mandans had never heard of Wales and to his greeting of 'Sut mae, gyfeillion?', they returned a non-committal 'How'. Worse still, their curious fertility rites would never have won the approval of the Gorsedd of the Bards of the Isle of Britain. Another Welsh dream faded.

There was one result of John Evans's journey which Iolo and the Gwyneddogion had not anticipated – Evans had made a series of splendidly accurate maps. These were used with great success by the Lewis and Clark expedition of 1804 which made the first crossing of the North American continent, eight years after poor John Evans had died forgotten in New Orleans.

Prince Madoc and America remind us that there was a second powerful driving force behind the Welsh eighteenth-century revival. The past was a stimulus but so was the Future. The intellectual wind of change that swept through Europe as the century progressed, touched Wales as well. The writings of Voltaire, Rousseau and other authors of the French *l'Encyclopédie*, a work which embodied the ideals of the century, circulated among sections of the rising middle class – the progressive dissenters, the better-off tradesmen and craft workers. The propaganda of the Age of Reason was even translated in some measure into Welsh. The American Revolution had been warmly welcomed in these circles, too, for throughout the Supine Century there had been a steady flow of emigration to America from Wales and a surprising number of those who signed the American Declaration of Independence in 1778 had Welsh origins.

One of the most powerful advocates of the American cause had been the celebrated Dr Richard Price, the greatest political theorist that Wales produced. Like so many of the progressive figures of the Welsh revival he came from the Vale of Glamorgan, a noted nursery of dissenters – Marcher country where, over the ages, Welsh and English had sharpened their wits as well as their swords on each other. Price was a close associate of Benjamin Franklin in London, and in his tract *Civil Liberty*, he gave the Americans a philosophical basis for their rebellion. He was one of the pioneers of the eighteenth-century idea of progress – of the heady doctrine of the perfectability of man. He was hailed by Condorcet as

one of the formative influences in the building of a new democratic society in
France. Edmund Burke wrote his *Reflections on the Revolution in France* in reply
to one of Price's sermons.

David Williams, again a South Walian from that fecund Vale of Glamorgan,
went even further than Price. He became an honorary citizen of the French republic
and helped to frame its constitution. He left just in time to save his neck, but
not before his earlier 'Liturgy' for a cult of Nature had served as a model for
Robespierre's own attempt to create a state religion with his Cult of the Supreme
Being. Previously, Williams had earned the praise of Voltaire, and Rousseau had
owned himself Williams's 'most devoted disciple'.

Advanced ideas were in the air, especially in London Welsh circles. In Wales
itself, Morgan John Rhys, a Baptist minister also hailing from that remarkable
radical area of the Vale of Glamorgan, gave these ideas a platform in his 'Journal'.
He, himself, was a remarkable mixture of religious and revolutionary fervour.
He betook himself to Paris where he set up a Bible depôt to convert the French
Catholics. He was typical of the many enthusiasts who felt that the French Revolution was also Wales's chance for a new start. They toasted the Jacobins and felt,
with the youthful Wordsworth, that 'bliss was it in that dawn to be alive'. They
were confident they were creating a new Welsh nation, firmly founded on the
glories of the past but which would surely move forward into the brave new world
of approaching universal democracy.

That move never took place. Relations between Britain and Revolutionary
France were steadily deteriorating. By 1793 the two countries were at war.
Immediately the political climate changed in Wales as well as in England. The
steel shutters of censorship clanged down. There would be no more toasting of
the Jacobins in Jac Glan y Gors's tavern in Southwark, no more odes to Liberty
from Iolo Morganwg. Such activities were suspect and would soon become highly
dangerous. Morgan John Rhys felt it safer to realise his dream of religious freedom
and universal brotherhood in America rather than Wales. With his usual enthusiasm he looked out over the 'unbroken grass' that then stretched westwards for
a limitless extent beyond the Allegheny Mountains. Here he vowed to create a
new Welsh national home, and build his 'sweet Beulah land'. He founded his settlement, but he suffered the disappointments that seem to lie in wait for all visionaries
before their time. His Beulah failed, as did the whole of the pro-revolutionary
movement in Wales itself. The dreamers of a new Wales found it safer to confine
their dreams to literature and history rather than politics. The final eclipse came
when the French, the harbingers of Liberty, actually landed on the soil of Wales,
not bringing universal brotherhood but with guns in hand.

On a February morning in 1787, two French warships were sighted off Strumble
Head, in north-west Pembrokeshire. They entered Fishguard Bay, and the little
fort that had been built by public subscription after the raid on Fishguard by John
Paul Jones in the American War of Independence, opened fire. The French ships
then withdrew around the point and landed a force of around 1200 men on the

rocky cliffs of Carreg Wastad. By evening the tricolour flag was flying over a tiny part of Wales. The French were under the command of an Irish-American, General Tate, who had previously intended to land near Bristol and march up through the Welsh border to Liverpool, creating confusion on the way. Presumably all this was intended as a diversion for the French adventures in aid of Ireland in revolt. It was an absurd scheme, and indeed the whole of the Fishguard affair has an air of farce about it. Tate had been flung ashore in a hurry by the captain of the warships, when he found that there was a British warship guarding the Bristol Channel. Poor Tate's command was, in the classic military term, 'expendable', and consisted largely of the sweepings of the French gaols put into uniform. His undisciplined troops were soon looting and getting drunk on the wine in the Strumble farmhouses, recently salvaged from a Portuguese wreck.

Tate was in no condition to resist when the Pembrokeshire militia came hastening up from the south of the county under the command of Lord Cawdor. There had already been some scuffles with the local farmers, shots had been exchanged and at least one Frenchman killed. A stout-hearted woman cobbler from Fishguard, Jemima Nicholas, rounded up thirteen Frenchmen with a pitchfork and became famous throughout Wales as 'The Pembrokeshire Heroine'. Tate had no option but to surrender. He led his men on to Goodwick Sands, where they laid down their muskets and were marched off to prison. The Last Invasion of Britain was over.

The memorial stone to Jemima Nicholas, in Fishguard

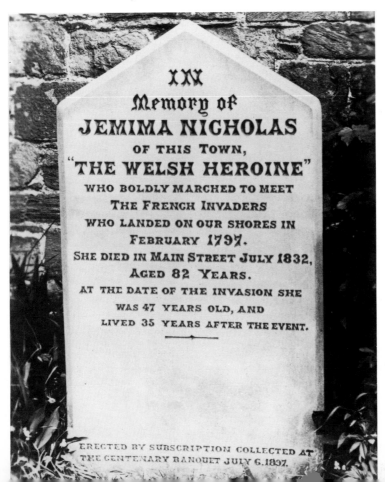

XXX
Memory of
JEMIMA NICHOLAS
OF THIS TOWN,
"THE WELSH HEROINE"
WHO BOLDLY MARCHED TO MEET
THE FRENCH INVADERS
WHO LANDED ON OUR SHORES IN
FEBRUARY 1797.
SHE DIED IN MAIN STREET JULY 1832,
AGED 82 YEARS.
AT THE DATE OF THE INVASION SHE
WAS 47 YEARS OLD, AND
LIVED 35 YEARS AFTER THE EVENT.

ERECTED BY SUBSCRIPTION COLLECTED AT
THE CENTENARY BANQUET JULY 6, 1897.

The shock of Fishguard killed any enthusiasm for revolution in Wales. There was no more talk in radical circles of a forthcoming Welsh republic. The next wave of political protest – when it came after the end of the Napoleonic wars – would come from a different quarter. It would be inspired not by the French but by the Industrial Revolution.

The term 'Industrial Revolution' is, of course, a convenient term of historical shorthand, for there was no 1789 in the development of manufacturing. The foundations of change had been laid down many years before, but most of the new techniques of iron-making and mining had been developed outside the Principality. Wales was still basically an agricultural country, yet there were some signs of things to come. Cardiganshire had long developed its lead mines, and as far back as the reign of Charles I, Thomas Bushell had been licensed to set up a mint in Aberystwyth to coin the silver he extracted from the lead. By the mid-eighteenth century, the great copper deposits were being exploited in Parys Mountain in Anglesey and the ore brought down by ship to Neath and Swansea, where coal mines near the coast made smelting cheaper. The slate of the wild mountains of Snowdonia was beginning to be known outside Wales, too, and a coal trade had already begun from the little ports along the Bristol Channel. Even in Merioneth, the roughest part of Wales, the country people met, in a sort of cottage industry, to knit stockings for export. It was the same at Bala and the valley of the Dee, and Welsh knitted stockings were in particular demand for the slave plantations in the West Indies. Weaving was carried on all over the country with wool from the mountain sheep. The woollen mills of mid-Wales were nearer to the midland markets, but they were being steadily outdistanced by the mills of Yorkshire.

Behind all this lay the one export activity that had never failed the Welsh since the days when the Tudors had at last brought peace to the countryside. Every year, the great herds of black cattle, together with sheep and geese, were driven

This page The open-cast copper mine of Parys Mountain, Anglesey

Opposite The great Penrhyn slate quarry at Bethesda, Gwynedd

from the mountains across the lowlands to the marts and Smithfields of London and the eastern towns. Archbishop Williams – at a time when the drives had been temporarily interrupted by the Civil War – described them as the 'Spanish fleet of north Wales, which brings hither that little silver and gold we have'.

The Archbishop had put his finger on one of the basic weaknesses of the Welsh economy. Wales had no big urban centre where capital could accumulate, a Bristol or a London, with merchant bankers experienced in international trade and in the risks involved in financing new industrial ventures. True, small country banks started to appear from the 1770s onward – one of the best-known early banks being the Bank of the Black Ox at Llandovery – and the master drovers acted as financial advisers to the scattered rural communities. But the big money and the technical expertise necessary for the new developments in Welsh industry had to come from outside, although the raw material on which the whole expansion depended lay waiting for the exploiters, hidden in the rocks of the Welsh coalfields. The Industrial Revolution depended on the application of coal-coke to the smelting of iron in place of charcoal. James Watt's improvement of the steam engine had given the revolution a new impetus. Iron in combination with coal now represented power. They were conveniently linked together in the Welsh mountains. It was not long before men of enterprise in the expanding world of iron moved in on Wales and on the opportunities it represented.

Isaac Wilkinson had set up his furnaces at Bersham, near Wrexham, using the technique of smelting iron-ore with coke developed by Abraham Darby at Coalbrookdale in nearby Shropshire. His son John, through his contacts with James Watt, made Bersham world-famous. The foundry house still stands at Bersham, although it is now used as a barn for the nearby farm! Wrexham, itself, grew rapidly and with its 8000 inhabitants was, for a brief moment, the largest town in Wales.

But the most spectacular industrial growth took place in the south. In the 1790s, the iron-works started to multiply along the northern outcrop of the south Wales coalfield, although there had been pioneers like Anthony Bacon who had already been at work in this wild country where coal, iron ore and limestone all lay in

Rolling mills at Merthyr Tydfil

close and tempting proximity. Places like Hirwaen, Merthyr, Penydaran, Tredegar and Blaenavon, mere hamlets or just points on the map, now became household names to an ever-widening circle of surrounding rural Wales, as did the names of the new dynasties of iron-masters – the Crawshays of Cyfartha, the Hills, the Guests and the Homfrays. They were all men of formidable dynamism and enterprise. They have received a bad press from recent historians and novel writers, and there is no question that they were driving, ruthless men, of the same stamp as many such entrepreneurs who were building the new industrial society in other parts of Britain. But their drive might have been given a harder cutting edge because they were operating in the most isolated and inhospitable of these new industrial development areas.

The furnaces at Hirwaen, at Dowlais and Blaenavon worked against a background of high moors that rose to nearly 3000 feet on the Brecon Beacons. Their product – the iron that would make the cannon balls that Wellington's men would fire in the Peninsula and at Waterloo, and the guns on H.M.S. *Victory*, as well as the rails that would soon be marking the ultimate triumph of the Industrial Revolution when they carried the steam engine – had to be carried down to the coast by canals constructed with enormous difficulty through deep, narrow valleys with gradients far exceeding those faced by their luckier contemporaries in lowland England. It was natural, therefore, for the iron masters to back the Cornish genius, Richard Trevithick, then employed in the Penydaran works, when he came forward with a revolutionary proposal to build a steam engine that 'would travel on its own account in any place where it was needed'. In 1806, the world's first steam train, carrying over seventy intrepid passengers and a load of iron bars, travelled amid scenes of great excitement for seven miles down the tramway from the Penydaran works in Merthyr to the canal head at Abercynon, along a route that is still walked in pious memory by railway enthusiasts.

Roads were also improved by the establishment of road trusts which – whatever they may have become some decades later – made a major contribution to the early industrial development of Wales. The most remarkable feat of road construction took place, however, not in south but north Wales. Encouraged by some government help to improve the route to Ireland, Thomas Telford drove his road through the wilds of Snowdonia and flung it across the Menai Strait on a suspension bridge that was one of the engineering wonders of the age. Telford's dramatic highway not only encouraged trade, it tempted the wealthy tourists to come to the wilds of Cambria in search of the now fashionable 'picturesque'. The Romantic revival had made mountains intellectually and emotionally fashionable. The artists had already gone on sketching tours, producing their series of pictures of the beauty spots carefully approved by such professors of the 'picturesque' as the Rev. William Gilpin. Turner himself did a series of tours through the Principality, and it was the scenery of Wales that gave him the inspiration to create his mature masterpieces. Turner concentrated on the waterfalls and the romantic ruins placed in their mountain landscape. Rowlandson concentrated more on the people. Here they are, in his drawings, in the market places or the inns, busy talking the Welsh which, no doubt, was incomprehensible to the artist.

How many Welsh people were now living among those mountains and in the little towns and villages linked by the rough roads that Rowlandson, Turner and their fellow artists had to travel over in search of the picturesque? The first census in Britain was organised in 1801, and only then do we have an accurate account and not an estimate of population of the Principality. The census gave the figure as 587,000. The second census, taken ten years later, showed that the population had increased to 673,000. There had been some small immigration from outside Wales into the new industrial areas, but the real increase had occurred inside the boundaries of Wales, above all in the rural areas. Something strange was taking place. For reasons that have never been satisfactorily explained, a similar population explosion was taking place all over Western Europe at the same time. The causes may have been obscure, but the results of this population explosion were soon to become only too obvious.

New, dangerous pressures were building up in the Welsh countryside and not all of them could be relieved by the extra population moving into the new industrial areas. Four-fifths of the Welsh population was still scattered through the rural areas. The Napoleonic wars had brought a degree of prosperity to richer farmers but once peace returned, prices came tumbling down. The censorship barriers that had appeared with the French Revolution weakened. Discontent could once again become vocal. The last half of the eighteenth century had seen the gestation of a new society; the first half of the nineteenth saw its birth, and the birth pangs were severe.

Birth Pangs of a New Order

The 'crowning carnage' of Waterloo in 1815 brought peace at last to Europe after nearly twenty years of constant warfare. The 'great disturber', Napoleon, was safely packed off to St Helena, and the crowned heads and diplomats returned to their Congress at Vienna to restore as much of pre-revolutionary Europe as they could, after those tumultuous times when the boundaries on the map had 'waved about like washing on the line in a windy day'. But as so often happens after wars to end wars, peace abroad brought strife at home. In the story of Wales, the years between 1815 and 1848 are years of social unrest, of riots and, on two occasions at least, something close to insurrection. Yet out of this turmoil, and perhaps because of it, a more equitable society eventually emerged, and that wider spread of prosperity which gave late nineteenth-century Nonconformist Wales its slight air of smug satisfaction – and its confidence in the future.

The years of turmoil had first to be endured, and in many aspects they were hard indeed. The abrupt change from a war to a peace economy is always painful. The iron works lost their best customers – the army and the navy. The re-opening of trade with the Continent sent the price of farm products tumbling. During the war years, unscrupulous landlords had taken advantage of the chance to change conditions of farm tenure. There had been a spate of enclosures, often at the expense of communal rights. Rural Wales seethed with discontent, which broke out again and again in violence. An example from Cardiganshire gives the atmosphere of these outbreaks.

In the 1820s, up on the bleak moorland of Mynydd Bach in the north of the county, the peasantry conducted a running battle against an English gentleman who, with the help of his grooms and even of soldiers, was trying to hang on to the 850 acres he had high-handedly enclosed. Six hundred men, disguised in women's clothing and led by the redoubtable Dai Jones, the local blacksmith, destroyed the fences and burnt the houses in what has passed into local folklore as 'Rhyfel y Said Bach' – The War of the Little Englishman. Popular feeling ran so high that the ringleaders had to be removed from Wales for trial. The Mynydd Bach 'war' can be paralleled by similar outbreaks in places as far apart as Anglesey and Carmarthenshire. They can be variously ascribed to fury over enclosures and the fall in corn prices, but behind them was one constant factor, the mysterious but constant growth in the sheer numbers of the people who now inhabited Wales.

Charles II

The artists and Wales:

ABOVE Cardiff by Thomas Rowlandson

LEFT Dolbadarn Castle by J. M. W. Turner

OPPOSITE ABOVE Snowdon from Llyn Nantle by Richard Wilson

BELOW Betws-y-Coed by David Cox

TOP LEFT The Bison Dance of the Mandan Indians. John Evans, financed by London Welshmen, had hoped to find them descendants of Prince Madoc. Their ceremonies seemed hardly suitable to an Eisteddfod

RIGHT Cyfartha Works from Cefn Bridge, Merthyr Tydfil by Thomas Prytherch

ABOVE The end of the 'Last Invasion of Britain'– the French surrender on Goodwick Sands near Fishguard, 1797

It has been argued that this population explosion was caused not so much by a rise in the birth rate as by a decrease in the death rate, and the doctors and sanitary inspectors were certainly the real heroes of the lengthening expectation of life as the eighteenth century developed. One wonders, however, how much medical care was available to sick farm-workers in remote valleys in rural Wales? There seemed to be ever more mouths to feed in the crowded country cottages, and limited resources with which to feed them.

The population problem became one of the great questions of debate in intellectual circles. With no reliable figures from a national census to guide inquiries, there were, inevitably, two sharply contrasting schools of thought in the eighteenth century. One influential group, represented by the celebrated Welsh political theorist, David Williams, maintained that the population was falling, with dire consequences for the future of the nation, while Arthur Young, a distinguished agriculturalist, would have none of this. He had travelled widely over all parts of Great Britain, including Wales, and preferred to trust the evidence of his own eyes. 'It is in vain to talk of lists of births, and tables of houses and windows, as proof of our loss of people. The flourishing state of agriculture, our manufactures and commerce, with our great wealth, prove the contrary.'

In 1798, a bombshell was thrown in to the academic calm of the debate by the publication of an *Essay on the Principle of Population* by the Rev. Thomas Robert Malthus. This inoffensive clergyman – in private life the most kindly and considerate of men – committed the most serious mistake, for anyone in holy orders, of applying cold logic to a hot political and emotional problem. He simply pointed out that the population was bound to increase in mathematical progression, and would always outstrip subsistence but for Nature's ruthless remedies of war, plague and famine. Some of his sentences fell upon his contemporaries with an icy but prescient chill. 'We are bound in justice and honour formally to disclaim the *right* of the poor to support. . . . A man who is born into a world already possessed, if he cannot get subsistence from his parents, on whom he has a just demand, and if the society does not want his labour, has no claim of right to the smallest portion of food, and in fact has no business to be where he is. At nature's mighty feast there is no cover for him.' These words were all the more chilling because they were written in an age when the only mentionable form of birth control was 'moral restraint'. Alas, history proves that 'moral restraint' is no substitute for the pill.

Malthus subsequently modified his views, and his book was certainly misinterpreted in some quarters. But Malthus's words echoed in the minds of far too many administrators when they came to tackle one of the most serious consequences of the population explosion – the increase of poverty in the lower sections of society. Every year the numbers of the needy increased – those poor people who had no right to a seat at 'nature's mighty feast'. Faced by these unhappy multitudes, the old system of parish relief was bound to break down.

The burden of looking after the poor had been placed on the parish as long ago as 1662, after the Restoration of Charles II. It had worked well enough when the population was small and the numbers of the needy not alarming; but its provisions were totally inadequate to cope with the conditions that prevailed after 1815. The parish authorities often resorted to desperate and cruel shifts to rid themselves of the burden. No question but that the whole business was in urgent need of reform, but when that reform actually came – after Parliament had reluctantly reformed itself in 1831 – the unhappy paupers must have felt that the remedy was much worse than the disease. The framers of the new Poor Law Act of 1834 no doubt honestly felt that they were tackling in the best way what they regarded as a serious social evil, but they went about their task with a clinical detachment. The Commissioners appointed by the Act were soon branded as 'concentrated icicles'. They seemed no longer to be dealing with the 'deserving poor' but with Malthusian unfortunates who had no natural right to sustenance. The new workhouses went up outside the country towns and were bitterly resented by the poor in Wales. No wonder that there was widespread protest and unrest among what a certain economist of the period called 'the lower orders'.

Many of these protests were bound to end in violence, for as yet there was no national police force. Peel's reforms lay in the future. The authorities might enlist special constables, but when faced with a boisterous crowd, a nervous magistrate would hurriedly read the Riot Act and thus call in the only available deterrent to disorder, the military – either the yeomanry or the regular troops, if there was a garrison town near at hand. Immediately, what could have begun as a high-spirited protest might be turned into a more serious affair. Was this the case in the celebrated Merthyr Riots of 1831? Or were they the result of a deeper malaise in the new and growing industrial areas of Wales, which found expression in the organised protests by radical and even revolutionary groups who were in the direct line of succession to the old Jacobin groups of the 1780s? They rekindled the torch of David Williams, Morgan John Rhys and Iolo Morganwg after it had been all but snuffed out in the Napoleonic Wars.

Professor Gwyn Williams, in his illuminating and challenging account of the formation of the Welsh proletariat, distinguishes three areas where the old Jacobin legacy was modernised and acted as an inspiration in the inevitable struggles that now rose between the possessors and the unpossessed in both rural and industrial Wales. One key area held the woollen towns of Newtown and Llanidloes, with Llanbrynmair and other smaller weaving centres of mid-Wales. A second strongly radical district lay in north Carmarthenshire and the immediately adjacent parts of Pembrokeshire and Cardiganshire. The third centre was the mining valleys of Monmouthshire, and the iron towns of the northern rim, especially Merthyr Tydfil. Professor Williams has christened these areas – if christening is the right word to use in a Marxist analysis! – The Radical Triangle; and it is certainly remarkable how many of the leaders of the protest movements, from Chartism to the Rebecca Riots, came from these parts.

It is surely no accident that Robert Owen, the remarkable pioneer of trade unionism, the co-operative movement and so much else that was to become an integral part of the future Labour Party, was born in Newtown. His career lay outside

Top Child labour in the mines

Above Working in narrow seams

Wales, in Scotland, England and America, and from one point of view it ended in failure. Owen may have been a bit of a crank, but he was a noble one. He spent his own wealth and health in the causes he so passionately supported. At the very end of his life he felt an overwhelming desire to return to his roots in Newtown. Return he did, only to die within a few days, and to be buried in his native town.

Trade unionism had some difficulty in establishing itself in Wales. Curiously enough, the first miners' unions were set up in the northern coalfield. In the south, communities were scattered through deep valleys and communication was hard. Working conditions were bad, the seams were difficult, and women and children struggled side by side with the men to drag heavily-loaded trams of coal through narrow tunnels. Many of the illustrations in the government's report on safety in the mines, which so horrified Engels, were drawn from south Wales. In these conditions, which were especially bad in the small mines of Monmouthshire, it is easy to see why the miners' resistance in Wales took on a violent, even sinister aspect.

The Scotch Cattle were an organisation whose leaders were wrapped in a veil of impenetrable secrecy but who conducted a highly sophisticated campaign of terrorism against blacklegs, unpopular managers, profiteering tradesmen and all whom they felt held the poor, hard-working miner in thrall. A visit from the Cattle was a frightening affair, and woe betide the workman who dared defy them. The warning notes themselves were enough to chill the blood. 'To all Colliers, Traitors, Turncoats and others, we hereby warn you for the second and last time'. If the victim still remained defiant, the Cattle then proceeded to deal with him using strange, ritualist and frightening justice.

The raiders always came from the next valley and made themselves unrecognisable with blackened faces, women's clothes and animal skins. Their leader wore a mask with bull's horns on his head. The herd approached in the darkness with a fearsome lowing and blowing of horns. Then the Bull – the Tarw Scotch – rapped formally on the door and gave the signal for action. The windows were broken, the furniture smashed and the occupants 'roughed up'. Then the herd melted away in silence leaving behind them another convincing proof of their all-persuasive power.

The 1830s were the years of Scotch Cattle power in Monmouthshire but, before this, political and social pressures had been building up in Merthyr, which were to lead to the most serious outbreak of violence in the history of south Wales. Merthyr was now the biggest town in the Principality. Its growth had been fast and furious, fuelled by the expansion of the great iron-works, which were soon to be supplying the whole world with the rails that launched the Railway Age. It was a town that had no deep roots in the past; it had created itself from scratch. The workers who poured into Merthyr from the Welsh countryside had broken the social mould in which they had been encased for centuries. The church had been slow to realise what was happening and the chapels had moved in on a big scale. The Methodists were no revolutionaries, but the chapels of the Old Dissent – the Baptists and, above all, the Unitarians, were far more radically-minded. The Unitarians exercised an influence in Merthyr and in the Radical Triangle far in excess of their actual strength. Many of the leaders in the vanguard of social protest in south Wales had a background training in oratory and in the marshalling of ideas in the chapels of the Old Dissent.

The opening months of the eventful year of 1831 had seen a sharp rise in the temperature of politics in Merthyr. Agitation for the Reform Bill was at its height. There were renewed protests against the truck shops – the system whereby the workers had to take their wages, or part of them, in goods supplied by the iron-masters or the coal owners. Crawshay had already abolished his own truck-shops, but few of the other owners had followed his example. At this time he was a radical, but that did not prevent him from lowering his colliers' wages during a poor year. Many of the miners were deeply in debt. All the materials for an explosion were assembled – a tradition of protest, leaders who could organise it and a cause to fight for.

In May 1831, Crawshay's men were marching through the streets in continual demonstrations. At the annual Waen Fair, held at the end of the month on the moors behind Merthyr, emotions boiled over. After a succession of fiery speeches, the red flag was hoisted alongside the white banners of the Reform movement, and the crowd marched down into the town shouting 'Reform for ever'. After sacking the local Debtors Court, they ransacked the town in search of sequestered goods, which they then restored to their owners. The authorities took fright and sent urgent messages for troops to be sent from the nearest garrison town of Brecon. The rioters had already announced their intention of marching on Cardiff and Swansea. The soldiers, from a Scottish regiment, arrived next day and took up their position in the Castle Inn, in the centre of the town.

The appearance of the soldiers set the town on fire. A huge crowd assembled outside the inn, led by the formidable figure of Lewis Lewis, known as Lewsyn yr Heliwr – Lewis the Huntsman. They launched a furious attack on the Highlanders and made a determined attempt to smash their way into the inn. This placed the soldiers in a highly dangerous position. They had no alternative but to defend themselves. The detachment drawn up in front of the inn lowered their bayonets and held off their assailants; those in the upper rooms opened fire on the order of their officers, who judged that their men outside were being overwhelmed. The attackers retired, leaving a score of dead behind.

In the cold light of History, the Highlanders could scarcely be held directly responsible for this bloodshed, but it inflamed the town. The iron-masters shut themselves in their houses as if in fortresses, and sent out desperate appeals for further help. Their messages reached Major Penrice, in charge of the Swansea and Fairwood Yeomanry and a Peninsula veteran. He acted with Wellingtonian speed and raced towards Merthyr up the Neath valley, with an advance guard. He had totally miscalculated the forces against him. The revolutionary fire had spilled out from Merthyr itself into the surrounding countryside. The workers at Hirwaen had dipped a sheet in calf's blood and, with this improvised Red Flag, were on the march. As Major Penrice approached Aberpergwm, near the top of the Neath valley, he found himself surrounded by thousands of men armed with muskets, pikes and scythes. He looked hurriedly around for the iron-master Guest, who was supposed to read the Riot Act before Penrice could open fire, but that gentleman had tactfully disappeared. The major and his handful of men were disarmed and retired disconsolately to the Lamb and Flag inn. The rebuilt inn still remains on the site at Aberpergwm.

What had begun as a riot was now assuming the proportions of an insurrection. It could not be allowed to continue. The yeomanry were brought up to strength and advanced again. More regular troops were brought in, but two pitched battles had to be fought before order was re-imposed on revolutionary Merthyr. The sequel is interesting. Lord Melbourne was then Home Secretary in the new Whig government of Earl Grey. He had the Reform Bill on his hands and had no desire to draw attention to some of the more unruly aspects of the proposed New Democracy. He made a deliberate decision to play down the events at Merthyr and to treat them as a riot, not a rising. The leaders had to be arrested and two of them – Lewis Lewis (the Huntsman) and Richard Lewis, known as Dic Penderyn, from his birthplace near Aberafon – were condemned to death. In the end, Lewsyn yr Heliwr was reprieved and then sent for transportation while Dic Penderyn went to the gallows, although Dic may not even have taken part in the attack on the inn, and he was assuredly not the stuff of which leaders are made. The whole of south Wales felt his death as a grave miscarriage of justice, and vast, mourning crowds followed his coffin to the grave at Aberafon. The Welsh working class had gained its first martyr.

Melbourne's oblivion tactics worked. The Peterloo Massacre and the Bristol Riots are in every English text-book. Merthyr is never mentioned. Yet Melbourne

Raising the Red Flag in the Merthyr Rising of 1831

himself, in a note he left to his successor in office, admitted that the Merthyr troubles posed the most serious threat to society that he had been called upon to deal with. Professor Gwyn Williams has carefully collected the folk-memories that still survive in Merthyr about the Rising, including the intriguing story that, as the Highlanders marched in, the women of Cefn shouted scornfully, 'Go back and get your trowsers on.' He finds it curious that Lewis Lewis, the 'Huntsman', should now be almost forgotten, while Dic Penderyn, in recent years, has been erected into a folk-cult figure. Are we, once again, in the presence of the Welsh predilection for the Deification of the Noble Failure?

Protest did not end at Merthyr in 1831. It simply flowed into new channels, above all into Chartism. The Reform Act of 1831 had proved a bitter disappointment to many of its most enthusiastic supporters. It was the middle classes who had benefited by it; and the new industrialists who could now share power with the old landed gentry. They had used the agitation of the artisans and the working class to gain their objective of the vote and now saw no need to extend the franchise. Indeed, extension might be dangerous.

The appearance of Chartism brought new hope to the disappointed. It opened a new field of fruitful action, and in no place did it receive a more enthusiastic welcome than in Wales. The Working Men's Association had been formed in London in 1836, and issued its Charter in 1838, demanding six major parliamentary reforms, including manhood suffrage, vote by ballot, annual parliaments, the payment of MPs and equal electoral districts. The Chartist manifesto seems highly reasonable by today's standards, but it appeared dangerously revolutionary to the Whigs who were now safely in power after the Reform agitation. Lord John Russell, in 1837, roundly declared that the Reform Act of 1831 was to be the final settlement, in spite of the warnings of Thomas Carlyle, the keeper of the mid-Victorian conscience. 'The matter of Chartism,' growled the Sage of Chelsea, 'is weighty, deep-rooted and far-extending; did not begin yesterday and will by no means end this day or tomorrow.'

The Chartists sent out their missionaries to Wales and they were warmly welcomed in the Radical Triangle. Branches of the W.M.A. were quickly established in the woollen towns of mid-Wales, and Henry Vincent, the 'Chartist Demosthenes', made a triumphal tour through the Monmouthshire valleys. A great Chartist convention was held in London in February 1839, at which the Monmouthshire delegate was John Frost, the radical ex-mayor of Newport. A furious debate raged between those who believed in 'moral force', in processions, petitions and political pressure, and those who advocate 'physical force', and who believed that only direct action would bring results. With the experience of the Merthyr Rising and the Scotch Cattle behind them, there was no doubt about the way the leaders of Chartism in Wales would turn.

The first troubles broke out in mid-Wales. The weavers of Llanidloes had been hard hit by the depression in the woollen trade and expressed their discontent in violent demonstrations. Extra special constables were drafted into the town. The

Leading Welsh Chartists – John Frost (*left*) and Zephaniah Williams

workers responded by attacking the Trewythen Arms, where the police were stationed. For a week the Chartists held control of Llanidloes, until the troops finally arrived from Brecon, accompanied by the inevitable yeomanry, and forcibly restored order. The leaders were transported, after a vigorous legal defence by Hugh Williams, a lawyer from Machynlleth who had now settled in St Clear's near the strongly radical town of Carmarthen. We shall hear more of him in other troubled areas.

The Llandiloes affair had alerted the authorities. They now took the provocative step of arresting Henry Vincent and of lodging him, under harsh conditions, in Monmouth gaol. With their idol in custody, the Monmouthshire Chartists now resolved on extreme measures. Under the leadership of John Frost they would march on Newport in a great demonstration of power. Their actual objectives are still obscure. Did they hope to release Vincent? Or was there a revival of Scotch Cattle terrorist methods behind it all? There were strange currents running under the tide of protest that surged through the Monmouthshire valleys in that eventful autumn of 1839. A secret meeting in the mining village of Blackwood in the Rhymney Valley on 3 October decided on a triple advance on Newport. One contingent would assemble at Blackwood under Frost. A second would march from Ebbw Vale under the leadership of Zephaniah Williams, who had already made his mark as a man of extreme radical views – 'The Infidel of Nantyglo', as he was known, seemed to be in direct descent from the old Jacobins of Iolo Morganwg and Jac Glan y Gors vintage. A third 'army' would set out from Pontypool, led by Thomas Jones, a man of lesser calibre than Frost and Zephaniah Williams – he was a beer-house keeper.

TO THE
Men & Women
OF
NEWPORT.

MY FRIENDS,

You have ever found me your consistent and dauntless advocate, I have a right, therefore, to expect you are my Friends.

I am informed upon unquestionable authority that your local rulers are anxious to arrest me to night. LET THEM TAKE ME. If their conduct be legal---*well!* If illegal, they shall hereafter rue it. At the worst my detention can but be for a few days---and as Philosophy is every thing, the jails of our tyrants do not appal me.

Efforts are being made to frighten the people by calling our meetings illegal.---I never attended an illegal meeting---and there have been none of an illegal nature held within the precincts of Newport, *save one held lately at Christchurch, where a man named Phillips told the mob to make their horses stand fire, and keep their powder dry!*

I am told your Magistrates are about to swear in persons as Special Constables. They have their reasons for so doing; I believe them to be bad ones, and will with your assistance, turn the mischief they may contemplate into an engine for their own legal destruction.

Meet me to night at Pentonville, where I shall do myself the honour of addressing you.

Keep the Peace I charge you!---The slightest indications of tumult on our part would afford our enemies a pretext for letting loose their Bloodhounds on us.

Keep the Peace
and laugh your enemies to scorn!

Your devoted Friend,

HENRY VINCENT.

APRIL 25th, 1839.

John Partridge, Printer, Newport

Henry Vincent's proclamation to the people of Newport, April 25, 1839

The Chartist attack on the Westgate Hotel, Newport, 1839

The three columns were to meet at Risca in the night of 1 November – a hint of Scotch Cattle methods, perhaps – and then march in formidable strength into the heart of the town. The ill-luck that always seemed to dog Chartist demonstrations decreed that the night should be cold and wet. The 'army' marched through driving rain; and not at full strength. The Pontypool contingent failed to turn up. When, at last, the bedraggled columns reached Newport they had an unexpected and unpleasant surprise: the authorities had been forewarned and had stationed troops inside the Westgate Hotel. As the demonstrators swarmed around it, the soldiers in the hotel opened fire. The surprise was complete and shattering. The columns broke and fled leaving their dead behind them. That volley was the Melbourne government's equivalent of Napoleon's celebrated 'whiff of grapeshot' that broke the revolutionaries' attack on the Convention in 1795. It had the same effect. Chartism, as an effective force, died in Wales. There were still enthusiasts who kept the debate going in the press and who rallied support for the movement on all occasions of dispute or discontent. But the fire had gone out of Welsh Chartism. Was the spirit of protest now dead in Wales?

In the month after the suppression of the Chartists at Llanidloes, a strange incident occurred in the lonely countryside on the slopes of the Preseli Hills on the borders of north Pembrokeshire and Carmarthenshire. On the night of 13 May 1839, the guardian of the toll-gate in the scattered hamlet of Efailwen was startled to hear the sounds of a large party approaching in the darkness. When he looked out, he was horrified to see a mob swarming up to his gate, with blackened faces and disguised in women's clothes, led by an imposing figure on a white horse, also in female garb. The leader pointed dramatically to the gate. Immediately the mob fell upon it and chopped it to pieces. The gate-keeper saw the scythes and sporting guns flourished by the attackers and fled with his family into the fields. He turned to see his gatehouse going up in flames. The mob melted silently back into the darkness, leaving the ruins of the gate and gatehouse behind as a reminder that a new force had appeared in the Welsh countryside. The strange rural revolt, known in Welsh history as the Rebecca Riots, had begun.

The authorities were caught unprepared, in spite of a dramatic warning of what was to come. In January of 1839 the workhouse ar Narbeth was burnt down in protest at the new Poor Law. In spite of large rewards being offered, no one came forward to give any information whatsoever. A deep veil of conspiratorial silence held the whole countryside. Attacks on Poor Houses were, perhaps, understandable, although the impenetrable secrecy of a whole community was disturbing. Turnpike gates, however, were another matter, for they represented road improvement – and improvement was the crying need of the whole of west Wales. The main roads west of Carmarthen were notorious for their appalling condition. As one traveller ruefully recorded, 'Nothing but a love of glory should tempt a man to pass along them.'

Under the old system, the duty of maintaining the roads had fallen upon the parish, and every able-bodied man was required to work on road repairing one day a year. The work was hardly performed with enthusiastic efficiency. In fact, the workers almost looked on it as a pleasant day off, and, in Wales, you will still hear the phrase, 'A day for the Queen', used to describe a happily wasted twenty-four hours.

The Reform Parliament, after tidying up the Poor Law, set its busy fingers to work on the roads. The Highways Act of 1835 abolished the corvée of compulsory labour, but missed the chance of making the business of road improvement a national charge. Instead, the improvement of the highways was placed in the hands of road trusts, who advanced the money and got their profit out of gates set up along sections of the road. In theory, the tolls were to be fair and not too onerous. In practice, trusts in poor areas tended to multiply their gates to increase revenue, and west Wales was certainly poor. The Whitland Trust, which had farmed out its tolls to a notorious operator, Thomas Bullin, not only multiplied its gates but neglected the upkeep of its roads. In late spring, the farmers in the upland area on the southern slopes of the Preselis made their annual journey to the south of the county in search of lime for their sparse farmland. The new gates now made the long journey cripplingly expensive. In accordance with the countryside code of 'natural justice' the gates had to go.

The Trust did not take the destruction of its gate at Efailwen lying down. They set up a new gate and swore in special constables to guard it. In vain. For a second time, a mob with blackened faces and dressed in women's clothes came out of the darkness. The 'specials' took to their heels, but not before they had heard, for the first time, the leader being addressed as Rebecca, as he called on his 'daughters' to proceed to the good work of sending the second gate the same way as the first. Nine days later the gate outside the village of Llanboidy was also destroyed. Rebecca now ruled at night in the lonely countryside south of the Preselis. But she had not sprung into action, new-minted for the occasion. She had her roots deep in the ancient traditions of the Welsh countryside.

She came from the ritual of the 'ceffyl pren' – the wooden horse. People who had broken the code of what the country folk regarded as decent conduct – grasping land agents, adulterers who did not stand by girls they had 'put in trouble' and the like – would be visited at night by a mob, with blackened faces and in women's clothes, carrying an effigy of the offender on a rough wooden horse. The effigy might be burnt in front of the offender's cottage, or, in bad cases, he might be 'roughed up'. Natural justice had been done.

It was easy to transfer all this to the destruction of the hated toll-gates. The new element was the name. Who was the first Rebecca and who christened 'her'? Folk memory maintains that he was a well-known character in the Mynachlogddu region – Thomas Rees, known from the name of his cottage as Twm Carnabwth. Twm was not a farmer but a farm labourer; however, in rural Wales, there was very little social difference between the small farmer and the men who might work for him. They worked and worshipped together on terms of equality which would have been incomprehensible to the substantial farmers of England. Twm had been a noted fighter at country fairs, and a popular figure in the ale-house, but that did not prevent him also being a pillar of Bethel chapel and the man who led the singing there. He was a man who knew both the excitements of the 'ceffyl pren' and his Welsh Bible. What was more natural than for him and his fellow rioters to seek their justification from the Scriptures? Verse 60, Chapter 24, of *Genesis* seemed to fit the bill perfectly: 'And they blessed Rebecca, and said unto her, "Thou art our sister; be thou the mother of thousands of millions, and let thy seed possess the gates of those which hate them".' Naturally the embattled farmers did not look closely at the following verse which declared 'and they rode upon camels'. Their first, unexpected protests were effective. The Trust took the hint and modified its policy for the moment in the foothills of the Preselis.

Rebecca had retired to the shadows. She remained there for the three following years – years in which the small farmers of west Wales, however, saw no real improvement in their lot. There was a series of bad harvests, all the more serious as the population continued to increase. Observant travellers, passing through west Wales on their way to southern Ireland, saw little difference in the condition of the countryside on either side of the Irish Sea. Not many years later, Ireland was in the grip of famine – the 'Great Hunger' followed the failure of the potato crop. In such circumstances, any renewed activity by the egregious Thomas Bullin was a recipe for trouble. He persuaded the directors of the Main Trust, which covered a wide tract of country from the borders of Carmarthenshire northwards to Breconshire and west into Pembrokeshire, that the time had come, once more, to improve their financial position by installing new gates. He selected St Clears for the operation, for this village was a road bottle-neck between Carmarthen and Haverfordwest which could not be easily avoided.

Nothing is more remarkable than the speed with which Rebecca now came

Rebecca leading the toll-gate rioters, 1839

back into action, as if a widespread secret organisation had been waiting for over three years for this very eventuality. The new gate at the Mermaid Tavern outside St Clear's had hardly been in position for a few hours when rioters reduced it to matchwood. The destruction of the St Clear's gate was the signal for Rebecca to begin a major campaign 'to possess the gates' of those who hated her. All through the early months of 1843 'Becca' and her daughters were busy at night, appearing and disappearing with bewildering frequency and speed, until not a gate belonging to the Main Trust, the Whitland Trust and the Taverspite Trust remained intact. Once again the authorities had no idea of how best to deal with the crisis. Special constables were enrolled, but they had a habit of disappearing as soon as the horns of Rebecca were heard blowing in the darkness. On one occasion, Royal Marines were marched out of Pembroke Dock, but Rebecca had no trouble in evading them. They tramped from gate to gate in vain. Rebecca destroyed the gate as soon as their backs were turned. They marched back dejectedly to their barracks.

Informers were equally unsuccessful. Even when rioters were brought to court, no one would testify against them. Rebecca, herself, remained equally mysterious and untraceable. There were, no doubt, a multiplicity of Rebeccas – each district threw up its own natural leader. The technique of gate destruction was, after all, simple and easily imitated. Rebecca and her daughters cleared the gates from a large expanse of country in south-west Wales. Her attacks did not end in serious violence, and many a country lad joined in for the sheer fun and excitement of the thing – a break in the monotony of rural life.

With success, however, Rebecca grew bolder and began to turn her attention to grievances other than toll-gates. Was some element of Chartism creeping in?

Certainly Hugh Williams, the Chartist lawyer, would soon be prominent in defending arrested daughters of Rebecca, and rumour credited him with being the secret organiser of the movement, although he was always careful to deplore any violence. Others were not so particular. Lloyd Hall, a Newcastle Emlyn attorney who was not unsympathetic to the farmers, warned the government; 'if this state of things is not repressed very shortly, the efforts of Rebecca will, I have no doubt, be directed to other matters . . . It is quite possible that they only want leaders to effect a thorough revolution. The people have thus discovered their immense power without knowing how to use it constitutionally.'

The people's power, and their uncertainty about how to use it, were dramatically demonstrated on the hot, sunny morning of 19 June 1843. Obeying the orders of Rebecca, posted up in every ale-house or pinned on the doors of every chapel in the countryside north of Carmarthen, a vast crowd had assembled at the Plough and Harrow Inn. In their centre was Rebecca herself, with a wig of golden curls and surrounded by an escort of three hundred horsemen. At her orders the 'army' moved off to the music of a band and preceded by a huge white banner inscribed with the motto, 'Cyflawndwr a charwr cyflawdwr ydym ni oll' – 'Justice, and lovers of justice are we all'. Other banners in the crowd demanded freedom and better food. Rebecca was certainly spreading her demands into wider areas of social discontent.

The alarmed magistrates of Carmarthen had already sent out a distress call and a detachment of the 4th Light Dragoons had already left Cardiff and were eighteen miles from the town as Rebecca's army approached the outskirts. Two bold magistrates had gone out to meet the Rebeccaites and did, at least, persuade them to leave their shot-guns behind in a barn near the inn. What would have been the outcome if the rioters had been armed? What happened was bad enough. The Mayor and his council were waiting in the Guildhall in the expectation that Rebecca would halt there with a peaceful petition. The demonstrators, however, were now joined by the town 'mob' and, in Carmarthen, this mob was notorious for disorder. They almost shanghaied the daughters of Rebecca into by-passing the Guildhall and making a full-blooded attack on the hated workhouse. The crowd smashed into the courtyard and started to loot and wreck the place. A desperate message reached the dragoons, who immediately put spurs to their horses and rode to the rescue at such a furious pace that two of their horses dropped dead when they reached Carmarthen. This did not stop the cavalry immediately charging the crowd around the workhouse with drawn sabres – the first charge in the history of the regiment. The next would be with the Light Brigade at Balaclava!

The rioters outside the workhouse scattered in all directions, many of them leaving their precious farm horses to make good their escape. Rebecca, herself, disappeared as usual, while the rioters trapped in the workhouse courtyard were all rounded up. The authorities congratulated themselves on crushing an incipient rebellion and an article in the press was firmly of the opinion that 'the presence of the 4th Light Dragoons will effectively stop Miss Becca's gambols for some time'.

The Rebecca rioters destroying a toll gate

This optimism was ill-founded. Rebecca and her daughters were shaken but not dismayed by the Carmarthen affair. They soon recovered their morale and started to spread their activities into an area which again startled the authorities. Attacks were now made on the gates in the western area of the coalfield and took on a more violent aspect. Two formidable leaders appeared: John Jones (Shoni Sguborfawr), an ex-pugilist, and David Davies (Dai'r Cantwr), who was a ballad-singer and a bit of a poet. Carmarthen did, however, have one important effect – it stirred the central government into action and it drew the attention of the country to what was happening in west Wales. As a result, two new characters entered the drama of Rebecca and both were to have a powerful influence on the future course of events.

The first was a soldier, Colonel James Frederick Love. Love had a fine army record and had fought in the Peninsula campaign and Waterloo. He had sub-sequently gained a great deal of experience in the suppression of civil disturbances and he was sent to Wales to lead the campaign against the Rebeccaites. He was no narrow 'fire-eater' – he realised that it was as important to get at the cause of the disturbances as it was to suppress their manifestations. He was one of the first to urge the government to send down commissioners to make a strict inquiry into the misconduct of the toll-gate trusts. He also had no illusions about the diffi-culties of his task, in trying to catch rioters at work, at night in a countryside where everyone supported them. As one farmer put it vividly: 'It is like firing a charge of shot into a swarm of flies.'

The second character to enter the scene after Carmarthen was a newspaper man and, as it proved, an exceptionally able and understanding reporter. Thomas Campbell Foster had been sent down to Carmarthen by *The Times* in the wake of the workhouse riot. He immediately began a series of vivid despatches which became markedly sympathetic to the farmers' cause. Like his fellow correspondent, the famous William Howard Russell in the Crimean War eleven years after Rebecca, Foster had the gift of making contact with the average man. In the end, the Rebeccaites came to trust him so completely that they invited him to their secret meetings. It was not long before he realised how completely west Wales was behind Rebecca.

Foster sent back a despatch describing a typical patrol through the Gwendraeth valley on the edge of the coalfield on which he accompanied Colonel Love and the 4th Light Dragoons. The military had been given false information and Rebecca had no trouble in leading them a pretty dance. Foster reported 'that though everything wore a peaceful aspect and there were few people about', it was clear that every move of the dragoons was being carefully watched. Rockets went up from the highest hill and, immediately, a series of bonfires leapt into life to mark the route taken by the cavalry. No sooner had the colonel and his dragoon clattered past a gate, and gone a mile or two down the road, then Rebecca was at work behind them, smashing with impunity every gate on the Carmarthen–Llanelli turnpike. Said Foster: 'The scene throughout was remarkably striking, the bonfires burning on the hills, the firing of the rockets, the explosion from the guns, the beating of drums and the blowing of horns! The surrounding country meanwhile being beautifully illuminated by the light of the young moon, it was very striking in the extreme.' It also indicated the degree to which the Rebeccaites had now perfected their organisation.

Faced with such a problem, Love soon saw that he would need more troops. He also stressed one other important point: 'Hitherto the military have been called upon to take the initiative instead of *support* the Civil Power, for the obvious reason of there being no Civil Power.' In addition to more troops, he asked for a detachment of the Metropolitan Police. The only police of any sort then in west Wales were the highly incompetent 'handful of coppers' at Carmarthen.

Colonel Love's despatches were important and influential, but the articles of *The Times* correspondent were more influential still. They shook the Home Secretary, Sir James Graham, and stirred the government into action. Not only did Colonel Love get his extra troops and his policemen, but the government sent down a powerful commission, charged with investigating the cause of the riots and the operations of the turnpike trusts. The commissioners began their work in October 1843, and not a moment too soon. The rioting had reached a climax in the summer months of the year, and the original purity of Rebecca's motive was being compromised. Just as the Carmarthen 'mob' had side-tracked Rebecca's entry into the town into an attack on the workhouse, so Shoni Sguborfawr and Dai'r Cantwr usurped Rebecca's role to establish a reign of terror over the coalfield area of eastern Carmarthenshire. In this countryside of small collieries and farms, it was possible to hold the more substantial farmers to ransom. Shoni and Dai

ABOVE A Welsh coal mine,
around 1780, by Paul Sandby

LEFT The arrival of troops at
Merthyr during the riots of
1816, Penrny Williams

OPPOSITE, ABOVE The splendours of Edwardian Wales –
Cardiff Civic Centre

BELOW Aberystwyth University

ABOVE Poverty in Merthyr in the 1870s – queuing at a
pawn shop

RIGHT The Investiture of Prince Charles as Prince of
Wales, Caernarfon Castle, 1969

TOP The steel works at Port Talbot

ABOVE The splendour of Wales – Ceri Richard's evokes the power of a Cardiganshire waterfall

ran an early-nineteenth-century version of a modern 'rent-a-mob', with a scale
of tariffs for every threatening job undertaken. The contrast between the 'Stag
and Pheasant Gang' and the true 'daughters of Rebecca' was strikingly indicated
by the dramatic events at Pontardulais in early September.

Pontardulais was a large village eight miles to the west of Swansea and, like
St Clear's, it was a road bottle-neck surrounded by a maze of gates, one of which
was under the control of the notorious Thomas Bullin. It was obviously a classic
target for Rebecca. The attack on the main Pontardulais gate was launched on
the night of 6 September 1843. The Rebecca was an intelligent young farmer called
John Hughes, known as Jac Ty Isha. The raid met with disaster. The authorities
had been alerted and an ambush of the newly-formed Glamorgan police was waiting. A pitched battle took place in the darkness. The rioters were scattered by
volleys of musketry and Jac Ty Isha and two of his fellow Rebeccaites were captured – Jac with his arm shattered by a bullet. He was the only 'Rebecca' who
was ever captured making an actual attack on a toll-gate.

A few nights later, the 'Stag and Pheasant Gang' attacked the Hendy gate. The
affair ended in the ruthless murder of the gate-keeper, old Sarah Williams. The
attackers disappeared untouched into the darkness but they had now gone too
far. A feeling of revulsion swept the whole area and there were men prepared
to come forward and give information to the authorities. Shoni Sgubowrfawr
and Dai'r Cantwr were arrested. Their reign of terror was at an end.

The behaviour of the arrested men provided a striking contrast. Young John
Hughes (Jac Ty Isha) remained true to the ideals of Rebecca. In spite of his inevitable
sentence of transportation at the Cardiff assizes, not a single word passed his lips
that might have betrayed his fellow rioters. He behaved with dignity and went,
silent if broken-hearted, into his bitter exile. Shoni and Dai were made of different
stuff. They denounced and betrayed every member of their gang, as well as the
farmers they had blackmailed and terrorised. Yet such is the vagary of history
– or perhaps of historians – that it is Dai'r Cantwr who is now remembered as
a symbol of the courage and defiance of Rebecca. Dai had the inestimable advantage
in Wales of being able to write a poem about his misfortunes. In the days when
he lay in Carmarthen gaol he wrote verses which soon became immensely popular.
Indeed, something like a Dai'r Cantwr ballad-industry developed and kept his
memory alive. Alas, no one wrote a poem about poor Jac Ty Isha!

The Pontardulais affair was the high-water mark in Rebecca's crusade in the
west Wales countryside. Sporadic outbreaks still occurred elsewhere – one, surprisingly enough, in Anglesey – but the fire had gone out of the movement and it
finally died when the report of the commissioners appeared, in March 1844. It
was surprisingly favourable to all that the farmers had striven for. The government
acted swiftly on the recommendations of the report. The trusts were unified and
the tolls made uniform, and even reduced in some cases. The remaining Rebeccaites
in gaol were given comparatively lenient sentences by the standards of the day,
and some were let off with a caution. Other measures helped to ease the tension
in the rural areas. An Enclosure Act made future enclosures dependent upon first

holding a public inquiry, and in 1847 a new Poor Law Board started its work of making the Poor Law more humane and acceptable. But behind everything lay the increasing growth of the coalfield industries. This would, in the long run, take off the pressure of the rural population explosion, and soon the railways would be pushing ever westward. The daughters of Rebecca could soon ride off to a different destination from the toll-gates.

The drama of the Merthyr Riots, the Chartist march on Newport and the night-rides of Rebecca capture the limelight of history. It is easy to see the story of Wales in the first half of the nineteenth century as a seething cauldron of fiery revolt, in which a new Welsh working class was forged. There is no question about the reality of that turmoil, but we must not forget that it did not involve every part of Wales or every section of the Welsh community. In north Wales, for example – strange as it may seem to many modern observers – the burning questions were religious and not social. These were the years in which the Methodists firmly established themselves in the north. They had finally severed their connection with the Church of England and, after the death of Thomas Charles, the new denomination came firmly into the hands of a remarkable and, perhaps, domineering personality, John Elias, described by his enemies as 'the pope from Anglesey'. There can be no doubt, however, of his preaching power. He was the first and greatest of those pulpit orators who were the power and the glory of the ever-spreading world of Welsh nonconformity. Later commentators have looked back on this striking religious development with some bewilderment. Emyr Humphries, in a witty summary of the activities of John Elias, suggests that he 'took the easy-going social habits of the natives of Anglesey, for example, and transformed them from being the Welsh equivalents of the cheerful poteen makers of Connemara into convincing imitations of New England Puritans, neatly ranged in pews rented a year in advance'. Historians on the left are even more disapproving. Here were the down-trodden peasants of rural Wales concerning themselves with religion and such impractical matters as the state of their souls – lapping up 'the opium of the people' doled out from the pulpit by the new race of preachers, when they should have been marching with the Chartists or out smashing gates with Rebecca. Was rural, and certainly Methodist Wales, retreating into a cultural 'lager', defended by language and religion? A gulf was opening up between two Wales, in which the countryside would remain Nonconformist and Welsh-speaking and the industrial areas would become increasingly Anglicised. The gulf is there to this day.

Yet out of this matrix came a vigorous, if narrow, cultural life. Publications in the Welsh language proliferated, and they did not confine themselves to the consolations of religion. This was the environment which was eventually to produce the young, revolutionary Lloyd George. Nonconformity and with it Methodism was compelled, almost in self-defence, to take the first, somewhat reluctant steps, towards political action. It was an indication of the subtle change that was creeping over the atmosphere of political life in Wales that, when the

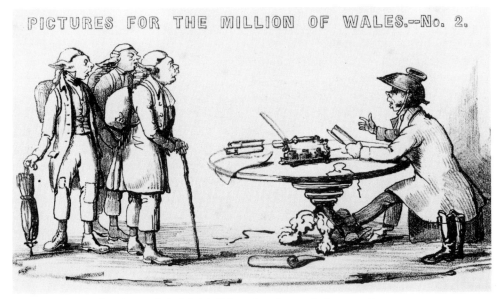

Sir James Kay-Shuttleworth briefs his Education Commissioners, 1844

next national turmoil took place, it was occasioned by the distinctly non-materialistic subject of education, and the battle was fought not in the streets but in the pulpit and the press. A mere three years after the last toll-gate had been smashed and the last Rebeccaite transported, the government published an exhaustive survey, in three bulky blue bound volumes, of the state of education in the Principality. Those Blue Books shook the entire nation.

Education in Wales was in desperate need of attention. The whole educational structure was a rag-bag of odd institutions from the old grammar schools in towns like Swansea or Haverfordwest down to the rough parish schools often kept in inadequate premises by such totally unsuitable people as old soldiers. The academies of Old Dissent still maintained their standards but they were few and scattered. New schools of a progressive nature had started in places like Merthyr and Dowlais in the growing industrial areas but were not enough to leaven the general mass. Two societies – the non-denominational British Society and the Church of England National Society – offered grants for the establishment of schools, but these had to be matched by money raised locally. The Nonconformists were reluctant to send their children to the National schools, where they would be taught their catechism, and many of them were too poor to take advantage of the British Society scheme. In any case, they had a deep-rooted fear of compromising their hard-won religious independence by accepting official or government grants. When it came to education, they were 'voluntaryists', especially in west and north Wales.

This was the position when the government sent down three special commissioners to inquire into education in Wales. Their inquiry was urgently needed, but the manner in which they carried it out was disastrous. The commissioners were all able men and incredibly industrious. They covered an amazing amount of ground in a remarkably short time, but they were young and above all, Anglican. The assistants they selected were also Anglican and they relied on the evidence, for the most part, of the clergy of the Church of England. When the report appeared in Blue Book form, it revealed only too clearly the parlous state of education in Wales. The facts were indisputable, but the conclusions the commissioners drew from them were felt as an outrage by the whole Welsh nation. They had stigmatised the Welsh language as a 'barrier to the moral progress' of the people, as well as a powerful handicap to their material success. But the passage in the report that gave the greatest offence was the commissioners bland declaration that Welsh country women were almost universally unchaste, and it was the weekend services of the Dissenters that offered them their opportunity to stray deliciously from the narrow path of virtue. The report was immediately named 'Brad y Llyfrau Gleision' – the Treachery of the Blue Books, on the analogy of the mythical massacre supposed to have been perpetrated by false Saxon mercenaries on the unsuspecting followers of Vortigern at the beginning of the Dark Ages, and remembered with loathing by the Welsh as 'Brad y Cyllyll Hirion' – the Treachery of the Long Knives. Even the very name of the conscientious civil servant who had drawn up the instructions for the commission, Sir James Kay-Shuttleworth, seemed, to Welsh ears, to have overtones of Hengist and Horsa. But after the shock came remedial action, and in the centre of it stood the remarkable figure of a young man from Anglesey, Hugh Owen, who was now well embarked on a brilliant career in London with the Poor Law Commission.

Hugh Owen is a new type of folk hero in Welsh history. Hitherto, the Cymric pantheon had been crowded with rebels against the establishment in church and state – Owain Glyn Dŵr, Howell Harris, Dic Penderyn. Hugh Owen was the first administrator to be accorded Welsh hero status. In the end, he received a knighthood and a statue on the Maes, the town square of Caernarfon, alongside that of Lloyd George. The contrast between the two statues is illuminating: Lloyd George is depicted with arm uplifted, in the full flood of his matchless oratory, Sir Hugh Owen stands calm and dignified, with a document in his hand. The careful official report, the formal letter of instruction, the minutes of committee meetings and the discreet call on the appropriate minister were the instruments out of which he built his career and which he used with such success to prepare Nonconformist Wales for the approaching Victorian heyday.

To Hugh Owen education was the key with which ambitious young Welshmen would unlock their share of the new prosperity spreading down through the classes with the continual advance of industry. The hungry Forties were giving way to the successful Fifties, soon to be celebrated in the Great Exhibition of 1851. Wales could not be left out on the edge of this triumphant development. In 1843, Owen addressed his celebrated *Letter to the Welsh People*. With the crisp clarity of a good civil servant, he shattered the cause of 'voluntaryism'. Nonconformist Wales should take full advantage of all official money available in the cause of education. Hugh Owen won triumphantly over the voluntaryists. In one sense, he was the man

Dame Venodotia (Wales) indignantly throwing out the Commissioners' enquiry into Welsh education in 1844

who prepared Nonconformist Wales for political action, the unsuspecting John the Baptist for the advent of Lloyd George!

He was also the first of the great 'fixers' — a man who knew his way about the corridors of power in London. Nonconformist Wales would need them as it advanced towards political control of the Principality, for the resident Tory-controlled M.P.s were there to represent the old landed-gentry Anglican connection. They were hardly interested in the problems and ambitions of the Welsh-

Lady Llanover in Welsh costume

speaking Welsh. Hugh Owen certainly knew his way around the Whitehall back-stairs. He even advised Disraeli on his Reform Bill, and Dizzy's wife Mary Ann – who, after all, had come from Wales – called him her husband's guardian angel. Left-wing commentators have another name for him. To them he is an Ambiguous Hero, leading the once nobly revolutionary Welsh into the bourgeois respectability of the Victorian high noon. But Owen was a man of deep sincerity, acting his best for his nation in the light of the standards of contemporary society, and his contemporaries felt that he had fully deserved his statue on the Maes at Caernarfon.

There were other prophets of respectability at work in Wales in the 1840s, especially in the cultural field. The enthusiastic patronage of Lady Llanover for poetry, music and indeed for all things Welsh, was a powerful factor in making the once rebellious culture of the Iolo Morganwg period socially acceptable. The series of eisteddfodau held at Abergavenny became important centres of encouragement to the guardians of the native tradition in poetry and song. Lady Llanover was the wife of Benjamin Hall, the grandson of the first Richard Crawshay and as Commissioner of Works, gained an unexpected immortality by giving the name of 'Big Ben' to the great clock over the Houses of Parliament. Lady Llanover also left an unexpected legacy to posterity. It was her advocacy that firmly fixed the female Welsh costume into tall black steeple hats, flannel shawls and skirts – the modern tourist symbol of Wales!

The old rebels – the Rebeccaites, the Chartists and the rest of them – now faded from the scene. They had no place in the new prosperous, respectable Wales which was now emerging. Most of them conformed to the new standards. Zephaniah Williams survived transportation to make a fortune in the coal trade. Others took refuge in cultural dreams and fantasies. Such a one was Dr William Price, ex-Chartist and now a fervent believer in the druidic cult of Iolo Morganwg. He stalked through industrial south Wales like a disconcerting yet fascinating ghost from the rebellious past. Nobly white-bearded, he received his patients in a green costume which he claimed had been worn by the Welsh soldiers of Henry VII on the march to Bosworth. He attended the National Eisteddfod in an even more fantastic garb, with a fox-fur cap and a tunic of Welsh wool decorated with bardic symbols, and carrying a wand with the horned moon on top.

When he was over eighty, he fathered three children on his young consort, Gwenllian, at Llantrisant, the hilltop village in the Vale of Glamorgan where memories of Iolo Morganwg, David Williams and Morgan John Rhys still lingered. In 1884, he burnt his dead infant son, Iesu Grist (Jesus Christ) on an improvised funeral pyre on a Llantrisant hilltop. These unheard-of proceedings led to a riot in which the white-bearded heir to the esoteric learning of the Druids was chased to his house by an infuriated mob. He was saved by the intrepid Gwenllian, who appeared at the door with a shot-gun in her hands. Dr Price appeared in court at Cardiff, where he made an impressive defence. Out of that strange fire on the hillside at Llantrisant came the recognition of the right to cremation in Britain. We can set the eccentric hero, Dr Price, alongside the ambiguous hero, Sir Hugh Owen, as a bringer of change. Rebecca, Lewsyn yr Heliwr and John Frost would have approved, even if the deacons of a thousand Bethels and Bethanias looked the other way.

The New Wales

The eventful years between the middle of the nineteenth century and the outbreak of the First World War were the years in which Wales rediscovered itself and the rest of Britain discovered Wales. For decades before, the Principality had been undergoing those dramatic changes which were the inevitable consequences of the Industrial Revolution. The great iron works had sent their smoke blackening the skies above the lonely moorlands of north Glamorgan and Monmouthshire. The foundaries roared around Wrexham and Ruabon in north Wales and the slate quarries were biting deeper into the rocky heart of Snowdonia. These astonishing centres of the new technology had, for fifty years past, been drawing recruits from the rural areas in ever-increasing numbers to tend their furnaces and dig their mines. By the 1850s the railways had pushed their way along the coastal plains of north and south, and the 'iron horse' was even preparing to penetrate the wilderness of Plynlimon and reach the sea at Aberystwyth in mid-Wales. The discontented sons and daughters of Rebecca had no need to cross the seas like the displaced Irish. They could 'emigrate' in their own country. They came willingly to the ever-growing industrial areas. They felt, rightly or wrongly, that whatever difficulties might await them in Nantyglo or Hirwaen or Brymbo, they were definitely improving their lot. They earned more money, even if they had to spend it at the company shop, and the Triangle at Merthyr gave them better housing than a leaking thatched cottage in the upper Teifi Valley. They may have been subsequently deceived, but the newcomers felt a sense of escape, of freedom. 'Tell it not in Cardigan, publish it not in the streets of Dolgellau', but the daughters of the Philistines were more approachable in Dowlais and Blaenavon.

Nonconformity moved even faster than the railways. By mid-century eighty per cent of the people of Wales were in a chapel and not a church on Sunday. A new Wales was rapidly taking shape. It was to be a radical, democratic Wales, and still, basically, a strongly Welsh-speaking Wales. The survival of the language and its strength among the majority of the people, made this new Wales increasingly conscious of its own individual nationhood. It was ready to flex its political muscle. There had been protest movements a-plenty before, from the Rebecca riots in the rural areas to violence in Merthyr and Chartist marches on Newport, but these were separate protests for separate causes. Now the whole of Nonconformist Wales was ready to make a serious bid for political power. Even the Methodists, whose leaders had sternly frowned on all protest movements from the romanticism of Iolo Morganwg to the Chartists, were prepared to consider participation in politics. Had not Henry Richard given the challenging slogan, 'Nonconformist Wales *is* Wales'?

There was little awareness of this growing ferment among the governing powers east of Offa's Dyke. The other countries of the 'Celtic Fringe' attracted far more attention. Sir Walter Scott had cast a romantic glow over Scotland's rebellious past. He had made Scotland not merely socially acceptable but fashionable. No more was heard of the Johnsonian diatribes against the pushful and poor Scotsmen on the make. Queen Victoria herself had taken up residence in the Highlands. Ireland may have remained a 'most distressful country', but retained her charm for even the most implacable English Tories. The Principality, alone, remained a Terra Incognita. There was no Balmoral in Wales.

When sturdy old George Borrow tramped through Wales in 1854, doing his steady twenty miles a day over hill and dale, he was an exception to the general indifference. He had actually taken the trouble to learn Welsh and could talk to the inhabitants. But even he felt that he was exploring a strange, exotic land, 'deserving,' as he said in the first sentence of his Introduction, 'more attention than it has hitherto received'. He called his book *Wild Wales*, and his readers may have understood the title in another sense than Borrow intended. Wales only hit the English headlines when the peasants destroyed toll-gates or the workmen defied the military. That leading Victorian intellectual, Matthew Arnold, had shown more understanding. He had attended the National Eisteddfod when on holiday at Llandudno, and although he had written woundingly about the ceremony, he was at least interested in the cultural traditions of the Welsh. He may not have understood all he saw and heard, for he coined that unfortunate phrase 'The Celtic Twilight', and pictured the Celts as impractical dreamers, unable, in contrast to

The expanding slate industry. Quarryman at work on the face at Penrhyn

the hard-headed, practical Anglo-Saxons, to face the dominance of fact. He made ample amends, however, by being the first to advocate a chair of Celtic Studies at Oxford.

Delane, the powerful editor of *The Times*, was scathing. He denounced the Welsh language as 'the curse of Wales' – the sooner it disappeared the better for the benighted inhabitants. Even as late as the 1880s, a bishop of St David's, no less, could talk of Wales as 'a mere geographical expression'!

As for politics, nothing seemed to have changed, on the face of it, since the days of the Tudors. Most of the parliamentary seats remained in the hands of the great landowners, whole families had held them for centuries. Rural Wales was still a land of great estates, whose occupants controlled the levers of power in London. Marriage with Welsh heiresses had brought Scottish and Irish aristocratic names to the Welsh social scene. There were Butes in Glamorgan, Londonderrys in Machynlleth and Cawdors in Pembrokeshire and Golden Grove. But there was still a Pryce at Gogerddan, a Powell at Nanteos and a Morgan at Tredegar. Above all, there was a Wynn at Wynnstay near Ruabon in north Wales. He was Wales's greatest landowner, with 148,000 acres to his credit. A Sir Watkyn Williams Wynn of that time could regard himself as 'the Prince in Wales', and he was still affectionately known as 'Old Syr Watkyn' to his tenants.

Although they were Anglicised in their speech and firmly Anglican in religion, these great landowners did not feel that they were interlopers who had been 'planted', like the Irish aristocracy, onto an alien country. Many of them were proud to trace their ancestry back to the old Welsh princes. They prided themselves, perhaps mistakenly, on their good relations with their tenants. There was no Captain Boycott in Wales, no burning of the Big Houses, for the owners of the large estates were not ruthless landlords. They supplied capital for agricultural improvements, rents were low and the tenant farmers felt secure on their land for generation after generation. By the 1850s, however, this feudal relationship was already out of date. It was soon to be subjected to unexpected strains.

The first sign of the emergence of a new spirit in rural Wales came in a series of elections, starting in 1859. A religious revival had just swept Wales, with all the singing and dramatic conversions that usually accompany these remarkable emotional outbursts. The Conservative member for Merioneth, W. W. E. Wynne, had been a strong supporter of the Oxford Movement and had introduced High Church ritual into Llanegryn church. To the surprise of the landowners, the Nonconformists put up a candidate against Wynne, who succeeded in making serious inroads into the Conservative majority. The Establishment took alarm at this unexpected threat to their authority. Certain tenants on the Rhiwlas estate, near Bala, had refrained from voting for conscience' sake. They were quickly evicted from their farms. A gulf had opened up between landowner and tenant.

It widened still further after the next election in 1868, fought after the Reform Act of 1867 had widened the franchise. In a memorable contest, a Liberal, George Osborne Morgan, captured one of the two Denbighshire seats which had always been the prerogative of the Wynns. Nothing is quite simple in Welsh politics and

Osborne Morgan was a churchman, although a very broad one, who had actually advocated disestablishment for Wales. He had the support, however, of the fiery and powerful Nonconformist propagandist, the Denbigh publisher Thomas Gee. Again evictions followed the election. The landowners were badly rattled and showed signs of losing their nerve.

They became even more worried when the ever-strengthening Nonconformist opposition turned its attention to the old and vexed question of tithes. The Anglican church was no longer, by any stretch of the imagination, a national church in Wales, but its clergymen and its buildings had still to be supported by tithes paid by Nonconformist tenant farmers. The system had been under increasing attack from propagandists of all denominations. By the 1880s the tension boiled over into action. The Vale of Clwyd, in particular, became the centre of the 'tithe war',

The tithe war in Denbighshire, an 1890 cartoon

when riots took place at farms where the property of Nonconformist farmers was being distrained for non-payment of their dues to the Anglican Church. The trouble did not end until the Tithe Act of 1891 transferred the payment of tithes from the tenant to the landlord.

But by 1891, the political map of rural Wales had been re-drawn. The Liberals were firmly in control, and most Liberal MPs could base their bid for power on the heady mixture of anti-landlord and anti-Established Church oratory. It was land reform and Disestablishment that sent the youthful and gifted Tom Ellis, of Bala, to Westminster as the MP for Merioneth. His victory over the Conservatives in the election of 1886 was widely regarded in Wales as the symbol of the victory of the peasantry over their landowning Anglican gentry.

This all-conquering march of Liberalism across Wales was bound to make an impression on the leaders of the Liberal party in England. It was surely significant that Mr Gladstone himself made a point of attending the National Eisteddfod at Mold, and poured forth his rotund oratory on the ancient language and proud history of the Principality. He soon became the favourite chapel 'pin-up'. No Welsh cottage was complete without its portrait of the Grand Old Man. Gladstone lived at Hawarden on the Border and knew Wales better than most English politicians, but he would not have been the skillful political manipulator he was if he didn't appreciate the strength of having a guaranteed block of Welsh MPs at his command. His old rival, Disraeli, is supposed to have quipped that he did not mind Gladstone having an ace up his sleeve, but he objected to the Grand Old Man claiming that the Almighty had put it there. In many crises of later Liberal governments, the Welsh MPs could claim to be useful stand-ins for the Almighty.

The new nationalism was not solely a political phenomenon. It began to permeate all ranks of Welsh-speaking society, and even acquired a compelling song to help it onwards. 'Hen Wlad fy Nhadau' – Land of My Fathers – with words written by Evan James, a weaver from Pontypridd, and music by his son, James James, was adopted as the Welsh National Anthem in 1856. It is a splendid air for mass singing, and the sound of it, fervently intoned by enthusiastic voices at the National Eisteddfod and the rugby battles with England at Cardiff Arms Park, is still the most satisfying expression of their nationalism for many Welshmen. But it is hardly a clarion call for revolution, like the Marseillaise, or even the Red Flag. 'Hen Wlad fy Nhadau' is eloquent about the warlike deeds of the heroes of the distant past but it does not urge its singers to take to the streets, sword in hand.

The new Welsh nationalism stayed within the accepted limits for political action. Its rallying cries were Disestablishment of the Anglican Church in Wales, land reform, education and even teetotalism. The first fruit of the alliance between Gladstone and Welsh nonconformity was the Sunday Closing Act of 1881, which kept the doors of the Welsh pubs tightly shut on the Sabbath and sent the thirsty over the English border in coachloads until the licensing changes after 1961.

More important was the new fervour for a purely Welsh control of education, the revival of the dream of Owain Glyn Dŵr of a separate university for Wales.

There is something deeply moving about the devotion of the early pioneers, who pushed the scheme forwards through all difficulties, with that old veteran of the educational battles, Sir Hugh Owen, spending his last days touring the country at his own expense to collect subscriptions. The first college was opened in Aberystwyth in 1872 and it could literally boast that it had been financed by 'the pence of the poor'. It was housed in a gothicised hotel on the sea-front purchased after the failure of a company that had been before its time in planning comprehensive holidays for the masses. The crowds of hoped-for students did not become available until successive education acts had re-constructed secondary education in Wales, but by the 1890s the concept of a Welsh university was firmly established, with colleges at Bangor, Aberystwyth and Cardiff, and, by 1921, at last in Swansea.

The professors and graduates of the young university created a new intellectual climate among the intelligentsia of Welsh-speaking Wales. Grammarians like Sir John Morris Johns, poets like Professor T. Gwyn Jones and historians like Sir John Lloyd, set new cultural standards, but they felt that they were building on foundations that were already there. The new generations who took their degrees, with much doffing of mortar-boards at graduation ceremonies, had come from the small farmers, the shop-keepers, the manse. They had a respect for the culture from which they had sprung – an almost mystical cult of the 'gwerin' – the highly idealised peasantry, avid for education, still guarding the long traditions of music and poetry, devout and fiercely democratic. It was to the 'gwerin' that Sir Owen Edwards, who had been an undergraduate at Aberystwyth but became a history don at Lincoln College, Oxford, directed a stream of publications in strong, elegant Welsh – from popular histories to the first children's magazine in Welsh. This was one-man mass education on the grand scale. He brought to the ordinary man the first fruits of the university renaissance. It was natural that, later on, his son, Sir Ifan ab Owen Edwards, should carry on his father's work in a new way when he founded Urdd Gobaith Cymru, the Welsh League of Youth.

Perhaps this dream of an educated 'gwerin' was a happy illusion. There was a narrow, restrictive side to Welsh popular culture, where the chapel was in firm control of the 'Nonconformist Conscience'. But there was also truth in it. From the chapel came the splendid choral singing, and the poet-preachers who had kept alive the ancient poetic traditions of the land. It was faith in the supposed virtues of the Welsh peasantry, combined with the revived feeling of national identity, that inspired the last two attempts to found exclusively Welsh-speaking settlements overseas.

The Rev. Samuel Roberts (always known from his initials as S.R.) was a man of restless and inventive mind, who knew from his own experience at Llanbrynmair the problems that beset the small Welsh farmer. He, too, had had his disappointments. He had conceived the scheme for the penny post, only to find his idea appropriated without acknowledgement by Sir Roland Hill. His mind turned to the U.S.A. where there was already a steady flow of Welsh emigration. Why should not the Welsh settle in one community, retaining their Welshness and their language? S.R. acquired land in Tennessee, but the perverse luck that always

seemed to haunt Welsh colonisation decreed that S.R.'s settlers should find themselves on the one patch of land that immediately became a battleground between
the armies of the North and the South, when the American Civil War broke out.
The dream faded as the guns opened fire.

Even more dramatic was the Welsh attempt to plant a settlement in Patagonia.
Here the driving force was Michael D. Jones, a leader of Nonconformity, and
again we find in him the burning desire, the hopeful dream that, this time, the
Welsh settlers would not merge into the mass of the population within a generation. As they built their Zion in the wilderness, they would keep their Welshness
– chapels, hymn singing, sermons and all. He received the permission of the Argentine government to found a settlement on the Chabut river in Patagonia – as far
away, one suspects, from central authority as was possible. But the Chabut country
proved tough and the local Indians even tougher. The little colony had to struggle
desperately for survival, and at one point was rescued with the help of the Argentine
government. It survived, however, to prosper and to this day there are still Welsh
chapels in far-away Patagonia and Welsh-speaking lads who were called up to
join the Argentine forces facing the Welsh Guards in the Falklands campaign –
surely the strangest outcome of the Welsh national revival in the nineteenth
century.

One salient fact emerges from the story of these ventures overseas, even though
some of them ended in hardship or failure. The Welsh people were now on the
move on a big scale, in ever increasing numbers. From the 1850s onwards, the
mass stirring of the population increased at an unprecedented pace. It was the Welsh
'diaspora', and when the stirring ended with the First World War, we find a new,
unfamiliar Wales displayed before us. The whole balance of the country had been
dramatically upset. Even by 1900, three-quarters of the population of the
Principality was living in the mining valleys and coastal ports of Glamorgan and
Monmouthshire. This 'stirring' process had a profound effect on the politics of
the people, their religion, their social habits, and even on the games they played.
Are we dealing any more with that idyllic 'gwerin', that ideal peasantry for whom
the enthusiasts had set about creating their university and their national library
and museum?

There had been migrations of the Welsh before. The iron works of Dowlais
and Brymbo, the copper and the coal mines, had sucked in workers from the
Welsh countryside. There had also been a steady flow of hopefuls to the United
States, and the inns in the little country towns carried many an advertisement of
the type: 'The barque, Cariad, Capt. William Evans, to sail from Portmadoc to
Boston, God willing, on Jun 23, 1840. Good food and prayers every morning'.
The urge to be on the move increased as the rural population increased. Pressure
grew on the limited land available. The shadow of Malthus fell on Carmarthenshire
and Cardigan and Anglesey. It grew stronger as agriculture in Wales faced successive crises. When the American Civil War ended the stage was set for the rapid
exploitation of the prairies of the Middle West. The invention of the combine
harvester and the frenzied building of railways sent a flood of cheap American

Michael D. Jones, the inspirer of the Welsh colony in Patagonia

grain pouring into the European markets. Wales shared this problem with the rest of Britain, and indeed with the whole of the Continent. The response in Europe was mass-emigration. The peasants left their own country for the lands overseas where there were new opportunities. The reaction in Wales was curiously different. Professor Brindley Thomas, by his meticulous analysis of the figures, has shown that Wales was the striking exception to the rule. It was the one area in Europe where immigration exceeded emigration.

The census of 1841 was the first to show a fall in the population of rural Wales, and the fall continued. But where did the people go? We know that 100,000 of

Two views of the Rhondda: *above*, in 1830 and, *opposite*, fifty years later

them were eventually located in the United States but the greatest number of them stayed in these islands, above all in south Wales. And the reason is easy to seek. The steam engine was now well embarked on its all-conquering march around the world. Sail was giving place to steam, even in conservative naval circles, and the best reserves of steam coal still lay untapped in the deep trenches of the valleys in the middle of the south Wales coalfield. The whole world was crying out for coal power to drive its steam engines. As Al Capone said about Prohibition America; 'Jeez, someone has got to throw something on a thirst like that.'

A 'coal rush' now took place in the valleys of the south. Above all, the two Rhondas became the 'Black Klondyke'. In 1850 the trout still leapt in the clear waters that ran through the deep woodlands of Llwynypia – the Magpie's Grove. Fifty years later there wasn't a trout or a magpie in the whole deep valley. Long lines of terraced houses choked the lower slopes. The wheels turned day and night over mine shafts dropping their cages over a thousand feet to the lucrative Rhondda No. 3 seam. The endless trains of coal trucks rattled down to the docks at Cardiff and Barry, where the ships of the world crowded the roads to wait their turn

at the coal hoists. This was the real Rape of the Fair Country, and at the beginning it brought profit to both miners and coal-owners. But of course, far more to the coal-owner.

The atmosphere of those heady days comes through strongly in the account of the sinking of the pit at Cwmparc in the valley of the Rhondda Fawr. The coal-owner concerned was the formidable and dynamic David Davies of Llandinam, the very prototype of the self-made Victorian industrialist. He would have earned the enthusiastic approval of Samuel Smiles of 'Self Help' fame. Davies –

A statue of David Davies outside Barry Docks

known as 'Top Sawyer', for he was always on top of everything he did – had made his money as a successful railway contractor, and came into the Rhondda at the time when he was already heavily committed to the construction of the new west Wales railways – and it is significant that, by the time the 'coal revolution' took place, there were already Welshmen who had made enough money to take part in financing it. David Davies sank his own money into the sinking of the new shaft, but there came a day of crisis. The shaft had not yet struck coal and Davies's money was pouring down it. He was coming to the end of his resources. He called his men together. 'Well, boys,' he said, 'I'm sorry to tell you that I cannot go on here any longer. I am very sorry, for I believe that there is some grand coal here and I believe that we are close to it.' He paid the men's wages and then added, 'That leaves just half a crown in my pocket.' A voice in the crowd shouted, 'We'll have that, too.' David Davies took the coin from his pocket and tossed it to the crowd. 'Take it,' he said and turned on his heel.

Pit women in the Rhondda in the 1870s

He went westward to face the problem of continuing his railway, but the men had been so impressed by his gesture that they voted to give him a week's work for nothing. On a memorable morning in 1866, Davies's foreman on the railway was surprised to see his employer rushing towards him along the embankment, excitedly waving a telegram. 'William, William,' he shouted, 'it's all right. I'll not take £40,000 for this bit of paper. They've struck the seam at Cwmparc.'

Far more than £40,000 was eventually extracted from those deep holes in the ground in the Rhondda. The steam coal of south Wales went out to the world. Pioneers like John Nixon had established contacts with foreign buyers. Coaling stations were set up around the globe. Newcastle coal, which created more smoke, lost ground to Welsh coal, and David Davies fought old-style capitalist battles to get his coal to the sea without passing over railways controlled by the Marquis of Bute. He created new docks at Barry, which, in 1913, even eclipsed Cardiff as the greatest coal-exporting centre in the world.

The price of coal: funeral of a victim of the great Senghenydd disaster in 1913

Wales was thus playing a leading part in the extraordinary expansion of British trade in the heyday of late Victorian capitalism, and coal was not the only commodity that Wales exported. Tinplate had become very much a Welsh monopoly and Llanelli, at the western end of the coalfield, became the tinplate capital. It created almost a rival national anthem in the song of 'Sospan Fach' – little saucepan – beloved of rugby crowds. Swansea remained the copper-smelting metropolis, and the old 'Cape Horners' sailed their barques to distant Chile to bring back the copper ore that replaced the exhausted deposits of Parys Mountain in Anglesey. A perpetual canopy of smoke hung over the suburbs of Landore, Llansamlet and Morriston, but it was a cloud that marked money and success. It was a symbol of the part that south Wales industry was playing in the expansion of the Empire. The valleys and ports were, on the face of it, optimistic places in the second half of the nineteenth century.

A closer look showed some dark spots on the sun of success. The south Wales coal seams were lucrative but they were difficult to work. There was danger from fire damp, and the story of the exploitation of some sections of the coalfield is punctuated by a roll call of disastrous explosions, culminating in 1913 in the most disastrous of them all at Senghenydd, where more than 400 men perished in a few minutes. There was certainly 'Blood on the Coal' in Wales.

Owners and miners clashed over methods of working and wages. There were bitter strikes and disputes, but the interesting thing about them is that out of these

Children digging for coal on a tip during the Cambrian strike of 1910

battles came the curious peace treaty of the Sliding Scale. In this arrangement, the scale of the miners' wages was linked with the selling price of the coal and the figures were arrived at by a joint committee of miners' representatives and pit-owners. The Sliding Scale brought a surprising peace in the coalfield for twenty years, which temporarily ceased to be Britain's main industrial battlefield. It also brought national prestige to one of its chief protagonists, the miners' leader William Abraham, known throughout Wales by his bardic name of 'Mabon'.

Mabon was the one figure from the industrial area who seemed to fit into the nationalist picture of the 'gwerin'. Nurtured in the chapel – like many Labour leaders after him – he was a splendid orator in both Welsh and English, a strong supporter of the National Eisteddfod and a lover of Welsh poetry and song. More militant miners felt he was too sympathetic to the mine-owners' point of view.

The Sliding Scale may have brought peace but not plenty. As the class struggle developed later on in the coalfield, Mabonism became a term of contempt, but it worked reasonably well at a period when the coalfield was still expanding and prosperous. The problems of industrial Wales lay mercifully hidden in the future. In the 1880s and '90s no one worried that south Wales was totally dependent on heavy industry and on export. The early pioneers did not foresee the disadvantages of coal mines in narrow valleys which prevented the growth of subsidiary industries around them. No Birmingham could develop around Brynmawr or Ton Pentre.

Instead, the mining towns and villages developed a unique, intensive culture,

William Abraham – 'Mabon'

a private world apart. Many years later, the English poet W. H. Auden was to write that,

Glamorgan hid a life,
Grim as a tidal rock-pool's in its glove-shaped valleys.

He knew nothing of the fierce community loyalties that held these mining villages together, their splendid choral singing, their pride in the local boy who 'made good', their avid demand for education and their deep loyalty to the local rugby team. Industrial Wales may not have fitted into the ideal concept of the 'gwerin', but it was stubbornly alive, a force to be reckoned with. After all, the money that was supporting the national cultural revival came from industrial and not rural Wales. Here lay the reality of power.

Nothing emphasised this more than the early career of David Lloyd George. The story of his rise to fame has passed into folk legend – the orphan lad brought up by his deeply-religious and remarkable uncle, his determined struggles to qualify as a solicitor, his first success as a fiery speaker in Welsh and English in local politics and his election as MP for Caernarfon Boroughs in 1890 after a dramatic recount. The new MP was proud to proclaim that he was a man of the people – 'The day of the cottage-bred man is at hand'. He admitted that he was driven by a fierce ambition. 'My basic idea is to get on.' But to get on he had to have a power base, and Lloyd George's power base was always too narrow to make him feel secure in his subsequent career. Like Tom Ellis before him, he drew his strength from the unswerving support of north Wales Welsh-speaking Nonconformity and their demands for land reform and Disestablishment. These, in the end, were not the driving forces of industrial Wales. Throughout his astonishing progress towards the centre of political power Lloyd George never really understood the mystique of the miners, the tin-plater workers and the steel men.

Tom Ellis might have been an early rehearsal for Lloyd George. He, too, gained office as a Liberal Whip under Gladstone, but Ellis had had the advantage of an Oxford education and died early. Lloyd George began from a lower starting point but rose incomparably higher. He possessed the one essential gift for success in politics in the days before radio and television – he was a superb orator, a master of the crowd from the platform. Even though he was a 'cottage-bred man', the satraps of Liberalism were bound to take notice of him.

Lloyd George entered Parliament when the conquering flood of Liberalism had met with a slight hiccup. Gladstone's last government had so small a majority that he had to rely almost completely on his solid, dependable Welsh block. But the Grand Old Man's retirement and death was followed by six years of Conservative control of power. This was, perhaps, the reason why the young and dynamic Lloyd George directed his energies in an unexpected direction.

The revival of Welsh nationalism in the second half of the nineteenth century had mostly manifested itself in such fields as education, Disestablishment, land reform and the control of local government. But, inevitably, it was bound to take

Minister and deacons in a Nonconformist chapel, circa 1900

on a more direct approach to politics than blind support of an English political party, even if that party was Liberal. Home Rule might be the next step. It was 'in the air'. Gladstone had been pledged to it for Ireland. Why not for Wales? Joseph Chamberlain had actually suggested 'Home Rule All Round'. Tom Ellis, in a notable speech at Bala in 1890, had demanded a separate parliament for Wales, but he shrank from direct action to obtain it. There were those who were more determined and founded a growing movement for 'Cymru Fydd' – Wales of the Future. They visualised the transformation of the Welsh Liberal block in the House of Commons into a body that would press hard for a form of Home Rule. Did Lloyd George toy briefly, at this time, with the idea of becoming a Welsh Parnell?

If he ever did so, he was soon bitterly undeceived. Welsh-speaking, rural Wales might support him, but industrial Wales was another matter. The realities of the new population grouping were ruthlessly exposed when he came to support the Cymru Fydd campaign in the south. The immigration into the coalfield was no longer mainly Welsh. A huge English influx had occurred in the eastern valleys, and the social climate had been transformed. The chairman of the South Wales Liberal Association was a prominent coal-owner, D. A. Thomas – he later became Lord Rhondda and served under Lloyd George as Food Controller in the First World War. He had originally supported Cymru Fydd but now turned against it. The English-speaking Welsh in the big towns were also alarmed. The Cymru Fydd supporters found them totally unsympathetic. To them, Swansea now appeared as a 'howling wilderness of Philistines'. Cardiff, Newport and Barry 'thought of nothing except making money'. In 1896, at a disastrous meeting of the Liberal association at Newport, the 'Newport Englishmen', as Lloyd George called them, swept him and the supporters of the Cymru Fydd movement off the stage.

Lloyd George was a realist, and an ambitious one at that. After Newport, Welsh Home Rule was dead for him, and even when he had supreme power, he never attempted to revive it. He never forgot Newport – the scene of his only humiliation in his career of ever-growing success which was eventually to carry him to the portals of 10 Downing Street. He turned back to the wider stage of British politics. His courageous opposition to the Boer War earned him the hatred of the jingoists, but placed him firmly in the centre of a future Liberal government. He was on his way to stardom.

Later Welsh nationalists have reproached him with failing to further the cause of devolution when he was in a splendid position to do so. They forget Newport but Lloyd George did not forget Wales. He had a Welsh-speaking household staff at Number 10, and his 'kitchen cabinet' was filled with promising young Welshmen. So much so that his enemies accused him of running a sort of Welsh 'Tafia' in Downing Street. When he was the Chancellor of the Exchequer, presenting the revolutionary budget that was the forerunner of the Welfare State, or Prime Minister leading the country through the agony of a World War, even Welsh Disestablishment had to take a back seat. It had always been thus, ever since the days when Henry Tudor opened the door to a wider stage for gifted and ambitious

THE PHILANTHROPIC HIGHWAYMAN.

Mr. Lloyd George. "*I'll* make 'em pity the aged poor!"

[August 5, 1908.]

PUNCH, OR THE LONDON CHARIVARI.—April 28, 1909.

RICH FARE.

The Giant Lloyd-George(richter): "FEE, FI, FO, FAT,
I SMELL THE BLOOD OF A PLUTOCRAT;
BE HE ALIVE OR BE HE DEAD,
I'LL GRIND HIS BONES TO MAKE MY BREAD."

Lloyd George as seen by the cartoonists – *left*, the philanthropic highwayman, introducing old age pensions and, *right*, the terror of the rich with his revolutionary budget proposals of 1909

Welshmen. Even those able men who stayed at home were not prepared to sever their links with an England on whose Empire the sun showed no sign of setting.

Yet as Lloyd George turned to higher things, there came the first signs that the sun was not going to shine for ever upon Liberal Wales. On the face of it, the Liberals had never looked stronger, but a new political party was in the making in the South Wales coalfield. The early development of the Labour Party coincided with the growing disenchantment over the working of the Sliding Scale. Mabonism, and all that it represented, virtually disappeared after the bitter defeat of the miners in the great strike of 1898. The leadership of the South Wales Miners Federation was violently challenged. The old leaders, like Mabon, were urged to 'get on or get out'. A more militant spirit appeared as the new century dawned. Curiously enough, it had been the quarrymen of north Wales who had struck the first blow at 'Mabonism'. In the dramatic Penrhyn strike of 1896, they had held out heroically against the dictatorial Lord Penrhyn. A further strike in 1900 lasted three years before the men were forced back to work on humiliating terms. The north Wales slate industry was set on its steady downward path. The quarrymen had been one of the prize exhibits of the 'gwerin' concept – the ideal Nonconformist working man, devoted to education and the solid backbone of the Liberal vote. With their eclipse came the eclipse of their party.

But it was the miners who were the pace-setters in the new industrial climate. It was they who threw up the new leaders and the theorists of this movement

The aftermath of the Tonypandy riots of 1910

to the left – men like Noah Ablett, one of the authors of the revolutionary pamphlet, *The Miners Next Step*, one of the most influential pieces of propaganda to come from any coalfield. The disputes in the coal industry now took on an aspect of class warfare, and the violence of the Cambrian strike of 1910 has remained firmly fixed in folk memory. In the rioting at Tonypandy, a man was fatally injured in a clash with the police and Winston Churchill, then Home Secretary, ordered the military into the 'disturbed district'. In the event, the soldiers did not actually open fire on the strikers but Churchill was never forgiven in the Rhondda. Even at the height of his war fame, there were still old miners who would remind you that, after all, Churchill was the man who had sent the troops not to the Normandy landings, but to Tonypandy. It was no surprise, therefore, that, when the decisive moment came, the SWMF should instruct the Lib-Lab members whom they had strongly supported, to leave the Liberal benches and sit with the newly-formed Labour Party. It was noted that Mabon was distinctly uncomfortable in his new position.

Yet, in spite of these deep-seated traumas, the distinguished historian Dr Kenneth

Returning from the Investiture, Caernarfon, 1911

Morgan, an acknowledged authority on late nineteenth- and twentieth-century Wales, can write of the period between 1900 and 1914 as Wales's 'Augustan Age', when the 'economic prosperity, national awareness, and political creativity of the Welsh people were most effectively deployed for the benefit of themselves and their neighbours'. Noah Ablett might not have agreed, but the Edwardian optimists could bask in the sunshine of their own approval. This was the period that created a brilliant, baroque-style Civic Centre in the heart of Cardiff, and celebrated the Investiture of the Prince of Wales at Caernarfon Castle in 1911 with a curiously unhistoric but delightful ceremony which gave social satisfaction to all concerned except the Prince himself. Above it all towered Lloyd George, new Chancellor of the Exchequer, a Welshman at last in the very centre of political power. Who knew to what dizzy heights he might yet ascend?

Those photographs and postcards from the era seem to exude an air of ease and confidence. The crowds fill the promenade at Llandudno. The charabancs set off for the circular tour of Snowdonia. The photographer records the departure of the Sunday School outing to Porthcawl. The family groups are posed before the snug country houses . . . They mirror the sense of security of Edwardian Wales, its buoyant hope for a prosperous future. You look closer, and you give a slight shudder of hindsight. The photographs take on a strange poignancy. Those young men between sixteen and twenty – the schoolboy with his first bicycle, the young graduate in the pride of his gown and mortar board, the forwards with proudly-folded arms in the annual snap of the rugby club – will they soon be among the hundreds of thousands destined never to see the future? Will their bodies hang on the wire of the Somme or be trodden into the mud of Passchendaele? That confident Edwardian Wales, like the rest of Edwardian Britain, was soon going to vanish for ever in the catastrophe of the First World War.

Through World Wars to the Future

Wales took its full share of suffering from 'The World's Worst Wound'. The four dreadful years of World War One wiped out all confidence in the national revival. It could never be 'glad, confident morning again'. A whole generation, the creative Welshmen of the future, was decimated. Such a loss is hard to accept in any society. It is doubly hard in a small community like Wales. The long lists of names of the lost are carved on innumerable war memorials in the small villages scattered among the hills. Who knows how many men of promise are among them? Let one stand as symbol of them all . . .

In the village of Trawsfynedd, on the moorlands of Merioneth, stands the statue of the shepherd poet, Hedd Wyn. He had entered his poem for the chair at the 1917 Birkenhead National Eisteddfod and the judges awarded him the prize. His name was called from the platform but there was no answer. Hedd Wyn had fallen in France the week before. The bardic chair was draped in black. Thereafter, the Birkenhead Eisteddfod was always known by the sad title of 'The Eisteddfod of the Vacant Chair'.

There had always been a strong anti-war, pacifist feeling in Welsh Nonconformity. Henry Richard had been the Apostle of Peace. Lloyd George, himself, had opposed the South African war – but now he became Minister of Munitions and then Prime Minister. A Welshman was at the heart of the war effort and its chief inspirer. This was Lloyd George's finest hour and no subsequent criticism or disappointment can take it away from him. Certainly he made the war acceptable to the majority of his fellow countrymen.

When the war ended, Lloyd George stood on a pinnacle of personal popularity attained by few politicians in modern times. He was 'The Man who Won the War', the charismatic leader who had brought the people safely through the wilderness to the Promised Land, The Land fit for Heroes to Live In. Unfortunately, the post-war Promised Land soon began to appear remarkably like a continuation of the Wilderness. There was a transient post-war boom, and then Britain had to face the real cost of the war; the price was an economic nightmare. This was a new world with which Lloyd George was not fully equipped to cope. Dr Kenneth Morgan puts the position clearly in perspective when he points out the contrast between the 'politics of status and social democracy', in which Lloyd George scored such striking successes, and 'the politics of class and economic democracy, which he seldom understood'.

THE NEW CONDUCTOR.
OPENING OF THE 1917 OVERTURE.

'His Finest Hour' – Lloyd George becomes Prime Minister. A *Punch* cartoon of 1916

And there was always the problem of the narrow personal base of his political power. All through his career, he had to make his way through compromise, private deals, and co-operation. His historic war-time government was a coalition, in which he was basically dependent on Tory support. His charisma could no longer work in those immediate post-war parliaments which seemed, in the famous phrase, 'to be filled with hard-faced men who looked as if they had done well out of the war'. They sang that 'Lloyd George knew my father'. Unfortunately he did not know enough Tory fathers! And even fewer Labour ones.

Inevitably, he was pushed out of power. From 1922 onward, he was to remain a frustrated but still fascinating figure off-stage, the Wizard in the Wings. He never returned to the centre of affairs. Was his whole career, therefore, a dazzling sky-rocket affair, which burst with glittering splendour in the political sky, and then faded to leave nothing permanent behind? After a long stay in the shadows of history, the figure of Lloyd George is beginning to receive more favourable consideration from historians. He stands out as one of the principal architects of the caring society that we feel is characteristic of our time. Welshmen, too, now see him in a more impressive light. Even his over-publicised amorous affairs have clothed him in a romantic light for a younger, more permissive generation. He may not have advanced the cause of Welsh Home Rule, but he surely advanced a general awareness of Wales in Britain and the world.

A distinguished Welsh historian has claimed that in the end, Karl Marx spoke more forcefully to the Welsh people than did Lloyd George. It is a pertinent and not a frivolous reply to point out that Karl Marx spoke no Welsh. In any case, Marx seems to have felt that the Celtic people had little to contribute to the dynamics of History. They were a grey people who were outside the main stream of development, destined to stay for ever on the fringe. Lloyd George certainly pushed the Welsh out of the shadows on to the stage in a way that Marx hardly foresaw. Perhaps, in the long run, Lloyd George was the most impressive product of the Welsh nationalist revival of the late nineteenth century. He gave a whole people a new pride in themselves. As one old collier put it, in grudging admiration, 'Well, boys, he showed them, didn't he? He showed them!'

When Lloyd George stepped down from power in 1922, the old Liberal splendour in Wales seemed to fade with his own failing fortunes. In election after election, the solid Liberal block was steadily eroded. The heirs were the Labour Party. The Liberal Party of the young Lloyd George had retreated to the rural areas. In the coalfield Labour's domination became absolute by the 1930s and the reason is not far to seek. The Welsh economy, so strongly based on export, had received a body blow with the collapse of the coal trade. The world had turned to oil and, in the long run, nothing could stop the steady closing of the pits that were once household names – Cambrian, Powell Duffryn, Nixon Navigation, the Ocean. Fewer and fewer coal wagons rumbled down the valleys to ports, where the world's fleets no longer queued up for cargoes. The miners endeavoured to fight with the only weapon in their hands, the strike, but in a climate of falling demand it was bound to break in their hands. They had stubbornly stayed out

Above A.J. Cook, the miners' leader, giving his slogan to the miners in the 1920s: 'Not a minute on the day, not a penny off the pay.'

Opposite South Wales hunger marchers in London, 1931

after the collapse of the General Strike in 1926, but to no avail. As the twenties passed into the thirties the Great Depression settled like a perpetual cloud over the mining valleys.

No one who knew them in those dismal days will ever forget them: the long line of once-proud miners waiting outside the Labour Exchanges for the dole, the women and children scrabbling for small pieces of coal on the tips in the winter rain, the young men keeping up their spirits by marching in gazooka bands or giving up the struggle and pulling out for Slough and Birmingham or Coventry, the general feeling of a whole community being thrown on the scrap heap and no one in authority caring. The Depression left a scar on south Wales that could never be effaced. The Labour Party was solidly entrenched and seemed on the way to become the party of the whole of Wales. It took on a crusading militant tinge and not for nothing was Mardy, at the top of the valley of the Rhondda Fach, christened 'Little Moscow'.

We are now a long way from the Nonconformist radicalism of the nineteenth century and the Edwardian nationalist revival. The Chapel in the Valley suffered in the Depression alongside the coal-mine and a man on the dole was not inclined to listen to sermons or join in hymns of praise. There were still some sections of Welsh industry which were not so seriously affected: the north Wales coalfield was more diversified and fared a little better, Swansea acquired an oil-refining industry, there was still a demand for tin-plate and for anthracite. But the centre of the coalfield and the eastern valleys remained a disaster area. Wales had seen Welsh industries suffer before. The old copper trade had faded in Anglesey and Swansea, the woollen mills of mid-Wales had been put out of business by Yorkshire and the slate quarries had started their slide before the advance of artificial roofing. But there had always been that ever-expanding coalfield to fall back on. Now the safety-net had collapsed.

The Depression altered the social structure of the country. Wales once more became a place of emigration and not of immigration. And that centuries-old gap between north and south, between industrial and rural Wales, seemed to be re-emphasised. It was to the Welsh-speaking areas that Liberalism made its last retreat, and it was from these areas, the stronghold of the 'gwerin', that there came a

totally different reaction to the stresses and strains that the Depression had brought not only to the economy but also to the cultural life of Wales. Plaid Cymru, the Welsh Nationalist Party, was the brain-child of a group of distinguished academics and protagonists of the Welsh language, who had become deeply disturbed over the ever increasing anglicisation of Wales. The eastern valleys of the South Wales coalfield had seen an English invasion at the close of the nineteenth century. In the early years of the twentieth, the coast of north Wales had been colonised by holidaymakers from Lancashire and Birmingham and by the retired businessmen of Liverpool and Manchester. It was becoming an appendage of the English industrial areas. The censuses showed a progressive fall in the number of Welsh speakers, especially in the south and east. It is a bitter and heart-breaking experience to see one's native language, the centre of one's early life and culture, disappearing in one's own lifetime. Those who have not undergone such an experience will find it hard to understand the anguish involved. It forced the dedicated academics of the Welsh colleges to leave their ivory towers and come out on to the hustings.

The most important figure among the founders of Plaid Cymru was Saunders Lewis. A Liverpool Welshman, he had fought in the First World War and been seriously wounded. He was an outstanding literary artist in Welsh, a fine scholar and a lecturer at the University College of Swansea. Frail in figure, he was yet imbued with an urgent sense of mission and fired with the conviction that Wales should look beyond England, back to her old links with the Continent and with European civilisation. Saunders Lewis had already joined the Catholic Church in 1922.

The Taff-Merthyr stay-in strike, 1935–6

The older political parties viewed the arrival of Plaid Cymru with something approaching contempt. Lloyd George, remembering his youthful experience with Cymru Fydd, declared that it would wither in the night, like Jonah's gourd. Labour leaders regarded Plaid as an unnecessary aberration. Aneurin Bevan, the most important figure to appear on the political scene out of Wales in the inter-war years, was imbued with Marxist internationalism. For him, an independent, Welsh-speaking Wales was a backward step in the all-conquering onward march of the working class. He expressed his opinion about the survival of the Welsh language in the same terms as Delane of *The Times*. It was an unmitigated nuisance. The sooner it went the better. It must be recorded, however, that other Welsh MPs, including James Griffiths, were more sympathetic to the cause of the language. Unfortunately, Liberal and Labour criticism of the infant Plaid Cymru seemed to be fully justified when the party made its appearance in a series of elections, in none of which it succeeded in impressing even a small section of the voters. Its hour had not yet come when it could appeal to the wider Welsh public.

It made most headway among young Welsh idealists in the universities and in the Welsh-speaking areas, but its pacifism seemed to place it outside the general tide of public opinion as the menace of Hitler started to loom over Europe. Re-armament seemed, to many members of Plaid Cymru, more of a threat to Welsh culture than Fascism. They were outraged when, in spite of general protest, the government went ahead with the construction of a bombing range in Lleyn, in the very centre of a deeply Welsh farming community, the heart-land of the 'gwerin'.

Aneurin Bevan speaking at a rally in Hyde Park, London

On a dark night in September, 1936, three of the leaders of Plaid Cymru –
Saunders Lewis himself, with the Rev. Lewis Valentine and D. J. Williams –
deliberately set fire to the construction hut on the site of the new aerodrome at
Penrhos. They then went to the nearest police station and gave themselves up.
While waiting to be taken into custody, they discussed Welsh literature and found
that they could not remember the last line of a certain poem. Whereupon the
policeman lent over and kindly supplied it. This seemed to be complete justification
for their action. Here was the popular culture they were defending. Amid scenes
of intense excitement, the case of the three arsonists was transferred to London,
where they were sentenced to short terms of imprisonment. Plaid Cymru had
gained its first martyrs. But did the majority of the Welsh nation really take notice?
The small fire in Lleyn was soon eclipsed by far greater conflagrations in Rot-
terdam, in London, in Berlin and in Saunders Lewis's own university town of
Swansea.

Wales, like the rest of Britain, went into Hitler's war with deep reluctance, but
with a conviction that this was a war which had to be fought. There were individual
conscientious objectors, but, in contrast to the First World War, Wales gave this
conflict more immediate and whole-hearted support. Churchill was forgiven –
for the duration! Swansea had its heart burnt out in a three-day blitz.

When the lights came on again in Western Europe in 1945, they lit up a scene
even more unfavourable to Britain than that which had followed the 1914–18
debacle. No war ever brings the results confidently expected by the combatants

The burning of the aerodrome at Penrhos, 1936. The Rev. Lewis Valentine, Saunders Lewis
and D.J. Williams

when they fire the first shot or drop the first bomb. The Second World War certainly brought an end to Hitler's monstrous dream of a Thousand Year Reich, but it also profoundly changed the structure of the British Empire and Commonwealth. The imperial position was no longer tenable. Britain – and France as well – had to face the harsh fact that, without an empire, it had to take a secondary place in the ranks of great powers. It had to find a new role on the world stage.

For the past three hundred years, England had been the driving force behind the expansion of British imperialism. Now the traditional governing parties had to undergo the traumatic experience of seeing the once indestructible structure of empire dissolve before their eyes. They faced the problem with success. They retained delicate Commonwealth links while they entered the arms of the Common Market. In the thirty years that followed the signing of the peace treaties, England succeeded in constructing a new national image.

Wales also faced a problem of post-war national identity, but it was the exact reverse of the English dilemma. England had to furnish itself with a new image. Wales had to safeguard and revitalise an old one. The Welsh economy and political structure was still firmly linked, even intertwined, with that of England, as it had been for the past four hundred years. Wales therefore endured exactly the same processes of reconstruction as the rest of Britain. There was one praiseworthy idea behind all the post-war schemes of both Labour and Conservative administrations – they were determined to make Welsh industry more varied, more capable of meeting the demands of a whole range of new industrial products. King Coal was quietly displaced from his proud position in south Wales. In any case, the geological structure of the coalfield was making mining increasingly uneconomic. Steel was a more hopeful affair. The big steel plants had long ago moved down to the coast from their original bases, such as Merthyr and Dowlais on the northern rim of the coalfield. Now the steel-making complexes at Port Talbot, and later at Llanwern, near Newport, expanded impressively. The Abbey plant at Port Talbot became the largest in Europe. Tin-plate was integrated with the steel production. The smaller units – those pack-mills whose chimneys had dotted the landscape between Swansea and Llanelli – were swallowed by the giant strip-mills. The doublers and the behinders no longer swung the red-hot plates through the rollers with matchless dexterity. The sturdy women no longer split the glittering sheets after they had come coated with bright tin from the Melingriffith pot. A whole way of life disappeared from the small towns and villages of west Wales. James Griffith, who was now MP for Llanelli, insisted that the strip produced with such impressive speed at Port Talbot should be finally processed at Velindre near Swansea and Trostre at Llanelli. Social politics were more important than economic factors.

A big petro-chemical complex developed at Baglan. The old munitions factory at Bridgend expanded into an enormous trading estate, and the same thing happened at Marchweil outside Wrexham in north Wales. A whole string of new enterprises showed promising fields for investment on a scale previously unknown in Wales. There were critics, of course, who looked on all these developments with a jaundiced eye. Wales, they claimed, was still a 'branch-factory economy', but the general air of the fifties and early sixties was optimistic. The Depression seemed to have faded at last into folk memory. Most Welshmen in the industrial areas would have tacitly agreed with Prime Minister Macmillan's celebrated dictum – quoted like so many other well-remembered pronouncements, out of context – 'You've never had it so good!'

On the face of it, Mr Macmillan's words seemed to fit the contemporary social scene in Wales. There were certainly more cars about, more people taking holidays on the Costa Brava and not in Porthcawl. Caravan parks multiplied along the coastline. Television aerials sprouted from every rooftop. Even in the valleys, living conditions seemed to have improved. The politicians of both major parties could claim that they had made Wales a better place to live in. But for whom? There were those in the Welsh-speaking areas, in the countryside and in what was left of Nonconformist Wales, who looked on this increasingly Anglicised world with doubt, even with dismay. The standard of living might be rising, but the numbers of Welsh-speakers were continually falling. Census after census had shown a steady decline. In 1911 a million people still spoke Welsh. By 1961, only twenty-five per cent of the population of the Principality could speak the old language.

Of course, in some parts of Wales, this problem was not new. Apart from areas like south Pembrokeshire and west Gower, which had been English-speaking for seven hundred years, since the Normans had brought in settlers from Devon and Somerset, industrial development had tempted non-Welsh immigrants, including the Irish, to come to places like Merthyr and ports like Cardiff and Swansea. Dylan Thomas, who was born in Swansea in 1914, once said of his birthplace, 'This town has more layers to it than an onion, and every one of them can reduce you to tears.' Thomas himself was the product of this mixed Anglo-Welsh environment. His parents were Welsh-speaking but he spoke no word of Welsh. But he spent his summer holidays as a boy in the deeply Welsh countryside of Carmarthenshire, and his memories of it permeate some of his greatest poems. Yet he needed the English language to give expression to them. Dylan Thomas was undoubtedly a genius, a magician with words, and, in some respects, probably the best-known Welshman, internationally, since Lloyd George. But Lloyd George was Welsh-speaking and the product of a totally Welsh community. To those who saw the language and Welshness threatened in the post-war world, Dylan Thomas's spreading reputation was hardly welcome. *Under Milk Wood* gave as much offence to the Welsh intelligentsia as J. M. Synge's *Playboy of the Western World* gave to the Irish. A great artist has the right to use his material as he pleases when he is creating a masterpiece, and time has mellowed the offence. After all, *Under Milk Wood* is a picture of the 'gwerin' seen from outside but with sympathy. The Reverend Eli Jenkins has the last word as he says his evening prayer,

> And Thou, I know, will be the first
> To see our best side, not our worst.

But as the 1950s progressed to the 1960s, Welshmen who had the cause of their

The poet, Dylan Thomas

native culture at heart might be forgiven if they looked on the worst side when they considered the state of the language. For what special quality would remain in Welsh society if Welsh itself disappeared? The threat to the language and the tension it produced now underlay every specifically Welsh movement in politics. Even when it did not come to the surface, it was the hidden factor in the attempts by politicians of all parties to get more recognition for Wales in the centres of power.

The Attlee government of the fifties, firmly committed to the virtues of centralisation for nationalised industries, had seen no reason to accord a separate Secretary of State for Wales on the lines of the Scottish model. Herbert Morrison felt that any such plan would be a 'dilatory nuisance'. The Conservatives made some gesture to the demand for more self-government when they appointed a spokesman for Welsh affairs, and the Labour administration went further and actually created a Secretary of State. The first holder of the office was, deservedly, James Griffith, who had always fought valiantly for special consideration for Wales in Labour's corridors of power. This somewhat reluctant concession could hardly satisfy Plaid Cymru or the defenders of the language. A political campaign for full self-government seemed to many to be the only solution of the Welsh dilemma. Others were prepared to adopt tougher methods.

A new impetus to this militant section came from an unexpected quarter. Saunders Lewis, the old leader of Plaid Cymru, emerged from his relative retirement from public affairs to deliver a powerful broadcast on BBC Wales in 1962 on 'Tynged yr Iaith' – the Fate of the Language. The revered hero of the 1936 protest against the aerodrome in Lleyn did not mince words. He made a powerful case for the use of 'revolutionary methods' if Welsh was not to disappear into the lumber-room of history. The survival of the language, he argued, was the key to the survival of Wales, even more important than any political or administrative reshuffling. What was the point of a self-governing Wales if it did not speak Welsh?

The broadcast had a powerful effect on Welsh-speaking youth. It gave them a cause, a rallying cry. Out of it grew Cymdeithas yr Iaith Gymraeg, the Welsh Language Society, pledged to direct action to gain a place for the language of Wales in Wales itself. Secret patrols went through the countryside at night blotting out English words on road signs. Slogans in large letters appeared on walls, demanding a separate television channel for Wales. There were sit-ins in the studios of the BBC and HTV (the commercial station for Wales). Transmitters were damaged, and the leaders of the campaign made constant appearances in court before magistrates who sometimes proved surprisingly sympathetic. Some activists – a mere handful as it turned out – were prepared to go further. They staged bomb explosions in public buildings and attacked the aqueducts that brought water from the Welsh hills to satisfy the big English conurbations, at the expense, it was claimed, of the Welsh consumer. There was even a short-lived fringe movement to form a Welsh republican army.

The Investiture of Prince Charles as Prince of Wales in Caernarfon Castle in 1969 had taken place in a different atmosphere from that of his great-uncle in 1911. Edwardian and pre-First World War Wales had been confident in its Welshness. The language seemed secure. Welsh nationalists felt no need for violence, for the steady march of Liberalism would give the nation all that was required. Now,

The police removing a Welsh language demonstrator

Welsh-speaking Wales was uncertain of itself and deeply anxious about the future. Prince Charles took the edge off the sharpest criticism by delivering a speech in Welsh at the Urdd Eisteddfod. He was the first royal personage to do so since Henry VII – if, indeed, the first Tudor really spoke the language.

The new militancy could claim results. The Welsh language was given legal equality with English for all purposes by the Welsh Language Act of 1973, thus reversing the much-resented clauses in the sixteenth-century Acts of Union. Later came the agreement to give the planned new television channel to a separate Welsh corporation, which would transmit programmes in Welsh at peak hours. The station went into action in 1982. All this was bound to have an effect on the fortunes of Plaid Cymru. Plaid had not done particularly well in the post-war elections and had dissociated itself from the activities of the Welsh Language Society and condemned the more violent actions of the extremists. It was firmly committed to the constitutional way. Progress in this direction had not seemed particularly promising. Then, in 1966, Plaid Cymru administered a shock to the complacency of the Labour Party in Wales, all the more severe for being totally unexpected. In a by-election at Carmarthen they captured the seat from Labour and, for the first time, now had an MP in Parliament to press Plaid policies.

Gwynfor Evans had been Plaid's secret weapon. He was also something new in the party. True, he had been educated at Aberystwyth and Oxford and had been a conscientious objector during the war, but he was not an academic. He was a successful market-gardener, living in the constituency, and an excellent speaker in Welsh and English. Handsome and courteous, he had a personal charm with special appeal to the young. With Gwynfor Evans in command, Plaid Cymru seemed set on a new, more successful path, and could turn to the non-Welsh-speaking Welshmen. It might even look at the industrial areas.

Some nationalists felt that such a look would be in vain. Things might have already gone too far. The best hope would be to retire, almost like Llywelyn the Last, into a redoubt of Welsh-speaking where the language could become the centre of community life. The Adfer movement aimed at creating a Welsh Gaeltacht, on the lines of Ireland. From this inner fortress of Welsh, the language could re-emerge strengthened for the future. Certain extremists were prepared to go further. English settlement in the Welsh Gaeltacht should be actively discouraged. Those who had acquired 'second homes', or converted country cottages that should have been occupied by Welsh young families, must be frightened away. At night, the flames of burning houses lit up the lonely parts of the countryside. Plaid Cymru set its face firmly against these extreme manifestations of anguish over the plight of the language. It stayed firmly on the constitutional path.

In the late sixties, this course seemed about to be triumphantly justified. In two by-elections in the Rhondda and Caerphili, massive Labour majorities, which had seemed to be impregnable, crumbled before the Plaid challenge. At Caerphili, a Labour majority of 21,000 came down to a mere 1874. Could Labour be facing the same anguish that had overtaken the Liberal party in industrial Wales? If Rhondda and Caerphili were not safe, what Labour seat was? The results set the alarm bells ringing throughout the Welsh Labour party. On the face of it, this was a different Labour Party from the old, fiery, militant one strongly based on trade unionism and the class struggle. Aneurin Bevan and Jim Griffith had given place to a new generation of lawyers, university lecturers and journalists – sincere, dedicated men, many of whom spoke Welsh, but who did not have quite the

Gwynfor Evans hailed by the electors of Carmarthen, 1974

same deep roots in the constituencies they represented. Plaid Cymru lost some
of its momentum in the seventies, but it did have three MPs in Parliament. It
could hope to become a credible alternative to Labour in the darker days that
now lay ahead.

The optimism of the Macmillan era was swiftly evaporating. In common with
the rest of Britain, Welsh industry was beginning to feel the cold wind of approaching depression. Were the dismal 1930s on their way back? The Labour government
would need all the support it could get in the hard times that now lay ahead.
It was prepared to make concessions to both Welsh and Scottish national feeling.
Both countries were offered national assemblies. The Scottish Assembly would
have far-reaching powers. The proposed Welsh Assembly was far more restricted.
Yet even restricted assemblies have a habit of growing in importance, of quietly
attracting more power the longer they are in being. The change such an Assembly
might produce in the Principality could be as far-reaching as that produced by
the Tudor Acts of Union. After its long marriage with England, Wales was being
offered, if not divorce, at least legal separation. In 1978 the Scottish and Welsh
bills passed through Parliament. Polling in the referendum, in Wales, to decide
if the Welsh people wished an Assembly, was set for the specially selected and
evocative date of St David's Day, 1 March 1979.

Was the youthful Lloyd George, in his Cymru Fydd days, looking down? Were the spirits of 'S.R.' and Morgan John Rhys, brooding over the scene? Were the deaths of Llywelyn the Last and Owain Glyn Dŵr about to be avenged? Alas, no. Scotland had already voted, and 45% of those who went to the poll opted for the assembly. The result in Wales was strikingly different. Only 13% of those who voted cast their vote for the assembly plan. Even in Gwynedd – the heart, as it were, of Welsh-speaking Wales – the pro-assembly vote only reached 21%. In Anglicised Gwent, a mere 6.7% opted for the very modest degree of devolution offered by the government's proposals. The result was decisive. The nation had reached a turning point in its history – and refused to turn.

In the post-mortems that followed, a vast array of reasons were evoked to account for this astonishing, and in some quarters totally unexpected outcome of the Devolution Affair. Welsh-speaking Wales may have feared permanent domination by the Anglicised south; the centuries old divide between the two sections of the country reappeared. There was anxiety about increased bureaucracy. The recent reconstruction, under the Conservatives, of the county administrative structure had not met with general approval. The old counties like Breconshire, Pembrokeshire or Denbighshire had been there for over four hundred and fifty years and had gathered emotional loyalties around themselves. People did not take kindly to seeing them swallowed up in large units created by anonymous bureaucrats and christened with titles like Dyfed, Powys or Gwynedd, arbitrarily resurrected from the distant past. Would the new assembly add another expensive tier to this already cumbersome scheme? Furthermore, Plaid Cymru worried that an Assembly would perpetuate a Labour majority. The Labour Party worried in exactly the opposite direction. A whole series of political currents swirled around the proposal. But there was a deeper current underlying them all.

Quite bluntly, most people in Wales, openly or secretly, feared that political devolution might bring economic dissolution. In spite of the well-researched and ingenious pleading by Plaid Cymru on the economic viability of small national units, the majority of people in the industrial areas were not convinced. They preferred safety in the economic arms of Britain to venturing out on the dangerous seas of independence.

The devolution vote offers a convenient moment for a historian to lay down his pen. Of course, Welsh history has not stopped or gone into cold storage since that St David's Day in 1979. In one sense, History is Now. As soon as a word is spoken or written, an act committed, it goes into the Past to become part of the collective memory of the nation, which it is the work of the historian to preserve but not to mis-interpret. The closer he is to the march of events, the more difficult it is for him to discern the direction in which they are moving, for he, himself, is an actor in the present scene. He shares in its anxieties and confronts it with his own hopes and fears, his own prejudices. It is wise for him to stand back a little and let the dust of battle settle before pronouncing on the struggles, successes and failures of his own time.

In 1979, Wales, for good or ill, decided to continue facing the threatening future closely linked with England and the rest of Britain. Plaid Cymru, the Liberals and the Labour Party all withdrew into their own heartlands – Plaid Cymru and the Liberals into rural and Welsh-speaking Wales, Labour into its industrial fortress. The Conservatives boldly moved in from the fringe – a political set-up which would have surprised Lloyd George. The economic scene would have been equally puzzling to those buoyant and ruthless optimists who had opened up the south Wales coalfield in the nineteenth century. Was Wales – with the rest of Western Europe – now entering a new, dangerous era; a world where the West was bound to lose its old industrial and political superiority, where modern technology would profoundly alter the conditions of employment and where the nuclear threat hung over all nations, great and small? In this vast and darkening scene, 'where ignorant armies clash by night', was the survival of Welshness, expressed through a people who now live to the west of Offa's Dyke, of vital international importance? After the old Scottish parliament had committed voluntary (and lucrative) suicide in 1707, and agreed on the union with England, Lord Seafield, the Lord Privy Seal, remarked complacently, 'That's an end of ane auld sang'. After the devolution vote, there were some Welshmen who were happy to confine all expression of their nationality to the singing of 'Hen Wlad fy Nhadau' at Cardiff Arms Park.

Yet no nation can escape its history, even if it tries to forget it. All through its troubled story, Wales has shown its strange power of survival. Even in dark eclipse, it has retained the secret power of revitalising itself, to add its own exciting note to the concert of Britain. In a world of insidious and spreading standardisation, this is surely the heart of the matter, the justification for the survival of Wales in its Welshness, its language and its culture.

In the end the historian must yield to temptation, forsake his strict discipline and risk looking boldly towards the future. For has not Wales drawn much of its strength for survival, not only on myth and legend but on prophecy. The defiant words of that brave Welshman of Pencader reach us from the distant twelfth century, when he confronted the formidable Henry II, King of England, with this ringing prediction of the future of Wales, come what may. His words are now engraved on stone in Pencader:

> Nor do I think that any other nation than this of Wales . . . shall, on the day of severe examination before the Supreme Judge, answer for this corner of the earth.

Further Reading

There is now a large and comprehensive literature covering every aspect of the history of Wales, but there are still few general surveys. This gap will soon be remedied when the new six-volume *History of Wales* is completed and jointly published by the Clarendon and the University of Wales Presses, under the editorship of Professor Glanmor Williams. The first volume to appear, curiously enough, covers the final period of 1880 to 1980, and Dr Kenneth Morgan has set a high standard for the series. There can be no question that the completed project will be the definitive account of the complex and romantic story of Wales. In the meantime, *Wales Through the Ages* (Christopher Davies) – a series of broadcasts on BBC Wales, by experts in each separate field – is a valuable general survey. Emyr Humphreys's *The Taliesin Tradition, The Quest for the Welsh Identity* is a stimulating and individual view of the continuity of traditional Welsh culture, while *Land of My Fathers* by Gwynfor Evans, (an English translation of his *Aros Mae*, published by Ty John Penry in 1974) gives a vigorous and challenging interpretation of Welsh history from the standpoint of Plaid Cymru, the Welsh nationalist party. On the opposite side stands Professor Gwyn A. Williams, whose *The Welsh in their History* (Croom Helm, 1982) is equally vigorous and persuasive in the presentation of the Marxist point of view.

There are several accounts of certain long sections of the history of Wales. Here, the classic work is Sir John Lloyd's two-volume *A History of Wales, From the Earliest Times to the Edwardian Conquest* (Longman, Green, first published in 1911). The earlier section has invariably been overtaken by modern research, by the later section is still an invaluable guide through the maze of Welsh medieval dynastic history. An equally classic and invaluable account of a later period is contained in *A History of Modern Wales* by Professor David Williams, covering the story from the advent of the Tudors to the present day and published by John Murray in 1950. Hugh Thomas's *A History of Wales, 1485–1660* (University of Wales Press, 1972) gives a valuable and clear-cut account of Tudor and Stuart Wales. Professor William Rees's *Historical Atlas of Wales, From Early to Modern Times*, was published in Cardiff in 1951 and is indispensable to anyone starting to explore Welsh history for the first time. There remains the *Welsh Historical Review*, published twice yearly by the University of Wales Press and edited by Dr Kenneth Morgan with Professor Ralf A. Griffiths as assistant editor. The review began in 1960 and is now the recognised channel of communication between all those who are at work in the

Welsh historical field. Again, this is an indispensable accompaniment to any serious enquiry into Welsh history. The following is a list of books dealing with separate episodes and arranged according to chapters.

Chapter One: *Out of the Mists*
The Origins of Britain, Lloyd and Jennifer Laing (Granada, 1982); *The Stone Circles of the British Isles,* Aubrey Burl (Yale University Press, 1976); *A Short History of Archeology*, Glyn Daniel (Thames and Hudson, 1981); *Wales, An Archaeological Guide*, Christopher Houlder (Faber and Faber, 1975).

Chapter Two: *Celts and Romans*
The Celts, T.G.E. Powell (Thames and Hudson, 1958); *Celtic Britain*, Lloyd Laing (Granada, 1981); *The Celtic Realms*, Myles Dillon and Nora Chadwick, (Cardinal, 1973); *The Druids*, Stuart Piggott, (Thames and Hudson, 1968); *The Druids*, Nora Chadwick, (UWP, 1966); *Roman Britain*, Malcolm Todd (Fontana, 1981); *Language and History in Early Britain*, Kenneth Jackson (Edinburgh, 1953); *The Roman Frontier in Wales*, V. E. Nash-Williams, revised by Michael G. Jarrett (UWP, Cardiff, 1969).

Chapter Three: *Into the Darkness*
Wales in the Early Middle Ages, Wendy Davies, (Leicester University Press, 1982); *A Celtic Miscellany*, Kenneth Jackson, (Penguin, 1951); *The Settlement of the Celtic Saints in Wales*, E.G. Bowen, (U.W.P., 1950); *Canuu Aneirin*, ed. I. Williams, translated by Kenneth Jackson as *The Gododdin*, (Edinburgh University Press, 1969); *Arthur's Britain*, Leslie Alcock (Penguin, 1973); *Gildas, De Excidio Britanniae*, ed. Michael Winterbottom (Phillimore, 1978).

Chapter Four: *The Age of Isolation*
The Laws of Hywel Dda, translated M. Richards (Liverpool, 1954).; *The Vikings*, Johannes Brondsted (Pelican, 1970); *The Beginnings of English Society*, Dorothy Whitelock (Pelican, 1952).

Chapter Five: *The Coming of the Normans*
The Norman Achievement, David C. Douglas (Collins/Fontana 1972); *Geraldus Cambrensis, The Journey through Wales and the Description of Wales*, trans. Lewis Thorpe (Penguin, 1979); *The Monastic Order in South Wales, 1066–1349*, F.G. Cowley (U.W.P., 1977); *The Norman Conquerors*, David Walker (Christopher Davies, 1980); *The Normans in South Wales*, N.H. Nelson (Austin, USA and London, 1966); *Mediaeval Wales*, R. Ian Jack (Cambridge U.P., 1976). *Geoffrey of Monmouth*, trans. Lewis Thorpe (Penguin Books, 1966).

Chapter Six: *The Age of the Princes*
The Mabinogion, trans. Gwyn Jones and Thomas Jones (Dent, 1974); *The King's Works in Wales*, Dr A.J. Taylor (H.M.S.O., 1974); *The Welsh Wars of Edward*

the First, J.C. Davies (O.U.P.); *The Welsh Church from Conquest to Reformation*, Glanmor Williams (U.W.P., 1962).

Chapter Seven: *Between Two Worlds*
South Wales and the March 1284–1415, William Rees (O.U.P., reprinted 1967); *Owen Glendower*, Glanmor Williams (O.U.P., 1966); *Wales and the Wars of the Roses*, T.H. Evans (C.U.P., 1914); *Lancastrians, Yorkists and Henry VII*, S.B. Chrimes (London, 1964).

Chapter Eight: *Tudor Triumph*
Bosworth Field and the Wars of the Roses, A.L. Rowse (Macmillan, 1966); *Welsh Reformation Essays*, Glanmor Williams (U.W.P., 1968); *Tudor Policy in Wales*, J.F. Rees, (Cardiff, 1935, reprinted); *Elizabethan Wales*, G. Dyfnallt Owen (U.W.P., 1962); *The Gentry and the Elizabethan State*, Gareth Jones (Christopher Davies, 1977).

Chapter Nine: *Stuart Tragedy*
Studies in Stuart Wales, A.H. Dodd (U.W.P., 1971); *A History of the Civil War in Pembrokeshire, 1642–1649*, A.L. Leach (London, 1937).

Chapter Ten: *Myth, Methodists and Machines*
Howell Harris, 1714–1773, The Last Enthusiast, Geoffrey F. Nuttall (U.W.P., 1965); *The Eighteenth Century Renaissance*, Prys Morgan (Christopher Davies, 1981); *Wales and America*, David Williams (U.W.P., 1962); *Madoc, The Making of a Myth*, Gwyn A. Williams (Metheun, 1980); *Iolo Morganwg*, Prys Morgan (U.W.P., 1975); *The Industrial Revolution in North Wales*, A.H. Dodd (U.W.P., 1951); *The Industrial Development of South Wales*, A.H. John (U.W.P., 1950); *Fishguard Fiasco*, John Kinross (Five Arches Press, 1974).

Chapter Eleven: *Birth Pangs of a New Order*
The Rebecca Riots, David Williams (U.W.P., 1955); *And They Blessed Rebecca*, Pat Molloy (Gomer Press, 1983); *John Frost, A Study in Chartism*, David Williams (U.W.P., 1939); *The Merthyr Rising*, Gwyn A. Williams (Croom Helm, 1978).

Chapter Twelve: *The New Wales*
The South Wales Coal Industry, J.H. Morris and L.J. Williams (U.W.P., 1958); *The Welsh Economy, Studies in Expansion*, ed. Brinley Thomas (U.W.P., 1952); *The Fed: The History of the South Wales Miners in the Twentieth Century*, David Smith and Hywel Francis (Lawrence and Wishart, 1980); *Wales in British Politics, 1868–1922*, Kenneth O. Morgan (U.W.P., 1980); *Lloyd George, The People's Champion*, John Grigg (Eyre Methuen, 1978).

Chapter Thirteen: *Through World Wars to the Future*
Aneurin Bevan, Michael Foot (Vol I: MacGibbon and Kee, 1962; Vol 2, Davis-Poynter, 1973); *The Welsh Extremist*, Ned Thomas (Gollancz, 1971).

To these accounts of the events of history, must be added assessments of the achieve-ments of the Welsh people in poetry and literature. The classic survey in this field is Professor Thomas Parry's *History of Welsh Literature* (trans. H. Idris Bell, Clarendon Press, 1955) and also the valuable *Welsh Poetry: Sixth Century to 1600*, Gwyn Williams (Faber & Faber, 1973). There is also an excellent collection of translations in the *Penguin Book of Welsh Verse*, edited and translated by Anthony Conran and J.E. Caerwyn Williams (Penguin, 1967).

This short bibliography contains only a small number of the important books that are now available to the student who decides to explore the fascinating field of Welsh history. The list has been made up with the interest in mind of someone who is coming to Welsh history for the first time.

Index